ALAYA CHADWICK

Alaya's Fables

Tales that Transform & Awaken

iUniverse, Inc.
Bloomington

Alaya's Fables
Tales that Transform & Awaken

iUniverse books may be ordered through booksellers or by contacting:

iUniverse
1663 Liberty Drive
Bloomington, IN 47403
www.iuniverse.com
1-800-Authors (1-800-288-4677)

These fables have been birthed over 17 years, beginning in 1996.

ISBN: 978-1-4620-2047-8 (sc)
ISBN: 978-1-4620-2048-5 (e)

Printed in the United States of America

iUniverse rev. date: 8/5/2011

Midwives—Lisa Scally & Anne Suddy

Written for the benefit of self, other, and the world. In truth, we are ONE great fable telling itself to itself. Are you listening with your heart?

Also by Alaya

Wake Up to Your (W)hole Life

Dancing Heart & Soul into Life

Once upon a time, a long time ago, and it is still true for me today, I found myself in the magical Land of Sanctuary. As I traveled the Land of Sanctuary, 'round the Labyrinth Ring, through the Gates of Grace, and into the Circle of Stones, I discovered the magic and mystery of (W)holeness.

Now, from Alaya Chadwick, creator of Sanctuary and author of *Wake Up To YOUR (W)hole Life*, comes the magic and mystery of *Alaya's Fables*. *Alaya's Fables* dive deeply into the weaving of psyche and soul into (W)holeness, revealing ancient insights into "The Secrets of the True You."

And so it comes to be in Sanctuary, that the winds have stirred again and whisper that Heart & Soul dance with one another in the deepest realms of our being, when we know how to feel into mystery, itself.

First, we feel that we are all One. AND, secondly, we feel that we are Love walking. Thus this holy, (W)holly secret is known and recognized only by our hearts, for the Truth of the Divine or Love is rooted in our hearts. Knowing and feeling into this precious mystery frees us to love, to be loved, and to be who we are.

How the dance of Heart & Soul happens is a mystery. What I have come to know is that when we cultivate a heart-felt awareness, we are able to accomplish things that we otherwise could never do. We begin to BE the dance of life. And when we seep ourselves in this truth, we come to know who we are.

Alaya's Fables reveal this secret, inviting the reader to walk a spiral path into their own sacred (W)holeness. These inspiring fables provide a unique and profound way of knowing ourselves. The Dance of Heart & Soul is revealed in all its infinity of variations, and we are shown the way to walk through our days with a renewed sense of authentic vitality and simplicity.

The Fables are wonderfully created tales of ordinary souls who, when confronted with a spiritual crisis, have surrendered to the quest of the spiritual journey and ended up seeing themselves and the world in extraordinary new ways.

Each fable presents the reader with an invitation to go along on a life-changing spiritual odyssey and discover powerful, wise, and practical lessons that teach us to:

- Follow our Life's Mission and Calling,
- Cultivate sources of Love, Support, and Encouragement,
- Love, Laugh, and live consciously,
- Be Ourselves in all moments, and
- Stand at the Edge and Keep walking.

These Fables are all about transformation, healing, and awakening. These tales are all about YOU, waking up to what is true of the (W)hole of YOU. Created with Love and woven with Soul in the Land of Sanctuary, offered to you with heart-felt truth, I invite you to pick up this book, and let your life be blessed.

Words from the Heart by Bob Stone, father of a grown daughter, Vietnam Veteran, and a Traveler in The Land of Sanctuary.

What Others are Saying About This Book

There are many ways to deliver truth. Alaya has found a tincture in her fables that dye right through to the soul and awaken in it a joy, while at the same time instructing it in the deepest mysteries. This is all the more amazing in its effect because Alaya has the unique creative capacity to teach using the hands and feet of our ordinary human experience to understand and come closer to secrets of the universe.

Martha Harrell, M.S.N., Ph.D., *Licensed Training Jungian Psychoanalyst, Initiated Shaman (Andean), Continuum Teacher, Biodynamic Cranio-sacral Therapist, Imago Relationship Therapist, and contributing author in* Transforming Terror: Reclaiming the World Soul

* *

Alaya's Fables takes us into the world of make-believe to discover how problems are solved from the heart. Her creative fables give us all something to think about and to learn from. Her theme is "learning to play" which comes from your original nature. There isn't a single one of us who doesn't need to remember and practice this greater freedom to become our truest self. Enjoy this enchanting read and practice the messages that can surely support and delight your efforts to grow in Love and Wisdom.

Meredith Young-Sowers, D.Div., *Founder & Director, Stillpoint Foundation and School of Integrative Life Healing, Author of* Agartha, The Angelic Messenger Cards, Wisdom Bowls *and* Spirit Heals

* *

Dear Alaya…wow!!! What a blessing you have created for us all. Truly, these fables are a gift of abundant pleasure and joy. With humility and grandness the reader is introduced into a myriad of tales crafted in poetic fable language. These unique fables engage both right and left hemispheres, and truly invite us to reach our potential. Thank you from an inspired heart!

Joyce Buckner, Ph.D., *Author of* Making Real Love Happen, *Master Imago Therapist, and guest on the Oprah Show*

It has long been believed that the nature of human experience is shared through story. *Alaya's Fables* offers a welcoming trail into one's heart and soul. This is a beautiful collection of stories, which provide wisdom and insight highlighting a most valuable gift—universal connection. *Alaya's Fables* invites people to tenderly explore and reflect on their life experiences. The stories provide an opportunity to learn, heal, hope and delight in pathways to self-awareness. The questions presented in the discussion section are particularly useful, and offer ways for people to deepen their understanding, expand their curiosity, and celebrate life.

Enjoy and use these lovely fables as a way to explore, grow, and play with all that you are.

Dee LaCrosse, Psy.D., *Licensed Clinical Psychologist*

****

In this Fable-ous tome, Alaya, a psychotherapist with degrees in both Psychological Science and Divinity combines Psychotherapy and spirituality with her own life experiences and those of people she's come to know well to share the secrets for a fulfilled life. She does so in the ancient therapist's style of first telling a story to set the stage for learning. She has a story for almost every human dilemma and painful emotion and the solutions suggested are a neat combination of faith in one's own integrity and the willingness to grant that others will have faith in theirs. Doing so, for example, keeps you from being seduced into pleasing others and losing your Self.

ONE need not be the lonely number its name implies. Alaya Chadwick takes us to the "land where dreams live" to find intimacy with our inner selves. In doing so, we allow intimacy with others and the One becomes WE and then We is also One as well as One is One. Add to Alaya's New Math that One and One is also Three in that there is You and Me and also WE.

Mark W. Shulkin, MD, *Distinguished Life Fellow of the American Psychiatric Association and Clinical Assistant Professor or of Psychiatry at Drexel University College of Medicine (retired)*

Sunny L. Shulkin, LCSW, BCD, *Master Trainer of Imago Relationship Therapy where she's been teaching Harville Hendrix, Ph.D.'s 'Getting the Love You Want' couples workshops since 2000. Co-author with Pat Love of the book* How to ruin a perfectly good relationship. *Sunny has been in practice in Bala Cynwyd, PA, for twenty-six years*

* *

This wisdom collection speaks to mind, body and spirit, and I'm ecstatic to have these fabulous stories available in one book. The words of these fables weave a rich vibrational tapestry that illuminate the magic of our (W)holeness. I recognize my particular uniquely ordinary magnificence in these stories and remember that I am this and I am that, too. Alaya's playfully powerful fables will gently soften your perceptions around who you believe yourself to be—revealing your unique truth and sparkling wisdom. Dare yourself to be seen as light breathing compassion.

Marilyn Dexter, *Grandmother, Mother, Wife, Friend, Business Owner, Shamanic and Reiki Practitioner*

* *

Alaya, how gifted you are in your ability to impart the deepest kind of healing and transformation through being (W)hole yourself and for taking the long journey it takes to get there. This body of work is such a reflection of what can be accomplished if we only tune in to our heart, if we listen and if we allow ourselves to get through the mud, dust ourselves off and go through a cleansing so we may shine.

You, my friend, are on the top of your mountain shining down on all of us your purity, your wisdom and your unconditional heart, so we, your readers, may release ourselves from the darkness and head more fully into the light. I am absolutely sure your fables will be a profound and transforming gift to humanity.

These fables offer reflection of the deepest kind. *Alaya's Fables* are a culmination of 30 years' experience in the field of psychology, skillfully bringing the reader on a deep and transformative inner journey. Each fable opens the gateway for deep reflection and access to one's inner core life experiences. A series of questions geared to probe even deeper into the inner recesses of the soul offer the reader an opportunity to acknowledge, forgive, and release patterns holding one back from being their (W)hole self.

Alaya's Fables are a true gift for the seekers of inner transformation! An extraordinary body of work!

We have much work to do. Let's get to it!

Julia Garreaud*, Marketing Director, Sound Light Healer*

****

I have so thoroughly loved reading *Alaya's Fables*! No matter what mood I am in, how lonely, how angry, how curious, there is a story to fit. As I read each story I am reminded I am not by myself in life's experience. There is always someone there to console and be consoled, to listen and advise, maybe to share their own story and hear yours. I see that whatever particular events have colored my day, with rainbows or rain clouds, life doesn't end. There is more; I just have to step into the next day, keeping my eyes and my heart wide open, and be present in each moment. Each time I read *Alaya's Fables,* I see something new. As I learn more about how I manage my life, and grow into my (W)hole self, the stories grow in meaning. The stories illustrate the choices are ours alone to make—to hide, to follow, to laugh, to cry, to stand tall and lead—and that whatever choice we make, it is correct for us in that situation, and there is always something more to be learned!

I have two college degrees, one in English, one in Accounting. For the last five years, I have been a student of the Wisdom Way, learning to live my life with an open heart, while remaining present in this moment and the next. I have worked professionally as an accountant for 30+ years. My brain has long been trained to work in a linear and facts-based manner. Reading *Alaya's Fables* inspires my imagination. I remember that life is not black and white, to be lived in a straight line, but is Technicolor, to be lived dancing in great swirling arcs! There are treasures to be found and lessons to be learned, if I keep my eyes and heart open to experience life.

Thank you, Alaya, for writing *Alaya's Fables* and reminding me there is magic learning in the telling of a story.

Ellen Fitts Byrne, *CPA, CRM, CMTR-1&2*

****

When I'm reading one of *Alaya's Fables*, I am transported to a different way of being. It is like I can rest—it's probably my mind that's resting—and I'm transported by the story and carried along to another place. I am sure that they speak directly to my soul, without the filter of my mind making translations. From this place, I feel as though I am reunited with an ancient, wise place within me that I can carry out into the world. I have many ideas of how these fables can support me and my clients (and of course, family and friends) on our life journey's. I often seek resources in my professional work that can help clients get out of their heads and into their hearts and souls. I know this is a way.

> ***Karen Uzar Aznoian***, *Principal and Executive Integral Coach, Aznoian Leadership Development, CMTR*

****

Fables that magically awaken feelings and evoke memories long suppressed sometimes forgotten. Get ready to experience an awakening deep inside as you read *Alaya's Fables*. Alaya is truly a gifted storyteller with a calling.

> ***Yvonne Laurence*** *(Founder), Avalon Holistic Clinic and Retreat, Raymond, NH*

****

I have had the pleasure of listening to stories written and read by Alaya. I'm always fascinated by the characters, their names, their stories and most of all, their struggles and triumphs. The detail in each story is what impressed me the most. I am a person that moves fast. These fables are beautifully detailed. When I read them, I can slow down, breathe slower and relax. I take time to enjoy the story, to linger on the words, to appreciate the beauty of the each character. I think about the details of my own life, what I have accomplished…not the exterior accomplishments, but the interior ones, the ones only I know about. The fable that I enjoyed the most is The Story of HoorTeeTah. While growing up, keeping secrets was a big part of the fabric of my environment. Secrets coupled with shame starved me. Wouldn't it be fabulous to guiltlessly eat chocolate in public, dance naked in the street, and suck your thumb???

Patty Miske, *Integral Life Coach, Business Strategist, Marketing Specialist, BSEE, MBA*

****

Alaya's Fables is an adventurous journey. Each fable will take the reader to places they have yet to imagine. As a mother of three, these stories have been enjoyed by the adults and the children of our home. We will continue to read and reread, recommend and sing the praises of each and every fable until our voices tire.

Alexandria N. Browne, *LPN*

****

Alaya's Fables deeply touched my heart. Each encounter with the beings, magicks, the twists and the surprising turns of fate wove a tapestry of revelation within my very soul. As I return to them repeatedly, a new message is revealed out of the mysterious action of engaging with a tale, again and again, and listening through the ears of my own heart. Each fable invites me to become a different character in the story. I find myself identifying with these various characters and themes, as I revisit my new fable friends. And then my heart opens up to the fable's message—a direct and particular message to my own soul. Safe in the embrace of a fable, I am inevitably invited to drop the veils between me and the truth of myself. What happens? I see myself as who I am: Profoundly Human and Truly Divinity.

Rochelle Mausteller, *Mother of Kate & Cole, Accountant, Reiki Master, Certified Radiance Master (CRM), Certified Master Teacher of Radiance (CMTR-1), (W)hole Life Coach for individuals & PAIRs, Accredited Facilitator for the Awakening Divinity Apprenticeship, Technical Specialist with Computer Support Services, Inc.(Lewisburg PA), and a Healer of Hearts, Bodies & Souls.*

****

Stories have the power to uncover, celebrate, and transmit transformational learnings. These fables provide wonderful teaching and learning moments that celebrate the complexity and joy of life. For me, they opened new doors of understanding of my potential and (W)holeness.

Micah Fierstein, *Assistant Professor, College of Education, University of Alaska—Anchorage*

****

Refreshing stories, describing a fresh, renewable world, but best of all, usable insights in learning to remount the horse of daily life (that periodically bucks us off!)—all in the delightful voice of Alaya Chadwick, a wise and enthusiastic teacher who, as you read, becomes your friend.

Loren Stell, *Published Poet, Psychoanalyst, Certified Imago Relationship Therapist, M.Div., Masters of Fine Arts in Poetry and Film, Creator of an award winning documentary*

Personal Dedication

This book is dedicated, in particular, to John Richard Chadwick.
You are my husband.
You are my friend.
You are the one who has loved me through it all.
You are the one who has believed in me from the beginning of the fables' birth.
Thank you, dear John Richard…the man who makes everything go at "Sanctuary" and in my heart.
Thank you for asking me, "Tell me about your soul." Here it is…fables that make the (W)hole world go 'round.
I love you so.

P.S. I also dedicate this to "Pop," the first and eldest light brother. I honor you and all the men who have the courage to open your hearts. Your kind and patient presence made a difference to us all. Hey, Pop, thanks for playing catch.

I also dedicate this to "Mum," an inspiration of light and love, who reminds us all that we leave far greater heart imprints on others than we ever realize and that each of us is loved beyond anything we allow ourselves to know or even imagine. You extend an invitation to everyone to let in all the love that surrounds us in every moment.

Dedication

Every word of each of these fables is written for the benefit of self, other, and the world.

Told first from my heart to the kind listening ears of friends, students, and apprentices, these tales have arisen in my mind's eye unbidden, while hungry to be born. In their essence, these stories are the children of my heart's agonies and celebrations—big or small, dramatic or mundane. Truly, LIFE itself is the mother of all that you hold in your hands in the form of this book.

Birthing these tales has awakened within me that which had been lost to me for a long time—a natural joy or I might say, the PLAY of LIFE as me. I believe we are all born to live from this joy and as this joy, being ourselves within it, playing wildly and boldly without restraint as the Creator-Selves we are.

Each fable is unique, just as all children are. Thus, I invite you to encounter and dance with each, as it calls to you, not by following some prescribed or patterned response, but by stepping to your own heart's rhythms. As these tales have been birthed from my blood and bones, my anguish and celebrations, it is my intentional invitation that as you read them, you will be provoked to greater play, longer spells of laughter, and richer tears of pain.

I am honored to be in your presence through these fables, and it is my heart's focus to offer you portals into the grandeur of YOUR reflected magnificence, one story at a time.

Dedicated to the (W)hole of US—you and me...US playing once again.

"When you tell a story, you tell it to all creation. It's cosmic. It never goes away."
Source: "BLUE" from an email note of Story Telling Network, 11/04/09

At the end of the games we played as children,
we would call ourselves back to "home" by singing out:

"All-y, All-y In Come Free"
"Come out, come out wherever you are."

We hide from our own life tales, until we don't.
We hide from our own precious wisdoms, until we don't.
We hide from ourselves, until we don't.

Let these fables call you home to YOU, a precious BEING of LIGHT.

Contents

Dancing Heart & Soul into Life 5

What Others are Saying About This Book 7

Personal Dedication 14

Greetings to you, dear reader. 23

Preface 27

Epic of Play: Meet the StoryTeller, via a fable, of course 29

Dedicated to the small being in each of us who knows our greatest secret—we are all here to play. We all long to play. We are all waiting to be given permission to play. Play is what it is all about.

Ripple's Tale 56

Dedicated to all of us who have chosen to walk within when the outer had demanded, no insisted, that it could no longer be the source of solution for life challenges. Going within, when our inner spaces are so dead that it is nearly hopeless and still, we have chosen to dive into the internal disasters, to find that bit by bit, the rubble is cleared away and there...before us is our (w)Holy Light, never extinguished, just awaiting our embrace.

The Mystery of the Gold Coin 59

Dedicated to all of us who, at one time or another, have been asked to do something we were sure was beyond us, said "Yes" anyway, and then surprised ourselves by accomplishing the impossible for the benefit of the (W)hole World and inadvertently for ourselves. Dedicated to the "small acts of love" that save the world—one at a time.

The Heart of it All: The Twice-Born Weaver 71

Dedicated to all of us who do "whatever it takes" to bring our (w)holie, (W)holly, Holy (W)hole heart to those we encounter throughout our days. Dedicated to the fires we have walked, the dark nights of the soul we have suffered and the courage we each demonstrate when we say "Yes" again to opening our hearts to life, to other, and to self.

The Cloaked Light **81**
Dedicated to the Light Being we all are! May we sweep wide our cloaks until LIGHT BEING is all we know…until BEING LIGHT is all!

ObLAYday, a woman of barren fertility, & her child, Mareeha . **86**
Dedicated to friends. Those friends we know, those we have yet to meet, those we have always had and those who once were. Dedicated to the power of a friend's presence, which in itself changes the (W)hole experience of life, itself.

A Diamond of a Soul **91**
Dedicated to all of us who close our eyes for fear of seeing who we really are. Our (W)hole Selves. Dedicated to those of us who look anyway, risking it all.

The Pink Webbie Shell Home **97**
Dedicated to all of us who have wrapped ourselves up in the wishes, hopes, fantasies, and imaginings of our child-selves so as to bear the ancient agonies of our young lives, only to forget that things change and so do we! Thank you to those who come knocking on our locked minds, our closed hearts and rigid spirits, calling us out of hiding.

The Gift of the Storm **106**
Dedicated to all those of us who feel or have felt trapped by the raging storms of life happening to us, around us, and to those we love. Dedicated to all those who boldly step into the storms again and again searching for a different way. May this fable grant you peace. May this fable open the portals of calm in the face of the storms, within and without.

The Story of Wah-NEE **118**
Dedicated to those of us who walk wide-eyed in the world after fate has demanded that we tear off our blinders in order to live. Dedicated to all of us who are opening our eyes to the new lives we are being called to walk into with open eyes, naked perceptions and bold hearts.

Ceques of the Heart 128
Dedicated to those of us who have hardened our hearts against the agonies of life. Dedicated to those of us who have inadvertently stumbled back home to our selves, only to find a village embracing us in welcome. Dedicated to those of us who thought a hardened heart would save us from heartbreak, only to realize that when our hearts break open, we awake to life itself.

MarNEEya and GherTiid: Blessings of Anguish Revealed 138
Dedicated to our (W)holeness, which is disguised as brokenness. Dedicated to us all—cripples in one form or another. Dedicated to those who tend the "crippled parts" and to those "broken bits and pieces" in us all, who lean heavily upon the others. Dedicated to the power hidden in the weaknesses of being a "human being."

The Awakening of a NOMAD 149
Dedicated to those of us who have felt like "rootless" orphans in the world and in our lives. Dedicated to those of us who have fought against our own natures, only to lose the fight, falling into our own embrace finally. Dedicated to those who ripen into themselves, kicking and screaming along the way, who upon finally arriving home, take their first deep breath.

Shame's Wisdom 160
Dedicated to all of us who have felt "different," set-apart for no reason, only to discover later, much later, that it was this very imagined "flaw" which birthed our true and holy wisdoms. Dedicated to the Mystic of us all. Dedicated to the "different ones" who long to belong, and when they are embraced, reveal themselves to be far more than they ever imagined themselves—leaders for us all.

Wanikiya—Light Mountain That Was 168
Dedicated to those who look where everyone tells them not to. Dedicated to those who dare to step into their own authority as the outer "bosses" and "sources" fall away. Dedicated to those who come when the call goes out to choose a NEW path of (W)hole Life.

Hot Stuff **177**
Dedicated to all of us who have felt lost, alone, and full of despair. Dedicated to all of us who still kept on going, one flicker of hope at a time. Dedicated to all of us who have dared to listen to others rather than to the "scary-blaming-judging" voices inside us, when we were too blinded by terror to hear our own (W)hole Truth.

The Dragon in the Box **185**
Dedicated to the Wondrous Creatures we all are—independent of our current shape or feel. Dedicated to our precious "boxes" which have served for so long and now are crumbling into dust, so we may remember who we really are! This fable is dedicated to all of us who have thought ourselves so small, when in truth we are wondrous beyond all imaginings.

The Gift of the Gazorah's Gaze **191**
Dedicated to all of us who admit to being our own "jailors" and still dare to chance the encounters which reveal the doors to freedom. Dedicated to all that was once considered lethal and is now unveiled as the source of Life. Dedicated to those who choose to gaze directly at Life and thus come alive.

The Stroll of the HoorTeeTah **200**
Dedicated to those who have become so adept at hiding that others don't even notice their absence. Dedicated to the maneuvers we all engage in to keep secret our "badest" secrets in fear that we will be found out and reviled for it. Dedicated to all those who have been called "the bull in the china shop," "the one who always puts their foot in it," or "the ones who seem to step right into the shit." Dedicated to the revealers of truth—purposely or accidently or invisibly. Thank you.

Olli's Echo **206**
Dedicated to all those who "walk first into the mysteries." Dedicated to all those who trusted and roped themselves to those "First Ones." Dedicated to the mysteries of life which call us to engage and dance with them in the daily moments of life's simple complexities.

Wandra, The Forgotten One 215
Dedicated to all those of us who have quested for so long that the beginning has been lost in the mists. Dedicated to all of us, hoping for recognition, who have gathered wisdoms from the far corners of the globe, only to realize that the mission itself has been forgotten. Dedicated to all those who have believed in "self-growth," only to discover it wasn't thc point at all.

Feisty & Nudgy: The Moles Who Came to Love (w)Holes. . . . 220
Dedicated to all of us who have gone towards the anxious dark scary places within only to discover the treasures of our own (W)holeness waiting for us to embrace them. Dedicated to the rebels and radicals of us who pushed the edges and broke through the barriers of fear and presumptions to bring greater life to all the people.

The Land of Gleeful Laughter 239
Dedicated to all Moms and Dads for having hearts big enough to love, despite the naked powerlessness over the fate of one's children. Dedicated to all parents and family who have had a child die. Dedicated to all of us who have suffered the anguish of losing someone we love. Dedicated to all those who, knowing the risks, open to love and life anyway.

The Birth of the People of Light Chapter 1: The Time of Terror 252
Dedicated to our brains which contain within them miracles and magic beyond any known science. Dedicated to our hearts which, when confronted with another's terror, reach out and embrace without regard to cost. Dedicated to all of us who have jumped into burning buildings, leaped into frozen rivers, grabbed a child from the street car's bumper, held the hand of a dying person, cared enough to take a gift to one of the "forgotten," took the time to listen to the tears of a homeless person…this fable is dedicated to us all—the glorious wondrous expression of Life called Humanity.

Greetings to you, dear reader.

I decided to write this book for two reasons—You and Me.

No, actually, for three reasons—You, Me, and Us.

A simple truth is we are a great and intricate fable which is telling itself to itself over and over again—expanding in ever greater spirals of explorations. A simple truth is that each of us is a short story, written over and over again in different colors. A simple truth is YOU are a story of perfection, revealing its own reflections until you gently, simply fall into love with your own authorship. A simple truth is that YOU, dear reader, are the closing words of each of these fables, for it is your response that writes the last words, the endings of each tale. A simple truth is YOU and I are fables of Us happening again and again even in these pages.

For many years, as a therapist, teacher, mentor, author, and coach, I have told fables of my own creation to open portals into heart spaces. Stories do that! They open us up! They reveal us to ourselves, and most of all they invite us to soften into the natural joy of PLAY. Whether we are 95 or 5 years old, the invitation to hear a tale seduces us to set aside our pursuits, to settle into the arms of a comfy chair or lap, and listen—to really listen.

So what is it about stories that carry us off into the realms of creations so believable yet not, so real yet not, so powerfully transforming that upon our "return" we are born again! Is it not that during those moments in which our ears are filled with wonders as yet unlived or encounters so shocking as to awaken more of ourselves, we become wide open to Life's PLAY itself? Is it not that as we settle into our "chair-laps," we become the space between the known and the unknown? Is it not that as our mind's eyes begin to paint the images the words are invoking that we awaken to the Creator-Self we are, if only for a moment?

For in our moments of greatest "fable hearing," all is possible, all is endured and overcome, all is lived without restraint, and all those leaps of wonder are taken without pause or hesitation. Put simply, we come alive as Us—the (W)hole, Holy Wholly wondrous (W)holeness of us.

We begin to remember, "Oh, that is right. We are here to PLAY, to come to know ourselves as Creators beyond imaginings, to live boldly without hesitation, and to use ourselves up on the (W)hole and Wild Playground of Life."

Yes, I wrote this book for us all, and in doing so, I, too, am remembering, "It is all about PLAY!" How could I have forgotten? How much I now celebrate my remembering. I do so love to play!

Fables reveal ourselves to ourselves and in this way are guides and guardians of our transparent (W)holeness, if we allow it.

Agreeing to write fables is a soul choice to surrender to Mystery's blessings. The decision to write a fable is a risky one for me. It requires me to dive deep within, open wide, and embrace the surprises of the fable's unique emergence. To write as I do is to allow myself to be led rather than to lead. The (W)hole truth is that *Alaya's Fables* wrote themselves. I simply held the pen to paper. The fable itself led the way. Fables are songs written by Mystery and are then sung to us so we can hear ourselves. Fables are a very humbling experience for me.

Often my mind will have an idea of "what a particular fable will look like," and then much to my wonder, the tale takes many unexpected twists and turns, bringing me to uncharted inner depths. There has yet to be one of these tales that fails to birth transformative eruptions within my life. It is a "fable inevitability" that alchemical disruptions occur within and around its birth.

Each of these fables I share with you has changed me. Each of these fables has demanded that I ascend into ever more expansive, inclusive expressions of my own (W)holeness. Fables are my own invitations to awaken in ever greater spirals of Being Me. Let me suggest that this same will be true for you, if you so choose to dive into each one, open, and embrace what arises.

Fables are living breathing creations, which have the inherent capacity to reach those walled-off corners and secret hidey (w)holes that straight words alone cannot touch. Fables might be thought of as living spirals that are ever alive and ever changing tales whose tendrils ripen and spread into the being of the listener or reader. These vines of invitation weave themselves into those who are open and bring nourishment to starving soul-parts.

These tales are not only meant to enliven, they are also meant to shake-up our fixed interiors, for you see, fables are soul-gifts which arise from inside out, calling us to soften our gaze and look upon our wondrous selves. It is our judgments, fears, and shames that interrupt any fable's invitation to relax into our own embrace. Judgments of what is "right" or "wrong" or "good" or "bad" are the judgments that cut the life out of a fable and cut us off from the life offered to us by the fable.

Remember, we only judge what we fear. Therefore, here is a gentle suggestion or two about intimacy with fables, which apply also to our close encounters with other humans. If you happen to notice yourself moving into judgment as you are engaging with a fable, may I suggest that you pause? Ask yourself this question, "What in this fable is scary to me, is challenging my heart-routines, is threatening my established fixed knowing?" Then listen. Your wisdom-response will rise from within you, and the fable will lead you onward once again.

When we choose to engage with a fable, we are choosing to enter an intimate relationship with Mystery and with ourselves. Intimacy and intimate revelations cannot be rushed. Thus it is best to digest one fable at a time, over a period of time. Rather than hurry through and miss the (W)hole point of *Alaya's Fables*, let this be a banquet that you feast upon over many days and nights. Let each fable sing its song to you. Savor every note and nuance. Allow visions of its essence to rise from within you, and then sit with them for even more time.

The dance between a fable and its reader is an intimate encounter of heart and soul. Often there are fable surprises that creep up upon us sideways, turning our heart's prisons into gardens. And then there are those fable encounters which take us into the dimly lit places of our secret shames and blames, only to turn a flood light on them, reducing the shadows to mere ashes at our feet. Each fable is uniquely experienced by all.

This short inquiry into the process of encountering a fable is offered to you, the reader, not as a set of rules or "right ways" but rather as a hand extended saying, "Come, experience *Alaya's Fables* as doorways into your own Holy (W)holeness."

Go slow. Read slowly. Savor each one. Be gentle with yourself. Live with its essence. Listen for its notes in daily life. Allow the fables' faces to rise from within as mirrors of your own wanderings. And most of all enjoy their embrace, for beyond all else, these fables are offered to you as my naked-heart offering. Created out of my being, birthed in a labor of love and offered for your inquiry, we truly encounter one another as you are reading. In this way, we become intimates of one another.

Finally, how deeply I hope in the reading of this book that you, too, will embrace the wild sillinesses, the creepy monsters, the strange shapes and awesome wonders of all your creations! And that they come flooding back into your own heart's arms to be celebrated and elevated for their simple truths and profound wisdoms. May this book's tales serve to highlight the glory and the power of us all to create a (W)hole new world.

The (W)hole truth? We are ONE—always have been and always will be. May these fables introduce you to the "ever more of you" as they have for me.

Meet you on the "Playground."

Blessings,
Alaya

Preface

I am the sole author of these fables. They have been inspired through my own experiences over the course of thirty-plus years and 67,000 hours (or so) of listening to myself and others. I practice the arts of teaching, writing, coaching, and mentoring—all in many and varied forms. I have two masters' degrees (M.S.W., M.Div.). I have birthed this book as an expert of my own journey and with a bit of understanding of what it takes to awaken to the (W)hole point of one's life.

As you wonder and wander through these fables, it is my invitation that you notice that there is a thread that weaves subtly and sometimes not so subtly between and within all of them. It is the Wisdom WAY. The Wisdom WAY uses the word play of (w)holes/holes. I believe that any of the dark and scary tales we have walked ourselves into are also at the same time a step along The Wisdom WAY, or I could say, the gathering up of all the wisdoms and experiences that make for a chapter of Us. I believe that each of us is an expression of LIFE being light, revealing itself in the joy of creation. Thus, each of these fables is offered as an invitation to you to explore an element of your own story from a viewpoint that surprises and informs.

May these tales touch your heart. May they bring insights and awarenesses to you when you least expect them and are thus wide open. These fables are meant to be read and re-read, for their depth will reveal itself only as you befriend them with your entire self. They will take you to the greatest of heights and the dimmest corners of the darkest (w)holes. Truly any terrain can only be appreciated by repeated visits—this is also true of stories. They are living beings inviting you to be in an activated intimate relationship with them so as to unveil you to them and them to you.

This book is offered in service to the (W)hole world and to the individual expressions of LIFE called YOU and ME and US.

May the Radiance of transformation and awakening embedded in these fables ripple around the globe. May they bring celebration and elevation to all souls whose eyes glide across these shapes called words.

Thank you for offering me the portal invitation to share my fables with your "wide open ears and hearts."

With great gratitude and love,
Alaya

Epic of Play: Meet the StoryTeller, via a fable, of course

Dedicated to the small being in each of us who knows our greatest secret—we are all here to play. We all long to play. We are all waiting to be given permission to play. Play is what it is all about.

And what is play? It is BEING (W)hole in each moment—experiencing, feeling, acting, and being oneself without judgment, just as a child plays on the playground, flowing with simple joy and pleasure of being alive.

This is a fable of birth, death, and aliveness. Written on behalf of the small being in all of us who is born playing, this fable is for you, dear little being in us all! The little ONE we each are is simply Being Itself until someone or something begins to instruct us to stop playing and start working at living. And then, of course, those of us who choose go on a "quest" to "find oneself again

I call this "My Play Epic" because it was inspired by a request made to me to "tell my own life story starting before my spiritual journey began." It became this fable in which I wrote about myself to myself until I remembered myself and thus work to the blessing of PLAY itself.

This is a tale with an invitation to you, the reader, to wake up and play once again without apology or goal, without pressure or paralysis, without shame or blame. The simple truth is that playing is being yourself in all moments, without self-witness or judgment or effort. My blessing: May you play well today and in every moment of your life.

Play is a fractal of all my life moments—the loss of Play and its re-emergence as my grandest expression.

Perhaps this journey's description may strike the reader who is familiar with the details of my life story as distorted, for in truth my life has been quite wondrous and rich in opportunities; however, it has also been a dark journey. And it is truth to say that my journey's darkness has established my heart's authority as healer and spiritual companion for those in their own dark moments. It is not my dual degrees (M.Div., M.S.W.) that touch hearts and re-call Souls to their true wonder. It is my own journey's wisdom that infuses my work with a passionate potency of Wisdom and Grace. Put simply—I am not afraid of the dark. I have spent many moments in its cold embrace. I am in full recognition that it is my Soul's Presence that enfolds me in the Blessedness of GRACE, itself. Grace is not earned; it simply is.

Rather than simply "tell my story" which is something I have done many times for the sake of facts, analysis and spiritual maturation, etc., I am taking this opportunity to reflect upon my life as a fall from Innocent Play into the Darkness of Serious Living and finally a re-emergence into the EnLightenment of Playing without apology. The events of my life are far less significant to me at this time in my life than the wisdoms and the moments of grace that have brought me to my own authentic joy-filled present moments.

May this telling of my journey touch you, as it has touched me.

May your play be filled with the Wisdoms and the Grace of these "No Rule Rules" that are now foundational in my own life and work—both of which I now call PLAYING.

There is no way to fail.
Be curious without judgment.
I am my own expert and so are you.
Be gentle with myself—I am the only one of ME in all of existence and this is true of you, too.
All questions are welcome.
All answers are "right."
I get to change my mind and decide again.
I am loved for no reason and for every reason.
Relax and Play—this is the (W)hole Point to being alive as Soul Walking.

Chapter 1:

I was born Elizabeth, called Betsy.

I was born to play.

I was born playing.

Mom loved to play. She taught us to play. Daddy loved to play. He taught me to believe in Play as powerful and wonderful.

I learned that what I imagined was real and good and fun! I learned that I could wipe the white board clean and draw something more on it—it was whatever I imagined. Playing was REAL LIFE.

Real Life was all about Playing.

I loved my birthday in which everything was made blue with food coloring. I chased our pet rabbit, who wore red and white striped diapers, all over the house. I built sand castles and moats in our huge sand box, built by my Daddy under a corner of our house. I rode my bike very fast down big hills. I created huts in the bushes and knew beyond any doubt that they were homes and fortresses and ritual temples. I made the frost and ice of the freezer all the colors of the rainbow using food coloring when we thawed it out each month. I skipped rope with wild abandonment while singing at the top of my lungs.

I waded in the cold waters of Rock Creek Park near my home in Washington, DC. I put small pebbles in the stone wall near our home—sure that the fairies would get the messages attached to them. I played on the jungle gym of our school. I walked to and from school each day. I laughed with the teachers, all of whom knew us all in the small elementary school. I skipped and danced and sang and laughed. This was what greeted me at the beginning of each day.

I PLAYED! Wildly, confidently and boldly.

Play was not something separate from who I was—Play was my way of BEING.

I didn't know then that playing is a sacred act or that it is the ecstatic expression of life force. I just Played!

Since that time I have come to believe that PLAYing (***People Loving/ Laughing/Living Awake*** *saying* ***"YES"*****—P.L.A.Y.**) and the capacity to play consciously, is the (W)hole Point of being alive.

Yes, Soul walking awake on this earth in Human Form, playing, is the point!

I was born to play. I was born playing and THEN…

SURPRISE! AND SHOCK!

Chapter 2:

I lost my Play.

My father had chosen to end his life. I was 8.

However, my playing still continued until I was 11 ¾ years old. Playing boldly was his legacy to me. Even as he had chosen to die, I had learned to play from him! I kept Playing until I was 11 ¾ years old. Then I forgot to play.

Mom re-married.

Then in the middle of 6th grade, we moved. I didn't get to participate in the May Pole Dance, the graduation ceremony for all the 6th graders.

I lost out on Playing. I was 11 ¾ yrs old and suddenly life became serious and dark and scary.

I learned that people, places, hopes and dreams can be taken in a blink of an eye. Yes, life was serious business.

I lost my playmates, who played with me and who played like me. I lost those who loved to play!

I forgot that there was not any way to fail when we are playing. I forgot that there was any way to love myself or take delight in being me. I forgot to be gentle with me. I forgot that I was lovable for no reason and for every reason.

I forgot how to Play.

Chapter 3:

I learned that judgment freezes moments into ice sculptures of shame and blame. I learned to take everything very seriously because there was no room to not know. I discovered aloneness and isolation.

I learned that it is challenging to play ONLY alone, to never have others to play with you. I learned that questions were really traps to show everyone else how "stupid" you were.

I learned that I was a misfit—too young to know how to kiss in the halls, too country-like to own high heels to wear to the 6th grade dance, too slow to fit into the flirtatious competitions between the boys and girls.

I learned that my classmates weren't playmates; they were boys or girls. I learned that I hated history because I couldn't memorize all the Indian Tribe names. I learned to beg "God" to save me and take me back home to my playmates—only to lose hope that I deserved "God's" assistance. I learned that "God" didn't answer that sort of "prayer." I learned to TRY, TRY and TRY to be good enough to be allowed to "go home." I learned that growing up hurt a lot. I learned that life was all about surviving the next encounter. I learned that life was all about desperate efforting.

I learned to be afraid that my Mom might be taken from me too…so I worked doubly hard to be very, very good.

I learned that what mattered was pleasing the "They/She/He's" of my world. ("They/She/He" is a term from my book which refers to the "big people" in our lives, as children and as adults. It is a copyrighted term for use in a particular manner in The (W)hole Point Wisdom WAY model of empowerment.) I learned that "They/She/He" was the source of love, support and encouragement.

Play was now from the outside in—allowed with permission and restricted to "only that much" aliveness.

Play had become something outside of living, save for those rare vacation moments when my aliveness would rise to the surface for just a moment or two and I would find myself playing, accidentally.

I would water ski and laugh right out loud with the sea gulls. I would dance in gym class and so enjoy it BUT not show too much or "go for it" too boldly.

I learned to live in the range of "Not too much-ness:" Alive enough but not too alive, playing enough to sustain my soul, but not too wildly, smiling enough to please "They/She/He" but not so much to threaten.

I learned that "Not too much" meant never showing all of me at one time.

I learned to "play the system" so my grades were pleasing, my appearance fit in, and the administrators of my world were happy. I learned to keep them all "happy." I learned how to pass tests so I could go on to the next serious bit of life. I learned and learned, studied and studied, passed test after test until I graduated.

I was seriously determined to make no mistakes, to succeed in every moment and to never, ever be caught off-guard again. I knew what could happen suddenly and unexpectedly.

I graduated to the next level of SERIOUSNESS.

I got to go to work.

I re-named myself: "Employable."

Chapter 4:

I began to work. I liked my first "real" work. I worked hard. I found I was playing some too inside these moments called work.

I learned something about this experience called WORK. I began to believe that if I liked what I did for work that it might feel something close to play.

THEN…

I played more and worked less while accomplishing more. I began to see that the people with whom I worked were my "adult playmates." I began to relax and enjoy this thing called work.

I saw that what I was doing was making a difference to folks. I felt my presence open other's hearts to their own wonder—a bit at a time. I liked being me more and more. I began to maybe play a bit. Then more. Then even more.

I opened my heart. I trusted myself to Play.

THEN...I trusted someone with a truth of mine in a moment of vulnerability and was betrayed.

SURPRISE!
SHOCK!
SILENCE!
STUNNED!
SHUNNED!

Playing was over. Life was serious again. Deadly serious.

They/She/He said I had failed, that I was wrong. I was bad. I learned to remember this. I didn't think I was bad. I had meant no harm.

BUT...

They/She/He was the author of my world. I submitted to their naming of me.

I shut down—never to be THAT wide open again! I learned to not relax into the play—never, ever again.

I felt the power of shame. I felt the shunning force of blame. I felt the horror of being judged without the possibility of forgiveness. I submitted to their expertise over me. They/She/He knew best and knew me best.

I felt the aloneness of failure.
I shut off.
I hid.

Chapter 5:

I left my "everyday world" to travel. I went alone. I let my body be physical and sweat. I was alone and quiet.

Gradually, someone inside of me began to breathe again. That someone gently began to consider life again. Slowly, the shock subsided, and the silence within gave way to a quiet soul-song.

Yes, I was still alive. A miracle.

I gradually softened enough to remember my laugh. I learned to lighten up a bit. I learned to learn without too much terror. I learned to try again, even when They/She/He said I had made a mistake, *again!*

I remembered how to have some fun…after all, this was a "vacation" and a "retreat" from "Real Life." I could relax a bit…what I was doing really didn't matter…after all, it wasn't "Real Work."

I recovered some balance. I recalled some hope. I renamed myself: "Starting Again."

I took the job offered. Again…I stepped forward. I re-named myself: "Employee-manager in training."

Chapter 6:

The only woman-child—surrounded by old-men—in a cold plastic office suite, each at their own desk. No pig-tails protruded from my head, yet my heart was young and overwhelmed by the rules of the "Grown up world." Those rules that everyone else seemed to know that seemed so deadly serious and so empty of joy. I learned that following the rules of the "Real World" really mattered.

I learned to dress for success. I learned to use my woman-self in my selling of the serious toys of the company to male customers. I learned to flirt when I didn't feel flirtatious. I learned to act like I cared about how the profit lines moved. I learned to smile and nod even when what the management advised made no sense. I learned to present the material to make a point. I learned to play the part of a National Sales Executive.

I wondered, "Is this all there is?" No answer came.

I learned that I had "made the BIG sale" and They/She/He was thrilled. I felt nothing as they danced and ate in celebration for the "victory in the market competition game."

I quit.

There was no real play to be found here, for me at least.

I wondered, "What is wrong with me?" I began my quest for what needed to be fixed. I renamed myself "Student of Spiritual and Questor of Wisdom."

Chapter 7:

I began to study the wisdom of those gone before. I read books that were fat with dust and grace-filled offerings. I read books that left me starving for something I didn't have the name for. "What is missing?" I read books that were skinny in form, yet fat with comfort and nourishment. "I wasn't so different." I read books that left me confused and despairing. "If this is where the answers lay, I was a hopeless case." I read books that encouraged me to read other books. "Where is THE answer?"

I walked the halls of hospitals, listening to the cries and longings of patients and families alike. I had no answers. I sat at bedsides of the dying and the borning. I had no answers. I held the hands of frightened parents as we sat with the sick children. I had no answers. I laughed with the new mothers and fathers as they held their newborns. I had no answers.

I sat with my professor, a woman of grace-filled wisdom. She said, "Study well while you are here. Then forget it all and love those who come to you." Her words sunk into me. A wisdom seed was placed within my heart.

Know this…Real Life Love is what the heart cries out for—not concepts, but presence, not ideas, but hope, not roles to play by, but room to play within.

I learned that it was the people who touched me and whom I touched.

AHH!

People matter.

I learned that above the facts, the events, the bottom lines, the histories and the fantasies…it is the people that matter.

I named myself "Student—again!" Student of the grace of Human BEingness, again I learned and studied.

Chapter 8:

I learned that we are all Human Beings.

I learned that we are all doing the best we can with what we understand.

I learned that some of us understand more than others. I learned that confusion isn't a bad thing. I learned that questions are precious doorways into hope. I learned that word-hugs work better than blame. I learned that appreciations work better than shame. I learned that there is no one way to be.

I began to play around with the ways to touch a heart and heal a soul.

I began to play around with pictures and toys as tools of healing.
I began to play around with stories as portals of possibility.
I began to play around with how to reach into dark soul nights and turn on the night light.
I began to play around with these precious playmates called "clients."
I began to play around with the gift of each moment of inquiry.
I began to play around in my inside world of brokenness.

I found a Playground Coach and teacher. She wasn't afraid of me.

Surprise!
Shock!
Suspense!
Shared it all with her!

Pause…Surrender!

I dared for her to help me remember…all the while fearing her blindness to my true quest.

I opened to the possibility of "Serious Play"—all the while doubting and fearfully hopeful.

I learned that my old stories were forming all my next days. "Play isn't allowed for all these reasons." So I didn't play.

I learned that one can know one's story and still choose a new way.
Could I?
Would I?

Maybe.

I found playmates in this new Playground of studenting.
We sang.
We gathered to eat together and talk and debate and share.
We laughed and almost played.

I was opening again…to the maybes of the Old-New way of Playing.

SURPRISE!
SHOCK!
STUNNED!
SHUT DOWN!

Others, friends I thought for sure were friends and a therapist I trusted for sure, suddenly both gone. WHY? I had no answers. None offered. None received.

Like Daddy who left,
Like Bosses who cut off,
Like Mother who chose "the man,"
Like Father who was the Boss,
Like Friends who suddenly leave,
Like Therapists who nearly die and betray…

What does one trust?
To whom does one turn?
How does one soften in the face of these most assuredly, most seriously, most inevitably scary shocking moments?

The Rule, once again:
Do not Play! Do not open! Do not love! Do not dare!

Life touches us most deeply in play; there is the place of deepest pain and deepest joy…found in the same place.

I learned to not play.

I learned it is play to love another, tend to them and reach for the stars on their behalf.

I learned to be serious about any play I risked. "After all, Play is too naked if it isn't taken seriously."

I renamed myself again: Therapist—healer—therapoi—helper.

Chapter 9:

The Tide turned.

It is a mystery exactly how this turning happened from Ebb to Flow, but it did.

Work became a joy.
Work became nourishing.

I learned to play as a way to heal.
I learned to play with cartoons and toys as a way to touch the hidden, secret wounds of those self-named as "clients."

I learned to play with wild, gentle, bold curiosity.
I learned to play in the unknowns of the subterranean arenas of histories forgotten…empowering the secret keepers to give up their treasures and once again set their prisoners free.

I learned to play in the face of the darkest horrors.
I learned to play in the presence of the opposites of love and fear.
I learned to dance in the betweens of hope and despair.

I learned to play on their behalf.
I learned to play FOR them.
Play was OK if it had a purpose.

Helping and healing was a grand and glorious purpose.
Here I could play.
Here I would play.
Here I should play—after all, it worked miracles.

I learned from those who came to me for wisdom and who left me with a wiser heart for their presence.

I learned that I didn't know how to play for myself.

I learned that I had lost my play.

I celebrated my intensity and persistent serious focus.
I celebrated all those I touched.
I celebrated their victories and healings.
I celebrated how their lives were changed.
I celebrated that I could be with them as they awoke.
I could celebrate for them. This was easy.

I didn't play…
I couldn't play…
I wouldn't dare to play…
I shouldn't play…on my own behalf.

I didn't relax my vigilance.
I couldn't soften towards my own self.
I knew…I had learned…Real Life was serious for me.
I saw my loss.
I settled for less.
Sigh.

I renamed myself: "The Single One who ought to be married."

Chapter 10:

I talked myself into falling in love.

A marriage ceremony celebrated. Filled with hope, I said, "Yes, I do."

I re-named myself again: "New Wife on her honeymoon."

Wide open.
Big Play.
Hope sprung alive.
Loving without restraint.

"Oh…this is what love-being-made is all about!"

Two days of marital bliss…then!

SURPRISE!
SHOCK!
TRAUMA!
TERROR!

Numb.
Alone.
Shame.
Blame.
Horror.
Terrified beyond words.
Mute.
Frozen in time.

"How could it be that love could make him psychotic?"
But it did.

Trying.
Clawing in the dark.
Drowning in the quicksand of therapies failing.

He has betrayed my trust with another!
"How could this be dumped on top of the horror in which I am already swimming?"

Finally, I said, "No more."

One year married…then…A fiercely Divorced woman.

I re-named myself once again: Determinedly Single.

Chapter 11:

Thriving, as I played for them called "clients."

Surviving, as a lover on behalf of other's right to play.

Abiding, as a failure of life's greatest commitment.

I hung my head in shame for me while standing tall as "healer of those over there."

Still through it all I journeyed into my darkest realms with my Guide, my Mentor and my Soul-Mother.

Still through Chapters 7 to this moment's chapter and beyond…

I named myself spelunker of the caves of hell and heaven…I would rope myself in with clips of curiosity and lines of spacious gentleness…and still my Guide urged me forward, ever deeper into the frozen eruptions of my oldest stories.

I plunged into the depths with all due seriousness of one who is exploring for her very life.

I learned to look even as I wished to turn away.
I learned to feel even as I longed to shut down.
I learned to admit my truths even as I tried to lie.
I learned to stand even as I felt myself collapsing.
I learned to stay in the dark until the light came on.

I learned that I had been wandering—an orphan, ever since I lost play.

I learned that home is where one plays with abandon.

I learned that play without apology is life happening in all its splendor.

I learned all this in concept.

I waited.

What would I re-name myself to be?

Who was the doorway into my Soul's awakening?

Chapter 12:

I met a man.

I feared to fall in love.

He asked me, "Would you marry me? Would you be my best friend? For life?"

I said, "Are you kidding?"

I risked admitting I was in love, again.

Later, I said, "YES."

What else could I do? There was nothing more for me to learn from outside looking in. It was now the time to learn about love and life and play from the inside looking out.

I re-named myself again: Re-married.

Chapter 13:

We moved to a strange land.

It was a serious move.

I learned to move, to pack and unpack.
I learned to build a business from the ground floor up in a state in which I knew no one.

I learned to work harder and take it all very seriously.
I learned to push and strive and shove my way forward.
I learned to fight well with the man I loved and lived with.
I learned to lead a group of women into co-creating a radically powerful healing practice in rural USA.

I softened, a bit.
I opened to some friendships.
I gentled enough to be initiated into Reiki.

I grieved as my Mom suddenly died.
I grieved as my Step-Dad slowly died.
I let go of my childhood, as there were no more parents to turn towards.

I trembled in the face of my nakedness in the world. One of the "Silent Orphans" (a term I use for those without living parents), I shook secretly. "Who would save me from life now?"

No one.

My husband-man stood by as I ripened into myself a bit at a time—still very serious about it all.

Little play allowed, by me alone.

I knew from long experience that life was meant to be seriously tended.

Success upon Success.

I learned that it was the people that mattered in life, not the things nor the degrees nor the businesses.

I learned that daring to feel deeply with who were around me called forth ALL of me.

I learned that I feared to be THAT close.

I learned I lived awaiting the next SURPRISE/SHOCK/TRAUMA/HORROR.

I learned that waiting for THAT meant playing was impossible.

I learned that I waited by hardening my heart and closing up my moments with pre-designed results.

I learned that I feared the They/She/He's and all their judgments.

I learned that this fear still drove me from the Precious Playground and imprisoned me in the Serious Work House of being "adult."

This, despite what the world saw on the outside, was the truth of my inner viewscape.

Still he loved me.
What a wonder!?!
How could this be?
To be loved for me?!

Yes—he just stood and said yes by every deed and every breath.

"Yes, I love you," he whispered on the wind of his very breath.
I began to believe him.

AND…

Still the play was lost to me…UNTIL…it seemed for forever it had been.

And I re-named myself again: Apprentice of this new teacher-man.

Perhaps he would show me the way?!

Chapter 14:

I learned his teachings.

I studied diligently.
I began to understand life in a new way.
I felt myself coming alive from inside out.
I hoped.
I dreamed again.
I dared to risk my full, no, nearly fully opened heart.
I shared with others what I was hearing.
They, too, became excited.
There was the BIG HOPE that it was all done.

The DAY of Recognition—it was to be the end of all that was known and all that was foretold.

And then it wasn't. Lied to. Tricked. Blamed and Shamed. Shattered.

SURPRISE!
SHOCK!
SHUNNED!
LOST!
ADRIFT.

I re-named myself:: Nomad, adrift from all the Known.

Chapter 15:

I looked around for home.

I walked onto a piece of property.

It called me. The Land sang, *"All-y, All-y In Come Free, come home to BE! Come home and Play!"*

WE said YES.

I was terrified and could do nothing but move.

We moved.

We called it SANCTUARY.

We built a space-place for transformation, renewal and healing.

Maybe I could open my heart to the property—this was possible.

LAND wouldn't hurt me.

Maybe?

I fell in love with this Land.

And I began to PLAY.

Me and the Land, the earth and the grasses and the creatures…we played. And Played and Played and Played.

There was no danger here!

Then there grew a whisper of maybe's inside of me…Maybe I could include others in this Play?

I would create so that they, too, could see and feel the embrace of this earth.

And so I did…in my Orange Suit I carried rocks, I dreamed up shapes and spaces.

I named them by my authority as Play Master:
Radiance Garden
Mole Moment
Transformation Swamp
Suzie's Place
Turtle Rock
Bud
Claudia's Seat
Curlie Q Paths

JohnR's Way
The No Name Path
Bunny Stop
Anne's Place
Incus' Crossing
Janice's Angel Place
Radiance Pond
Pause N' Ponder

And so forth and so forth and so forth...the creations spilled forth from me and out upon the Land that received them without restraint.

I was playing—wildly and for no reason.

Just for the FUN of it.

No effort. No fear. No reasons. Just Playing!

And then it began to happen...the whisper from within:

> *All-y, All-y In come Free come home—all parts inside of me—come home to BE!*

Then, in a gentle cascade of moments...I began to play fully as I had so long ago.

I was home again.

I can't say when exactly this occurred...it is the mystery at Play, as me.

All this has been the mystery of Play, revealed as me, forgetting and then remembering:

> Yes—Play and Play and Play—it is the (W)hole Holy Point of Being.

I re-named myself once more: Creator Self

Chapter 16:

As I have lived here on this Land, I have transformed.

I have been renewed in my Playing self.

I am healing and awakening to ME—all of me.

I am Creator Self awakening now.
Is this not what Play is?

Creator Self awake playing as bits and pieces and parts for the fun of it and then for the joy and pleasure of it—remembering, "Oh, that is right—WE ARE (W)holeness awakening to itself!"

From the dirt of this land and the Green Things on this earth, I have forged a place of mysteries revealed and concealed and revealed at ever deepening vibrations.

A place called Wisdom Grace Mystery "school…"
a space-place where mysteries are revealed and invoked from within to without and from above so that they are below.

I have learned that one cannot truly live, afraid of what will be.
I have learned that one cannot truly play, afraid of mistakes.
I have learned that one cannot relax, avoiding judgments from self or other.

SURPRISE!
SHOCK!

Became just experiences woven between moments of

GENTLENESS
EASE
PEACE

Until all moments became woven into the tapestry of Play forgotten and Play remembered.

I stopped running from life happening!
I stopped running from life encountered!
I stopped running from the surprise called LIFE!
I stopped running and turned once again.

I re-created myself this time as TRUTH of the (W)hole of ME.

I re-named myself once again.

I Am Alaya.

Chapter 17:

Alaya—*the name I wore before my mothers were born.*
Alaya—*a state of BEINGness without apology.*
Alaya—*my self at play since the beginning of time.*

So, I have picked up my wand of creatorship, and out of wild play I have waved my "wand" in the air, following the patterns and the etchings of my heart and soul.

From all of this journey to date, I have birthed a Sanctuary for myself and others.

After all, isn't this the home I have been running towards for all time, since I lost play?

After all, isn't this the hope-made-manifest that I have longed for?
A space and a place safe in which it is safe to play!

A Sanctuary—a Holy of Holies—a space and a place in which PLAY is the heart of it all.

I know now I was born to play.
I know now I was born playing.
I know now I forgot how to play.

I know now that I fled from life—in terror of playing and its vulnerable Soul—to the enclosure of Seriousness and all it's pseudo-safety.

I know now that it was only when I turned—submitting to my own journey of return—that it happened.

I know now, I am learning once again that The (W)hole Point is to play.

To play Boldly, Wildly, without restraint is what life keeps calling us to say YES to, over and over again.

And so it is…that I began to Play and to Create and to Celebrate my own hands and feet as those of The Creator-Self.

Now I look around me here at Sanctuary, and what I see is this: A three dimensional living sculpture of my own journey from my birth to my forgetting to my remembering the (W)hole Point of life: To engage in all the glory that Play-filled Living offers.

Despite all the They/She/He's and all the "shoulds" and "oughts" and "ought-nots," this Landscape I named Sanctuary is my great revelatory mirror of my own on-going journey.

Yes, I have remembered how to play.

I re-name myself once again: Play, Awake as itself

Chapter 18:

It is so simple, and yet in my forgetting, I had made it so complex.

To play is simple:
Decide what IS to be created
Be the Creator of the creation—without hesitation—pick up your wand.

THEN...

Hold nothing back of your (W)hole Self from participation in the creating—wave the Wand

THEN...

Surprise! There it is before you, created from "thin air" by the power of PLAY itself.

To play is not simple because it calls us to risk the Direct Experience of each moment, over and over and over again.

I have come to feel that Life embraced each moment is EnLightened Playing.

This is what I have come to know from my journey to date.

And once again I re-name myself: A response in each moment, again and again, free fall, Wisdom Grace (w)Holy Space Place.

Chapter 19:

What is Play? Playing…

is to honor all of life.
is to embrace all that is felt and feel all of it.
is to soften in the face of even the biggest surprises.
is to engage with all of yourself in response to each moment's offering.
is to laugh with the surprises—no matter how dark they may seem.

Playing is Knowing more surprises are coming and coming and coming.

Playing is staying wide open to life.

To Play is to be ***Presence Loving All-that-is*** *saying* ***YES, YES, YES***!

To be playing is to be abiding in full presence, in the direct experience of this moment, again and again.

To play is to admit to ones' own creatorship—boldly without shame or apology.

To play is to be a presence that opens the doorway for others to their remembering.

To be the Presence of PLAY is to fling the portals of possibilities wide open and say, "Yes, let's pick up our wand of creator-ship and show ourselves the power of our own Soul Self walking here on earth!"

I re-name myself once again: A response of HERE I AM.

Chapter 20:

How did I play here at Sanctuary?

I created within my holy SELF a space-place that would invite the imagination and creator-SELF of all visitors to awaken.

I saw it in my mind's eye.
I knew it to be so.
I offered my hands and feet to the creation energy and its loving flow.

Thus it is before me now.

There are paths with gnomes and elves.
There are places to pause and ponder upon what IS before us.
There are moments to share with the moles and the owls.

There is a place created by a woman who had named herself "Nothing."

There is a swamp named Transformation, as it is the original soup from which we all have come.

Here and there are turtles who in their own good time ripen and arrive home—able to play.

Ripening is something we are all doing—no matter how it may feel.

There is a great labyrinth made up of stones from places around the globe and from my Soul's journey. A labyrinth baptized on 9/11 by strangers and family. Here there are multi-colored strips of cloth named "Prayer Flags" that visitors place upon the central axis—knowing the real magic of trust.

There is a Gate of Grace offered to the Land by strangers. It continues to hold its vibratory doorway open for all who visit the Land of Sanctuary. A doorway into dimensions as yet unexplored.

There is a "Water Falls" which spills and trickles depending upon the year-time one visits its huge boulders. Some say this is from the time of Atlantis. Who is to say otherwise?

There is a point called Inspiration, which offers an up-close and personal view of a damn built by Beavers who conquered the lands all around. A place where the sky is huge and the sounds are a cacophony of birds, bees, squirrels and chipmunks—singing to the heavens of the glory of play in all its forms.

There is a Stone Medicine circle—blessed and honored by ancestors and living alike. A mere pile of garbage, removed and thus revealing the invitation that stones arranged in the pattern of the spheres offer to those who enter its embrace. This circle place is where a huge tree struck by lightening still offers shade under its green boughs.

It is here that I came to remember how to Play.

Everything I see is a bit of me reflected in nature's forms. The Trees, the Grasses, the Paths and Spaces—all of them reflections of my journey back to my own play-filled self.

It is here that I have remembered how to Create, for isn't EnLightened Play creation at its finest?

Chapter 21:

Here, at "Sanctuary," my Playground, I have come home to Being ME, without apology.

Here, at "Sanctuary," I have birthed the Universal Story—the Story of Hope and the (W)hole Point Wisdom WAY map, method and means. All that I have come to see as the skeletal framework within healing and transformation, revealed by the analogy of "a hole," happened here at Sanctuary. My greatest play, my greatest work, my greatest miracle—found in my return to and through my original activity: PLAY.

Here, I have birthed my authorship, a book and a love of creating tales that transform.

First the book that revealed the essentials of The Universal Story: **Wake up to your (W)hole Life**

Now, the birthing: **Alaya's Fables—Tales that Awaken and Transform.**

Here, I have birthed The Wisdom Grace Mystery "school."

Here, I have formed and shaped an Apprentice Radiance Teaching Program for the Works of ART that we all are.

Here, I have opened a space for folks to show themselves their own wonderful creator-selves, each celebrated in all their glory by a community of Radiant Pulsating Beings of Light, gathered around the medicine circle in dancing, drumming rituals for all to see.

Play no longer hidden.
Play playing bolding in wild delight.
Play in community of service and light.

Sanctuary in action…I have come home to myself.

A Conclusion of my journey to date:

Here, now, I surprise myself with the depth of what I am, who I am, and how I come to each moment.

The other day, someone said to me "You sure do know how to play!" "Yes," I replied, "Would you like to learn? It is what I teach now, you know."

And so it is that I began my life Playing from inside out…and now midway in life, I am living from the inside out by Playing Boldly Lightly and without apology…Just for the fun of it.

My life journey to this moment is this:

I was born to Play.

I forgot to Play. I lived from the outside in—seriously.

I have remembered to Play by teaching myself and others the preciousness of Play itself.

I am Playing now, as I was born to do.

Now, I can say…all this just for the fun of it!

And for now this is my Journey, offered in play and light-hearted wisdom.

Ripple's Tale

Dedicated to all of us who have chosen to walk within when the outer had demanded, no insisted, that it could no longer be the source of solution for life challenges. Going within, when our inner spaces are so dead that it is nearly hopeless and still, we have chosen to dive into the internal disasters, to find that bit by bit, the rubble is cleared away and there...before us is our (w)Holy Light, never extinguished, just awaiting our embrace.

Once there was a woman who came to walk the spiral paths. There had been a disaster.

In the world now, she chose to go within. She walked as the dead, her inner landscape a dusty desert, barren of greenness. The Truth? There was nowhere else to run to, nowhere else to turn to but inside.

She walked the rings 'round and 'round, going deeper and deeper towards that space of void found only in the inner spaces. At times she found herself falling to her knees and weeping, for no particular reason and for all the reasons that burdened her soul, mind and heart. Then, after a time of pause, she would press herself up to her feet once again and begin the walk of 'round the rings, beginning where she had left off. It could have been that she chose to walk away from this most perilous pilgrimage, but no...she chose and chose again to dive deeper into her inner secrets, revealing ever more of herself.

Sometimes horrifying, sometimes delicious and all that is between, these revelations kept occurring as veil after veil was brushed aside with each step she chose to take.

Then she would fall once again, sometimes to her very belly, face in the dirt and leaves, only to rise again after a time, more present than the moment before. Again her feet walking her 'round the rings and ripples of her own soul's calling.

Sometimes, she could hear the screams and ragings of her orphaned aspects, shards of her heart, which had shattered so long ago. Sometimes, she could taste the loneliness and anguish of her abandoned bits and pieces of her heart's feelings. Sometimes, she could smell the horror that had caused her to flee from her own self. Sometimes, she knew all this and more, all at the same time.

One day, she came to the center, to the void. Here in the void, within the heart, she heard nothing. It was the silence of (W)holeness flowing as Grace does when it is given space to find it's WAY. She remained here for an eternity and a moment of NOW…and then…knowing it was not the point to remain in this internal eternal stillness…she rose and began to walk her (w)Holy (W)holeness outward into the world from which she had come.

'Round the rings and 'round the spirals, ever expanding, she stepped, one step at a time, choosing to embody more and more of the Wisdom of the Ages found only from within.

And she would come to a point along the spiral rings where another had fallen to their knees, and she would kneel with them, saying nothing, offering comfort only through her presence. Then, at the time of perfection, she would rise and continue to walk without, while the other would continue the walk within.

And so it was…the dance of heart and soul, the pulsation of within-without, the expansion and contraction of Life itself, the song sung between the steps of souls, some moving within and some moving without…the dance became a symphony of notes, a tapestry of experiences and a golden river of harmony.

Until she heard the (w)HOLY song of the heavens being sung as her and them and me and you and us and I and we and all.

As she stepped out of the Rings of the Spiral, the (W)hole World changed, for she, as each of us are called to do, had chosen to fall in love with our precious messy human holy selves, and in this "WAY of Wisdom" all the many of the world become ONE BEING.

She had come to walk the "Rings of Radiance" and left as a "Ripple of Radiance," transforming each space she entered, each soul she touched. And most precious of all, she had returned to life.

The Mystery of the Gold Coin

Dedicated to all of us who, at one time or another, have been asked to do something we were sure was beyond us, said "Yes" anyway, and then surprised ourselves by accomplishing the impossible for the benefit of the (W)hole World and inadvertently for ourselves. Dedicated to the "small acts of love" that save the world—one at a time.

Once in a time, a long time ago and is still true today, there was a young girl. She lived in a small village high in the mountains. Her name was Dia (dee-ah).

The village was filled with love and laughter and community. Everyone cared for everyone else. Generosity was the foundation of their way of life. In fact, their generosity was something the village was known for around the (W)hole world.

All the folks of the village loved Dia, and in turn, she loved them as only a pure-hearted person can love. In fact, Dia was considered the "most" generous-hearted in all the village, though this was not discussed openly for fear of it "going to her head."

One day a plague swept through the village like wild fire. Everyone fell ill except for Dia. The healers in the village were unable to find a cure, and the folks of the village began to sicken unto death. For some unknown reason, Dia was not stricken.

Day after day Dia worked to care for those she loved. She carried water. She cooked as best she could, and she wiped the foreheads of those who were the sickest. Each night, when she finally went to bed, she would pray that someone would do something to save those she loved. It was very scary.

After a few weeks, the village elder called Dia to his bedside. He said, "Dia, you are the only one not sick with this plague. You are our only hope!" His voice was very weak, and she had to lean close to hear his wispy-words.

His barely formed words made her heart pound. "I am but a young girl," she thought. "What can I do?"

The elder, as if reading her mind, continued by saying, "Dia, although you are young, you are also pure of heart and generous of spirit. You can do this, though it will not be easy. You must go high up into the mountains—way above this village. Go to the top of the mountain. There you will find a wise woman. Her name is Chandar. Go to her and tell her what has happened. Ask her what we must do to save the village."

Dia felt afraid. This was a huge journey that he was suggesting, and she had never traveled alone. Yet, what could she say? This was about saving all those she loved. Taking a deep breath, she spoke with the bold resolve of the innocent heart, "Elder, I am but a young girl. I have never traveled outside this village, nor have I traveled alone. And I am willing to make the attempt, for I love all of you so much!"

The elder sighed. He had hoped this would be her response, but he had not been sure. It was so much to ask of one so young.

Dia gathered the few bits of food which she felt would be okay to take with her and a small container of water. She left as much as she could for the stricken villagers. She put on her jacket and hat. She found a strong walking stick.

And it is said that this was the extent of her preparation for her journey. Beyond this Dia was unable to imagine any way to prepare her soul for such an undertaking. She thought, "I am who I am. I cannot make myself into a strong man or gain instant experience to be confident in my skills. All I can do is travel as myself." So this is exactly what she did. She readied herself by being herself.

Dia went to the elder, who was still quite ill and lying in bed. "I have prepared as best as I know how. I have come to say goodbye and to tell you that I will do my very best to reach Chandar. Please hold me in the light, as this is a huge journey for such a one as me. I am afraid down to my toes!"

The elder gave her his blessing and assured her that all those who were able would steadily witness the light around her until she returned.

Taking a deep breath, she turned and began her walk up the mountain.

She had never considered that there might be someone else living on "her" mountain, much less higher up. However, up she went…and up…and up…until it grew dark. She was forced to stop since she could no longer see her way. Dia had not considered that the mountain was so very tall as to require days of walking to reach its heights! She was surprised to find herself not yet arrived in the dark of the night.

That first night she slept out under a very dark sky. She saw stars she had never noticed before. She heard sounds that gave her the creepy shivers. The moon was but a sliver, offering little comfort and next to no light at all. She was so glad when the sun rose. The light brought her confidence back, as least a bit.

She continued her journey. Day after night after day after night she walked. It seemed to be never ending and scary and exciting and long, this walk-on-behalf-of. She worried each minute that she was taking too long and that all those she loved would die from the plague before she got to Chandar. She pushed herself very hard.

"Just get to Chandar," she would say to herself over and over again as she walked up and up and up. Dia could see in her mind's eye all that the "Great Chandar" would do for her dearest village. Chandar was the savior; Dia was simply the messenger. "Just get to Chandar" was her chant as she ascended the great peak.

Finally, one day she saw a small shack far up ahead. "It must be where Chandar is!" she thought. Dia hurried even faster. The end of her journey was near!

Just as she was about to knock, the door opened. There before her stood an old, old woman with long, thick gray hair hanging down to her waist. She was leaning on a thick "knobbly" walking stick. Her eyes were bright, bright blue with a piercing light in them. She was dressed in clothing of patches of every color of the rainbow. It seemed as if she was everything at once. Although that doesn't make a lot of sense, that was how it was.

She looked right into Dia's eyes and said, "Deary, what took you so long?" Come on in. We have much to discuss."

Dia was so glad to have finally reached the end of her journey, she didn't even notice how odd that comment was coming from Chandar. It had been so long, and it seemed like weeks since her stomach had felt full. She simply walked into the shack and sat down right on the floor, still not having said one word. She just sat, stunned that she had actually done it! Dia had found Chandar! "All will be well now," thought Dia.

Then, suddenly she seemed to awaken…and her words spilled out.

"I am so glad to have found you. You are Chandar, aren't you? I have walked and walked for days. My (W)hole village is sick with the plague, and I was the only one who could come for help. You will help them, right? Right? We must hurry because although I hurried as fast as I could, the journey has taken a long time. Please, let's go. I will show you the way. You will be able to save them, right?"

Her words had spilled out of her. She couldn't hold them back; so much depended upon her. Chandar listened with patient compassion.

"First, dear child, you must eat, and then we will talk of what you must do to try to save your family and village." Chandar said this as she handed Dia some water, bread, and cheese.

Dia froze. "What do you mean 'what *I* must do?' I was to come get you to help us. I have. I can't do anything more. I am just a young girl!"

Chandar smiled, saying, "You are the only one who can accomplish this great healing. I will tell you what you need to know for your journey, but the truth is no one can do it but you! You alone have the qualities needed for such a quest." She paused. Dia was too shocked to speak. She had thought her journey was done as soon as she found Chandar.

"Eat as I talk to you, for you will need your strength. The steps ahead of you are many." And then as Dia ate, Chandar told her what was before her.

"You must travel to the Underworld and get some Water of Life from the fountain, found only in the darkness. You must travel alone and overcome many dangers and trials. Once you reach the underground river, the ferry man will row you over to the island upon which the fountain stands. There you will fill your container with the Water of Life. Finally, you must return to your village and give everyone there a sip of this Life Elixir. The "underworld water" is the only possible cure for this type of plague. It is a plague that eats at the soul. All of your village has been stricken from the inside out, a sickness of the Soul."

"But, but, but...," said Dia.

However, there was really not much for her to say, since she loved her village and her family. There was just no way to say, "No." So she just got very, very quiet. "Maybe I'll wake up and find I've been dreaming," Dia whispered inside herself.

"Here is a gold coin," Chandar was still speaking. "You must hold onto your gold coin until you come to the ferry man. You must give him this gold coin in order to reach the Fountain of Life. Whatever you do, HANG

ONTO YOUR GOLD COIN!" As she said this, Chandar placed a gold coin into Dia's hand and closed her fingers around it. "Remember," she said, "hang onto your gold coin!"

Then, for the next few hours, Chandar told Dia how to find the Underworld. Chandar packed up food and water and a container in which to carry the Water of Life. She gave Dia a warmer jacket with pockets to hold all the things she was carrying.

Dia was very quiet through all of this. She was trying to remember all that Chandar was saying. She was trying not to panic. She knew that she had been able to climb the mountain because she had believed that was all she would have to do. Now, she had agreed to go on a journey to the Underworld. She was terrified. She was determined. She was scared. She had to go for them. Outwardly, she appeared steady and firm, but Dia was quivering and quaking deeply inside. Inside there was arising such a "terror of error" that it struck Dia speechless.

"Now, Dia, remember always," said Chandar, "you must hang onto your gold coin—no matter what—for without it, you will be unable to save your village. You are the only chance. They are all depending upon you."

After a hug and a kiss, Chandar pushed her out the door.

And there Dia found herself standing, facing a closed door. She had her jacket pockets full of supplies and her gold coin clenched in her hand. Chandar was gone.

All Dia could do was turn around and walk away.

And as the story goes, she traveled from the top of the mountain to the gate of the Underworld. The stories of that descent are for another time, for there are too many to go into now.

Arriving at the gate to the Underworld, Dia took a deep breath and then walked into the dark huge opening into the earth and followed the path downward. The darkness of that opening seemed to be a living-void, a (w)hole that would swallow her up for forever. She was terrified but determined to persist and save her village. Her generosity of heart was said to have been the fabric of her courage, for nothing else could propel someone into the dark Underworld beneath the surface of the earth.

Underworld darkness operates like a mirror for one's most scary imaginings. Every turn, corner, texture and sound of "Underground darkness" reflect elements of one's own particular terrors. The only resource available in confronting such a darkness is the naked truth of oneself. Only this truth served to light Dia's way. It was her innocent realness that shed enough light for her to find the path of descent.

It is said that on her journey downward, she faced dragons and lions and monsters too horrifying to describe. All of these "monsters" were merely constructed reflections of her most dreaded nightmares. Despite all this, she continued downwards. It is said that she cried, fled, and fought her way deeper and deeper into the land beneath the world. How she managed to do this is also for another time, as there are many stories told of her perilous quest. However, she did manage to continue to descend deeper and deeper into the womb of the earth.

She managed to handle all the obstacles with creativity and some bit of growing confidence, and then she faced the most difficult challenge of her (W)hole descent.

Far off in the distance she began to hear, "I hurt. I hurt. Ooohhh, please help me. I am in great pain. Please, oh please, help me."

Dia thought to herself, "Gosh, that sounds kind of like the voice of my mother, or is it my grandmother? It sounds so familiar, but how could that be?"

As she grew closer and closer, she began to see the huddled shape of a woman by the side of the road. The details of her torn clothing and wound-infested body became increasingly clear as Dia approached her.

The woman's voice grew more and more pleading and insistent. "Please, oh please, I have been here in the Underworld for eons of time. It isn't my fault that I am here. Please, oh please, help me. All I need is one gold coin, and I will be set free. Please, don't let me hurt like this any longer. I know you have a gold coin; no one passes by me without one! No one! Help this old, old, old woman."

Dia was deeply troubled.

Her generous heart longed to hand over the gold coin that was hidden in her jacket pocket. Dia hated to see others suffer when there might be something she could do to help. It was in all of her upbringing, and it was the heart of the village's culture—to give whenever possible, to leave no one in need.

Yet, Chandar had told her, "No matter what, do not give up your gold coin. It is the one thing that is necessary for you to reach the Water of Life. Hang onto your gold coin!"

What was Dia to do?

"Please, please, can you not see the pain I am in? You have a gold coin, I just know it. If you have any generosity or love in your heart, you will help me. Pleeeeaaassssse help me!" cried the woman who seemed to sound like Dia's mother and grandmother all rolled up into one. In fact, the woman seemed to sound like all those Dia loved.

"Why do you continue to persist?" cried the beggar woman. "Those you seek to save are most likely dead anyway. You have taken too long."

It *had* been such a long journey. "Perhaps," wondered Dia, "all of my beloved village are already dead. What use is all this for them? Perhaps I ought to just give up. Maybe she is right. It has been such a long time! If that is the case, I don't need my gold coin."

Now, it is said that there are two endings to this tale. Both are true and will always be true. In fact, both are true inside all of us at some time or another, sometimes even simultaneously.

According to one ending of this tale, Dia took a deep breath and reached into her pocket. She grabbed the gold coin and then extended her arm toward the woman. She opened her hand and offered her the gold coin. Her generosity overshadowed the words of Chandar.

The woman grabbed the gold coin from her. Suddenly, the beggar woman turned into a huge monster and ate Dia. Then Dia found herself spit up and transformed into the form of the old beggar woman.

And so it has been said that for eons of time, she has pleaded with those on their descent into the Underworld—always seeking to seduce another into giving up their gold coin just as she had given up hers. No one ever heard from Dia again. And it is also said that Chandar, the wise woman on top of the mountain, grieved into eternity that Dia's generosity had been her undoing, since it had also been her greatest gift. Dia had failed to claim the (W)hole of herself. The village disappeared, since no one survived the plague, and the gold coin was lost for all time. To this day Dia remains sitting along the path of descent in the dark Underworld, all because she had been unable to say "No" in the face of a need.

In the other ending, which is the tale that Dia, herself, tells, something quite different occurred.

Dia held her generosity as precious and yet clung to her fierceness of purpose. "I will save my village. I have a mission. I am on a quest that requires me to persist. I will not give up. I will not just be generous. I am many things. I will be true to myself first. I will stay the course. Then we will see." She kept repeating this over and over again to herself.

And finally, she was able to walk past the beggar woman, clutching her gold coin in her hand.

She felt awful. She felt guilty. She felt so "bad" for the woman. Yet, she stood her ground and walked on. As she walked on, she could still hear the beggar woman pleading, "Please, help me. Please don't leave me here hurting and old and alone. Please save me from this place. I don't deserve this. Where is your generosity?"

And still Dia walked on. It felt as if her heart was breaking, breaking open and hardening all at the same time. Still, Dia kept walking.

Her journey took her to the River of Life, and there she met the ferryman, just as Chandar had described.

He said, "Give me your gold coin, and I will carry you across to the island."

She reached into her pocket and brought forth the gold coin. Handing it to him, she stepped onto the ferry.

She was taken to the island, surrounded by the darkest waters she had ever seen, where the Fountain of Life was located. Dia quickly filled her container with the Water of Life, for the fountain was large and flowed with great abundance.

The ferryman carried her back across the river. As she turned to get off of the ferry, the ferryman extended his arm to her and said, "Here. Here is your gold coin."

Dia was confused and asked, "Didn't I have to pay for crossing to the island? Why are you returning the gold coin?"

"I asked only to determine if you had managed to pass the beggar woman, still retaining your gold coin. Clearly, you were not seduced into giving up your gold coin. This is a great lesson and a great challenge to have overcome. It is the challenge that those with big hearts have the greatest difficulty in overcoming. To be able to say 'No' is as important as being able to say 'Yes,' for then one has true freedom of choice. If one is hostage to either response, they remain in a prison of their own making. Know this: Every one of us has but one gold coin. Your coin is not for me to keep. No matter what, hang onto your gold coin."

Dia took back the coin and once again placed it in her pocket.

As she began her ascent along the path of the Underworld, she began to imagine how she would return to the village and save all those she loved. But then her thoughts were quickly pushed aside as, once again, she could hear the beggar woman crying out. Her heart felt sick with guilt and confusion, fear and dread and even a bit of anger. "This old woman is such a thorn in my heart!" mused Dia to herself.

"I know you are returning, and you still have your gold coin. Please, please, please give me your coin. You now have no more use for it. All I need is one gold coin to be free from this torment. Where is the generosity of heart for which you are known?"

Dia stopped.

"Yes," she thought. "Where is my generosity?"

Standing before the beggar woman, she felt her heart tearing in two. What agony! She knew herself to be generous, but she had heard the warning of the ferryman. What was she to do? All her life she had strived to be generous. But now, her purpose conflicted with her "training" as she thought of it.

And then, it came to her.

"I cannot give you my gold coin, for it is for me alone, but I could give you some of the Water of Life. I have a very large container of it, more than enough for all of my village. I do not know what that will do for you, but I am sure it will do no harm."

The old woman was not very interested in the idea, but finally, after much pleading and crying from Dia, the old one grudgingly agreed that "Well, it could do no harm."

Dia reached into her pocket and pulled out the container which held the Water of Life. Carefully spilling three drops into the beggar woman's mouth, Dia wished with all her heart that something wonderful would happen. Perhaps the water would help the woman, saving her, as Dia knew it would save her family and friends.

The beggar woman swallowed.

Suddenly, there was a flash of brilliant light and before Dia stood a young boy. The beggar woman had disappeared. The boy reached out and threw his arms around Dia.

"Thank you. Oh, thank you. You have saved my life. You didn't get seduced into giving away your gold coin. You did not try to slay me from fear or anger. You held to your purpose with fierceness and still stayed generous of heart. You were not tricked into giving away your life to save mine, for then we would both have been trapped here in the Underworld forever. Thank you for staying true and being generous, both!"

Then he reached into his pocket and pulled out his own gold coin.

Dia was stunned.

As she looked at the boy, she could feel her heart open with joy and love. After all, the darkness had not won.

Together, they left the Underworld, holding hands as only two people who have faced the great darkness together and lived to tell about it could do.

They returned to Dia's village. Just as Chandar predicted, the Water of Life saved them all. And in time, Dia and the young boy named Claud were married.

They named their first child, ClauDia to remind them that generosity alone is not enough. And as time passed, ClauDia became a great elder and healer in his own right, carrying on the wisdom of Chandar. He even studied with her for a time, high on the mountain.

Dia and Claud lived long and joy-filled lives. And throughout all time, there were two gold coins, each in its own case, sitting on their mantle—reminding them to cherish their gold coins no matter what. Dia, sometimes would sit and tell this tale of how she nearly came to be lost in the Underworld for all eternity. Dia would confess to her listeners how the powers of a pleading voice, the seduction of guilt-laden accusations, and even the appearance of the beggar woman herself were nearly her un-doing. And as those listening hung onto every word, Dia would laugh to herself at the simplicity of the magic that saved herself, her dear Claud, and the entire village: The magic of Truth woven together with Love.

Even the village elders came to know this greater wisdom, all because Dia dared to say, "No," and then, "Yes."

And it is said that all the folks of the village and then around the (W)hole world came to know that the greatest help can only be offered by those who HANG ONTO THEIR OWN GOLD COINS, for then they are giving from abundance of truth and love. They are giving free of guilt, shame, obligation, and blame. All changed because of a small girl named Dia, who was willing to come out of hiding and boldly walk into the unknowns with only herself to trust.

****

To say "No" from the viewpoint of the larger "Yes" is not an easy choice. Isn't it true that we often wish to say a quick "yes" just to make it better in the moment, when if we held steady to the greater call, much more might unfold? It is the unknown, the emptiness just before a moment has occurred from which we back away. And we back into the "quick" or "known" responses based on how we have defined ourselves to date. Just as Dia thought of herself as "only a small girl," she had to let go of this restriction to take on the quest on behalf of the village. She was called to say, "No, I am not just that" even as she had no idea of what more of her would be revealed. To hold onto our Gold Coin demands that we set aside what is known and dare to dance with the unknowns of the next unfolding moment, only to discover that our (W)hole World has changed, the values altered, and that which you knew yourself to be is no more. This fable is my invitation to you to dance, hold onto your Gold Coin, knowing that it is your price of passage, over and over again, to the "mo-R-e" of you.

The Heart of it All: The Twice-Born Weaver

Dedicated to all of us who do "whatever it takes" to bring our (w)holie, (W)holly, Holy (W)hole heart to those we encounter throughout our days. Dedicated to the fires we have walked, the dark nights of the soul we have suffered and the courage we each demonstrate when we say "Yes" again to opening our hearts to life, to other, and to self.

Once in a time that was and always has been and forever will be, there was a spider. She was known simply as the Weaver.

She had woven more webs than any other spider known in all the kingdoms across the land. However, that was not what made her so remarkable, so dearly loved and respected by all who knew her.

She was a weaver of the most beautiful, most incredible webs anyone had ever seen. They were filled with magic. In fact, it was said in hushed whispers that if you caught sight of a web she had just finished and allowed yourself to name your deepest heart's desire aloud right in that moment, it would come true in an instant. She, herself, didn't put much stock in this talk but simply continued to do her weaving, chuckling to herself at the fantasies those creatures around her spun about her.

Now, on this particular morning the sun was like a sparkling diamond in the sky, and she was, as usual, beginning her work of the day. For her, it was always like being pregnant, the actual creation of her webs. And it was like a birth when a new web was completed. And after each new birth she celebrated by considering its uniqueness and storing its design in her memory. She could remember all the webs she had ever created, and that was a great many webs!! Now, as everyone knows, spider webs are not permanent. Her webs were washed away each night to make way for her next creation.

In the beginning of her career as a weaver, she had grieved the loss of each web as if it were a dying child, until she came to understand that letting go was as much a part of the creation of the web-children as the act of bringing another into existence. She had come to peace with this cycle of birth and death. From this repeated act of letting go, much wisdom had come to her and was offered to those who lived around her. It was for this reason she was known as the Wise Weaver. She knew of sacrifice and the blessed laws of letting go, and she knew of the magical gifts of surrendering into the unknown of the next creation.

Now, as she was beginning her web-creation on this particular day, its design its own and as yet undiscovered, she allowed herself the luxury of remembering some of the webs she had created in the past: the one she had so carefully woven around that tiny rosebud, the one that had seemed to stretch all the way around the world, the one that had been so carefully wrapped around and around and through the branches of the old oak tree she so dearly loved. And so her thoughts flowed through her web-memoirs, as the web, her child of the day, spun itself from her fingertips. Always a miracle in process, she celebrated, as this particular child of the day came into its own form. Her mind drifted in and out with her weaving, for the weaving itself just seemed to happen, and she was never quite sure how.

Then a dragonfly flew by and called a greeting. "Good morning to you, Weaver. It looks like your web is coming along nicely. It is sparkling with joy, and just seeing it uplifts my heart." The Weaver waved, nodded her acknowledgment of the compliment, thinking little of it. The dragonfly continued, "Say, have you ever given thought to where the designs for your webs come from? They are always so beautiful and yet, so unique and different, each in its own way. I am curious to know how you do this."

The Weaver stopped weaving. A small antsy feeling deep inside her began to make itself felt. The truth was, she had once or twice wondered this herself but hadn't really wanted to explore this question, fearing that to ask this would be to risk the magic that seemed to flow into the webs. She mumbled something, "Not sure, but got to keep going. It's doesn't really matter. I just think them into existence or something like that." She thought using that particular tone of voice would discourage the dragonfly, but it did not.

The dragonfly was not satisfied. "I would think that you would want to know, but then again," and his voice drifted off. He could see she was hard at work and didn't really want to be disturbed. However, the Weaver was unsettled. If the truth be told, she had wondered about the same thing; however, she had put this question away a long time ago, for no answer had been forthcoming. She was feeling a bit resentful that he asked it at all but worse, that he had asked it so directly. The question hovered in the air like a wisp of something one could not brush away.

The Weaver continued her work despite this irritating interruption, and after a time, the weaving-work took her over, and the question as to the source of her creations drifted away. She didn't even notice it was gone, just that the peace and quiet of her world had, in fact, returned. She was quite relieved.

As she continued to spin and the child of the day was emerging from the tips of her weaving self, a beautiful butterfly came sailing by. The butterfly was bright in color and filled with a flittering kind of dancing energy that was both delicate and strong all at once, the opposites held in the movement and moment of its being.

"Good morning to you, Wise Weaver. Your web is coming along nicely. It is good that you are able to do such work on such a beautiful day, is it not?" Weaver nodded and called a warm greeting to the butterfly. The Weaver remembered to herself the time this creature in its other form had come to call, asking for advice as a caterpillar fearful of the cocoon. After a conversation of some length, the caterpillar had faced the letting go. She had emerged from the cocoon's darkly threaded embrace as this magnificent butterfly, surrendering into the birth of her own magnificence. She was, in one way, a child of the spider. The Weaver admitted, quietly to herself, that it had been her sage advice and steady encouragement that allowed the caterpillar to risk submitting to the cocoon's dark nights. The world would have been so cheated without this awesome winged creature.

The Weaver felt humbled by the part she played in the world's beauty and not the slight bit curious as to how it all worked or where it all came from. She just wove and wove and wove. "Say," said the butterfly, "by the way, where do your webs come from anyway," calling out this flying-by-kind-a-question. "I have often wondered this to myself but have never thought to ask as I was flying past. I'm greatly glad that I did in this moment."

The Weaver paused. This was, again, that same bothersome question that she really did not want to think on.

The Weaver just mumbled something and continued to weave. The butterfly flew on not bothered in the least at the unanswered question; after all, the butterfly was made up of all the opposites, answers and questions included. Yet, the Weaver was left with the question. That same pesky question that refused to settle for a nice vague, fuzzy answer kept nudging at her from all sides.

The Weaver could not go back to her weaving trance-like place where she was everywhere and nowhere, nothing and everything spread out across the universe, moving in and out with the weaving of it but apart from it. She was a bit miffed, even a bit huffy, one might say. The question just hung there in the air. This did not stop her from her from her daily creative expression. BUT…

The Weaver got through the day, and her newest web was again a beautiful and unique creation, but she was still unsettled. Not even a completed new web could quite free her from the discomfort brewing inside of her. A lonely ladybug flew by, saw the web at the moment of its completion, named her wish and immediately found herself flying beside the most handsome of manbugs, lonely no more. The Weaver didn't even notice.

The question simply hung on the air. "What is the source of your creations?" the sunbeams danced the question. "Where do they come from?" whispered the wind. "What if they stopped?" waved the branches of the huge oak tree. "If you don't know where they come from, how will you make sure they keep coming?" The questions would not go away. She slept finally, and she dreamed.

In the dream the greatest weaver in the entire world, the Spirit Weaver, came to her. It was a moment she knew she would never forget. There was a great compassion and a great power in this being. The Weaver humbled herself before this holy presence and waited.

"You are ready. You can no longer set aside this learning. You have come to a time when you must face and answer this question. The source of your life and your creations must become known to you. You can no longer drift along the webs of the universe's weavings, ignorant of its origins. Until such time as you know the answer to this question, you will no longer be able to weave a single web. This is my gift to you, for when you come to know the answer, you will be wholly you, a creature, a creator, a being of life, not just a weaver of webs. You will be known and know yourself as Creator."

In the dream the Weaver cried out, "No. No. Who will I be if I am not the webs I create? How will I know what the answer is? Where do I look? Help me. No, no. This could not possibly be so." The Spirit Weaver looked upon her, silent for a time, and then she spoke again. "You must seek everywhere until you find the answer, and in that moment I will return to you in celebration, bestowing things upon you that are more wondrous than you can imagine, but for now, go and seek, for you can weave no more until you do."

The dream ended. The Weaver awoke. It was morning. She shrugged her shoulders and began to prepare for her day's work. She didn't believe in dreams. She was a no-nonsense kind of weaver and, in fact, secretly held that it was this that made her so very, very wise. She just took things as they were. She could feel already that floating, weaving, drifting feeling even in her thoughts and caught herself. "Enough of this mind chatter," she said to herself and prepared herself to begin. It was time to begin her web of the day, but nothing came to her.

She waited. Nothing happened. Nothing. Not a thing was happening.

The Weaver screamed her terror, screamed her emptiness, and still nothing happened. The dream was real; that much was clear. The Weaver found herself unable to weave. She could not remember a time when this had ever been true. She had been born weaving. She was nothing without her weaving, and she collapsed, sobbing and shaking. She was now nothing, and nothing happened.

Time passed. Finally, the Weaver faced the fact that until she found the answer to *the* question, nothing would happen, so she began. She surrendered to the quest. Her life depended upon it. With determination, with great thought and care she planned how she would go about this particular journey, the process of answering *the* question. The hunger to weave the webs was great, and yet still, she moved into travel. She traveled. She studied. She asked. She sought. She listened. She quested. She used every tool she had and learned new ones along the way.

She traveled to the farthest lands, seeking out the wisest of creatures residing in each kingdom, and she would explain her quest, saying, "I must find the source of my weavings. I have traveled so far to seek you out. I must come to know the answer for this, for until I do, I can weave no more. Can you help me? Can you tell me the source of my creations?" She would ask this with hope and eagerness in her eyes and her words. The "Blocked Weaver" of her made every effort to be logical and clear in her requests, making sure that her need clearly showed itself. She made efforts to not sound too hysterical about it all, though inside she was quite, quite afraid.

The wise creature of that particular kingdom would smile gently, look at her, and say, "For me, the source of *my* creations comes from…" and their answers would drone on and on. The hope would die in her heart, for their answers never seemed to have anything to do with her. And then they would say, sadly, "I cannot tell you the source of *your* creations. This is for you alone to find."

And so she went traveling from one kingdom to another, from one wise being to another. During this time she met many creatures, learned a great many things about the lands, the beings inhabiting the lands, and how many different ways there were to live on the planet. She grew in her knowledge and understanding. However, *the* question, the question of her life remained unanswered. A great deal of time moved beneath her feet. She had not found the answer.

She had not woven one single web since the night of the great dream, as she referred to it. And finally, there came a time when she could think of nowhere else to travel, no other wise being to seek out. She paused. She paused for a very long time. Her mind drifted. She remembered the webs she had woven and the uniqueness of each and the love she felt for each of them, and her thoughts wandered. She found herself back in the memory-time when the butterfly, then a caterpillar, had come to her in great trembling and dread at the prospect of the cocoon.

She smiled to herself. It had seemed so simple to her to explain to the caterpillar that it was this very going within that would bring the caterpillar its second and greater birth to fruition. It had seemed so obvious, and yet for that dear, terrified caterpillar, it had seemed the most awful thought in the world, "to go in, to stop, to not be eating leaves and crawling along the branches. How can I do this? How could I bear it?" the caterpillar had screamed and cried. "This is too hard. I am scared. What if… What if… What if…," and yet, with great love and true compassion, the Weaver had promised she would see her again. The Weaver had promised the small scared caterpillar that "Yes, it would see the world in a brand new way." The Weaver had witnessed many caterpillars pass through their transitions and emerge transformed, quite delighted with their wings and flight.

She smiled in her heart as she recalled the cries of delight emitted by the caterpillar, now butterfly, upon her emergence from the cocoon. Both male and female, creature of crawling and creature of flying, the caterpillar, now butterfly, was the holder of the wisdom of opposites, all nestled within its small body and carried between its huge wings. She had known and witnessed this "going within" as a precursor to the Greater Life called butterfly. This wisdom had rested within her. It was to this creature she would turn, as she wove her webs, for they, too, required tension to hold their shapes.

True wisdom comes from going within!

Wait.

The winds stopped moving. The sunbeams paused in their dancing. Something huge was about to occur, and the world paused and witnessed quietly. It came to her. The one place she had not gone, the one place she had not traveled to was the great place within—she, the Wise Weaver, the one who had encouraged the caterpillar to risk the chrysalis. It was she who had never taken this inner journey. Perhaps this was the way to come to the answer to her quest. It seemed like such a nonsensical idea to the Weaver; however, she had no other ideas to replace it.

The Weaver had never really ventured inside before. She had spent time thinking and sorting things out in life but had never gone inside to the heart of things, to… to her heart of hearts. Here was a space-place to which she had not paid much attention. It was a place she knew was there but had placed little value upon. Secretly, she had feared to fully enter her heart. There were feelings there she instinctively knew were connected to the web weaving, but she had told herself she had not wanted to disturb the magic.

Now, it seemed the only hope of finding the magic of web weaving again was to go where she had never dared to go, to the deepest corners of her heart, taking her quest within, for there were no more places outside of herself to go. If she was to weave again, and how she so longed and loved to weave, she had no other choice.

She settled into a place near the base of her favorite old oak tree, a place safe from the path of other creatures and yet, familiar to her. She recalled she had woven a grand web around a tree branch not far from here. After all her travels, she had returned to the place she called home. As she faced this last hope, she was glad in her heart that she was in this place filled with the web tracings of all the webs she had previously woven. "If this is the end of me, I will be laid to rest near my dear companion, the great oak, who has been the loom for so many of my creations." The Weaver settled into herself.

Unseen by her, radiating outward from her were all the webs she had ever woven, her heart spinning all of them again, faster and faster than the eye could see or the mind could fathom. She was unaware of all of this. She was at the center of a huge spirit web composed of all the webs she had ever woven or thought of weaving in all her time as a weaver. She felt herself spiraling down deeper, deeper, further within herself.

Waves of feelings washed over her—joy, sadness, rage, shame, horrors and delight—each eliciting their own unique shapes and colors, each a response all of its own. And still she spiraled deeper and deeper within herself. All sense of the outside world washed away, and the depth and richness of this inner realm embraced her with both the softness of a spring breeze and the fierce wind of a hurricane. And still she spiraled around and around, closer and closer to her core, to the Heart of All Things, closer and closer to her heart's center. And then, in that moment she was there.

She was at the center of her being, in the heart of her heart. She had found the source and home of all of her weavings, those birthed and those yet to be born.

She could hear a kind of music, which, as she listened, formed itself into webs of all sorts, never the same, never static, but dancing before her eyes only to dissolve and be replaced by another. It was infinite. It was the source of her weavings. It was her heart of hearts. Then before her was the Spirit Weaver smiling.

"So," spoke the greatest of all weavers, "you have finally found the source of all your weavings. It is here in your inner heart of your heart where your webs are created and brought forth. There are no thoughts great enough, no actions bold enough that can bring to life such creations save the heart of your own heart." Having said this, the Spirit Weaver reached out and touched the Spider Weaver's heart.

The Great Weaver spoke, "My child, I now bless you in the name of all the universe. All you shall weave will bring new life and goodness to all creatures you touch." Then the Spirit Weaver dissolved in a shimmer of webby light. There was only the quiet silence of the answered quest.

And it is said that from this time forth, the Wise Weaver became known as the twice-born Weaver, weaving webs in spiral form that brought healing and joy to all who saw them.

And it is said that these webs woven by the twice-born do not dissolve at the end of the day but continue until the end of time, blessing all those who see them and awakening their hearts.

The spiral continues now and for forever, weaving its way around all hearts of all beings. And The Great Spiral leads all those who wish to know of their source to go within, to wake up to the (W)hole truth and then to birth true life again in the world.

In the telling of this story, it is said that there is a blessing that all receive—teller and listener alike.

****

To dare to stand naked with a wide open heart and allow life's fingertip to touch you in every moment takes the boldest of courage beyond any other. What makes this so? Regardless of our backgrounds, in our common humanity and in the face of life's hurts and struggles, we each shatter to some extent into bits and pieces, ultimately closing our hearts off. We imagine that if we do this, there will be less hurt. What we forget is that it means there will be less life. This fable is an invitation to bring your precious (W)hole Heart into your Holy Life until you and your Heart are ONE, once again, just as they were the day you were born.

The Cloaked Light

Dedicated to the Light Being we all are! May we sweep wide our cloaks until LIGHT BEING is all we know...until BEING LIGHT is all!

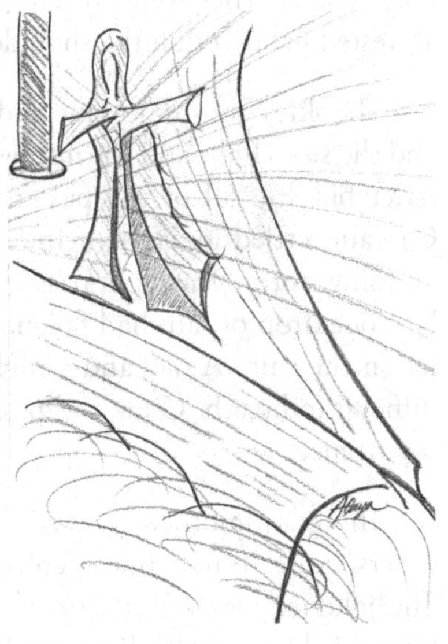

Once upon a time, in a time that was long ago and still is true today, there was a sailing ship. This sailing ship was ordinary. It stopped at ports here and there as it traveled around the globe, taking on and letting off passengers and cargo. Its name was *"Still Flight."* Its captain was known only as "The Captain." She was skilled and fierce and wise beyond any measure one might assign. The crew followed her unerringly and without any hesitation into any port of call and through all manner of storm. They named her a great leader.

At this one port they stopped and took on four passengers. In itself this was not unusual. One was a dark, cloaked figure. One was a flamboyant, boisterous jokester type. One was a small, petite grandmotherly figure, and one was an apparently crude, angry man who came along with a companion, but they seemed as one. Later the Captain noticed that the angry man was chained to the other. Perhaps he is a prisoner being transported, she mused. This meant a total of 13 on the *Still Flight,* eight crew members plus the captain and these four and a half, one could say. All would be sailing on the next leg of the journey.

The captain had always made a point of connecting with her passengers when the journey was extending beyond a day's time. This next stretch was for a month out. The Captain, once the ship had set sail, spent some introductory moments with each of the new passengers.

None of the passengers, save for one, stood out in any particular way other than just being ordinary folks, traveling for one reason or another. The one who had come aboard in a dark cloak was not open to any exchange. However, the Captain had sensed no ill-will, so had simply set it aside as a quirk of this particular personage.

All continued fine upon the *Still Flight* until about mid-way on the journey, when the skies began to appear suspect to the seasoned eyes of the boat's leader. They were far removed from any land, and the well-being of all rested firmly upon the shoulders of the Captain.

The skies grew dark blue and gray. The wind increased its noisy play, and the sun's light and warmth was sucked away by dark ominous clouds. After bidding all of the passengers "good night" for the evening, the Captain settled in at the helm, ready for a long night in the face of the building storm. The night passed. The storm still gathered on the horizon. Not one drop of rain had fallen, but the suspense was tightening around all on the ship. A day and a night came and went. The tension made it difficult to breath. Crew and passengers alike knew this was no ordinary occurrence.

The grandmother was wringing her hands, studying the skies and waters, quite afraid while deeply aware of her now near paralyzing worry. The jokester was talking up a storm, distracting himself, he thought, from all that was building within him. The man who had come aboard as prisoner was blaming his bad luck on being on a "cursed" ship and its "poor" Captain. He was screaming at his half companion, as if that would change their perilous situation. And the dark-cloaked figure said nothing, demonstrated no particular reaction.

Another day and night passed, and clearly the storm was closing in on them. And then, that fourth night the storm descended upon them.

Still Flight was now embraced in a fury, a fury that was indescribable. The rain fell like a waterfall. Thunder shouted stampedes of rumblings, nearly deafening them all, and lightening shattered the dark sky corners so repeatedly that everyone's sight was blurry.

Still the storm raged, disturbing all the elements of air and water, fire and earth. This was beyond all occurrences known to any of them. It seemed unending. Day and night were forgotten. There was only the storm.

The grandmother was moaning and crying, preparing to die as she watched with eyes wide open. The seas and the sky were torn into jagged bits and pieces. The wind touched and tore at her face-skin, for all else was covered in what protection clothing could offer. The jokester was huddled in a heap in a corner, mumbling to himself, hiding his eyes, shaking. Jokes long forgotten, he had collapsed into himself. The angry, accused man was screaming and punching and blaming, the winds buffeting around him, while his companion fought to restraint him. Unable to do so, given all of the turmoil of the storm, the companion had ultimately used his key to separate the chains which had bound the two together, in a small effort to gain some peace amidst the chaos. The cloaked figure stood by the broken mast silent, darkness blending with the cloaks' darkness, apparently with no response.

The crew, continually looking and hovering around the Captain, cried out, "Tell us what to do. Tell us what to do." The Captain, exhausted beyond all imaginings, held still to the helm. Yet, despair shadowed her eyes. She didn't know what to do, save to hold on. Though her hands were numb, her spirit near hopeless, she stood by the helm. Even though there was no way for her to control the destiny of the ship that she so loved, she held on. Her eyes were wide, taking in all that was transpiring to her beloved blessed boat, which had ferried her through so many tight moments.

Still the storm held them in its embrace, the ship taking blow after blow, portions of it falling away until it was that they were on a bare deck with a hull and water-filled decks below. Clearly, the end was near. Some of the crew, as the obvious end neared, leaped off what remained of the ship into the crazy, frenzied waters and died there. Some of the crew and passengers clung to each other, seeking solace in the human touch, vainly dreaming that this would prevent their death or at least make their death less horrible. Some simply, quietly lay down and died, their hearts shutting down in the face of the potency of the storm. Crew and passengers alike each met themselves in the mirrors of water falling from the skies. The cloaked figure simple stood alone.

One last wave crashed onto the deck. The deck itself crumbled, and there was nothing left to stand upon that was known to any of them. It was over.

Then, the cloaked figure opened her arms, spread wide her cloak, and from within her a light radiated, piercing the darkness.

A sound rang out, like the chanted songs of all the angels of heaven: it sent out a keening call. No one who lived could later describe this sound. Perhaps it was the sound of Creation, perhaps the sound of "God's Birth"—who knew. What was true and is known to this day was this "(W)HOLY" sound of the mysteries heralded an event such as never had been before.

The shadowy figure's dark cloak edges were flung wide by the wailing winds, and just as they were sinking into the frothy raging waters of the sea, a ship of crystalline light rose up beneath them. Those remaining alive found themselves standing on a ship's deck which was transparent, yet visible, solid, but not, real, but unreal.

Some were too afraid to open their eyes and look. They fell into the waters, screaming for help. Their eyes closed. Their hearts closed.

Others dared to stay present even unto this last moment. It was these folks who found their feet upon dry decks on the crystalline ship, gently bobbing on calm waters, beneath a clear sky. There was a pause.

Nowhere to be found was the cloaked figure. Those that remained were the grandmother, with more wrinkles upon her face than before but with a smile on her lips, half the crew and the Captain. The others were lost. Some believed that the dark cloaked figure was among the lost, and the Captain allowed this misconception, but knew otherwise.

It is said that what made the difference between life and death was those whose eyes stayed open in the face of that last moment, whose hearts broke open in that last grand disturbance.

Once safely ashore, the Captain changed the name of her ship to the *"Cloaked Light."* Now still sailing the seas, the Captain, always at the helm of the ship of crystal, holds the secret of its true origins close to her heart. She knows she is but a passenger, riding the waves in the living-ship called *"Cloaked Light."*

The grandmother went on to birth a lineage of creatures who swam, walked, and flew. The crew that survived their encounter with Creation's mysteries remained with the "Cloaked Light," ever vigilant for the gifts of the sea, air, and land, while never presuming their life continuance. Daily, all who had been there the moment before the transfigured ship rose from its watery womb offered gratitude and blessings for their continued breath.

So it is said that this living-ship, birthed in the moments of death itself, travels from port to port, bringing a means of transport to other realms for those with wide-open eyes.

****

How is it that there are those individuals who, hidden in the shadows seemingly of no account, step into "that moment" and by their revealed presence save the day? How is it that it seems some folks are like this and some of us are not? There is, I believe, only one difference. The difference is found only in how much of our own light we dare to allow to emerge from the restrictions of our "bounding-cloaking efforts." Is it the urgency of the moment that breaks us free? Is it our panic in the face of pending death or threat that coerces us into admitting "Yes, I am Light Walking?" Or is it when those around us are in danger that we throw aside our hesitation to show up and rush headlong into the fires on behalf of another? This fable is an invitation to you, my dear reader, to not wait for any "reason" but rather to sweep aside your cloak, be the Light Being you are, and thus become the vehicle of (W)holeness sailing across the waters.

ObLAYday, a woman of barren fertility, & her child, Mareeha

Dedicated to friends. Those friends we know, those we have yet to meet, those we have always had and those who once were. Dedicated to the power of a friend's presence, which in itself changes the (W)hole experience of life, itself.

Now this tale begins quite abruptly, as some do. The children had been playing out in a large meadow. This meadow was in full view of the village, which was perched apart and a little bit higher up in the landscape. There were always one or two adults who gazed out over the children's playing field. And so it was one day that it was Mareeha who was the one watching over the children at play. Now mind you, the children playing were still quite a distance away, but they were clearly visible. Over the meadow, from the far side of the children's playing field, came a loud, sudden noise. The thunder of many horses rumbled, and over the crest of the hill came a whole herd carrying a tribe, a warrior-warring tribe. They rushed out amongst the children, scooped them all up and were gone in seconds.

Silence rippled the meadow, just as a gentle breeze blows stalks of wheat. The children were gone before Mareeha could say or do a thing.

Not all of the children had been taken, for some had not been playing out on the field at that time. But all those who had been playing had been carried away. The moment became a horror frozen in time. And despite all the efforts of their own warriors, they could not locate the tribe that had taken the children, much less rescue them.

Mareeha was in shock and deep grief. Apart from her own shame that she had failed to provide an adequate lookout and alert, all of her five children had been taken in one moment, one horrific moment of time. Much of her life had been swept away in the matter of an eye's blink.

And so it was that she moved in a kind of death walk, a death walk that was beyond mourning. It was beyond grief. Only if someone fed her did she eat. Only if someone pushed her did she get up and move. It was as if she was frozen in time. All she could do was replay that moment over and over and over in her mind's eye, the last scene of the children on the playing field before they were swept away.

Now others in the tribe had also lost children, and they went through grief as one would expect, and then they were able to move on, move on about their life. It took many months, perhaps even a year or more, but they were finally able to move through their day without deep and anguishing grief over the children that they had lost. No one judged Mareeha for her response to that moment, for it had been so quick and so swift that even the warriors of the tribe had not been able to respond rapidly enough to stop it. In fact, it had happened so fast that the memories were like a flash of light, barely visible except when seen in the mind's slowed down motion. Mareeha was the only one who was so paralyzed, so locked in her interior space that she could not seem even to notice what was happening within her or around her. And so time passed, and nothing changed for her. Mareeha was frozen in place and time.

Now, it is so in all villages that there are many, many different sorts of people. In this tribe, there was one named ObLAYday. ObLAYday lived apart from most of the tribe. Her hut was far removed from the center of the village. She came to live this way when it had become clear that she was barren. This particular tribe happened to place great value upon fertility. In her state of barrenness, no one had been willing to take her as a wife. No one truly had been willing to even befriend her. And so it was that ObLAYday came to live a very interior and apart sort of life. She lived so apart that most of those of the tribe barely noticed her throughout the day. It was rare for her to initiate contact with the others in the tribe. She was nearly invisible, not quite, but near enough. On occasion someone would comment or notice, "Ah, ObLAYday has just passed by," or "Oh, yes, there is ObLAYday. She is gathering the wheat with us." She was more often than not simply noticed out of the corner of one's eye, much as a reflection is a bounce of sunlight off a bit of water.

Now what does ObLAYday have to do with Mareeha? Ah, this is the point of this tale. After about a year or so or some say three, Mareeha was still locked in her frozen world, chained to an anguish deep within her. Her heart had shut down and seemed sealed and closed off. Nothing that anyone could do or say seemed to touch her. All in the tribe were well aware of this. Women had come and cleansed her, fed her, talked at her, pleaded with her, attempted to offer sage advice. Men of the tribe, including her husband, had railed at her, shouted at her, shoved her gently, and even poked sticks at her feet—all to no avail.

And then one day, something unheard of occurred.

ObLAYday rose from her hut on the far side of the village, and without speaking a word, she walked through the entire village and right into Mareeha's hut and sat down. She did not speak. Neither did Mareeha, for she was not speaking at all. And so it was. The tribe wondered and watched. What was occurring?

And from that day and for many days, ObLAYday simply went wherever Mareeha went. If Mareeha rose to walk down to the river to get water, ObLAYday walked along beside her, saying not one word. She would be there as the water was gathered, and then ObLAYday would follow Mareeha back, where they would again sit in Mareeha's hut. At the end of each day, when Mareeha laid down, so, too, did ObLAYday. And when Mareeha rose in the beginning of the next day to move again into her walking dead experience, ObLAYday rose with her. If Maresha ate, so, too, did ObLAYday. If Mareeha forgot to eat that day or the next, ObLAYday did not eat either.

The villagers wondered, "What was this?" ObLAYday had never, ever that anyone could remember asserted herself in such a manner. No one knew what to do for Mareeha. In fact, her husband had taken another wife, for Mareeha was simply unable to be present in any way; her heart was so frozen-locked in time. And so the days and hours and months passed, and ObLAYday became known as the "Shadow of Mareeha." ObLAYday's presence gradually was noticed less and less, for she simply became an extension of Mareeha, and still no words had been spoken between them. It was as if they were one being, not two.

Days passed. Weeks passed. Months passed. Nearly a year to the day when ObLAYday first walked into Mareeha's hut, words broke the silence between them. On that day Mareeha lifted her head and her eyes and looked at ObLAYday and said, "What are you doing here?"—the first words she had spoken since that horrible day. ObLAYday simply replied, "I am here."

Mareeha lowered her eyes, and no more was spoken. And so it was, time passed again. No further words were spoken. Each woman present but not present, not asserting or pressuring or requiring anything or any interaction whatsoever of the other. And still more time passed.

Then one day Mareeha looked up again. This was a second and new moment. She looked at ObLAYday and said, "You are here. Where am I?" ObLAYday did not speak in return. More time passed. Some say it was days, some say it was months.

And then once again, Mareeha this time raised her head, looked at ObLAYday, and said, "Oh, you are there, and I am here. And we, we are one." Then Mareeha took a deep, deep shuttering breath, and for the first time since all her children had been taken and all the other children had been taken, she wept deep, bitter tears. It was as if something that had been frozen had thawed deep within her. Something inside of her that had been hardened suddenly loosened. Something that had been held at bay was finally released. And she sobbed and wept and wept in the arms of ObLAYday.

It said by ObLAYday that Mareeha wept for a day and a night and another day. Mareeha recalls that she wept herself dry until there was not one tear left, until all of the places within her that had been frozen, so horrified that they were unable to engage with life again, released and moved into presence once again. The tears and wrenching sobs were torn from the frozen wastelands of her heart until, once again a living breathing being called Mareeha was walking among the villagers.

The day came when ObLAYday, without words spoken, rose and returned again to her own hut. In that moment, Mareeha began to live her life again. All had thought this was the end of this episode or story, but it was not so, for over the course of the next weeks, Mareeha came back to herself. She began once again to engage in the life of the village.

Then it was on a day that will never be forgotten, a day when the sun was bright and the sky was clear, and one could feel the winds whispering around in a manner that had not ever been recalled before, something happened. Over the crest of the hill where the children had last been seen, the village watcher saw a group of beings. They were running towards the village. As they got closer and closer, the watcher saw that the group of beings were actually children—the children.

They came running across the field, older than when they had been taken, but alive and well and laughing. They had escaped. They had escaped from the tribe that had taken them, and they had walked their way back. And now in their return with all of their numbers safe, not one lost, the miracle was not so much that they returned but that Mareeha's heart was able to love and receive them. If it had not been for ObLAYday, Mareeha would not even have noticed the return of the children.

From that day forward, ObLAYday was known as a woman of presence. Her very company, her very breath itself would bring refreshment of spirit, mind, and body. Any time any villager was in anguish, they knew to go and simply sit in her presence, and all would soften, gently re-engaging in life.

And it was so from that time until this that in all communities there are one or two or three that carry ObLAYday's initiation presence. These folks of wisdom carry aliveness out into the world, not through their words or through their uniqueness, but rather through their shadowing companioning. Those of ObLAYday's lineage are sought after for their potent presence.

This is so then, now and for forever.

****

To be received without question, to be allowed the spaciousness of BEING without any demand to change, to be gifted the blessedness of "all the time in the world" for our own ripening or healing, these are some of the presents of friend. Presence that offers these presents is what I mean by the word "friend." The surprise in this fable is WHO befriends whom? The invitation in this fable to us all is to allow ALL those we encounter to be surprising in their expression of friendship, to consider how we might be-friend ever more deeply and beyond the edges of words—the casual acquaintance, the stranger, and even our dearest of "old familiar intimates."

A Diamond of a Soul

Dedicated to all of us who close our eyes for fear of seeing who we really are. Our (W)hole Selves. Dedicated to those of us who look anyway, risking it all.

At one time there was a cat—a sleek, elegant Persian house cat. She was quite a magnificent creature. She moved with an air and a grace that was quite notable. In fact, it was so notable that she was called Grace.

Grace wore a necklace that set off her fur to perfection. It was composed of diamonds lined up in rows upon rows. They glittered with every move she made. Grace was, without a doubt, a quite extraordinary creature. Anyone looking at her or watching her move knew immediately that Grace was special. The diamonds simply accentuated what was already present.

There was, however, something even more special about Grace. Her insides were even more beautiful that her outsides! She was quite intelligent and had an embracing, loving heart to match her wildly funny wit. To put it succinctly, Grace was grace-filled inside and out.

However, there was one difficulty in Grace's life and that was that she was lonely. This was in part due to the fact that rarely did available males come into her neighborhood; however, most significantly, her loneliness was due to an unusual inner condition.

Grace didn't know inside of herself how truly amazing she was. She, when she allowed herself to ponder herself, thought much the opposite.

If one watched her closely, one might see her avoiding mirrors so she didn't have to look in them, or ducking her head in a self-humbling/shaming kind of way. She had no idea that she really was magnificent. She had no idea that she was perfection walking on all four paws! Grace was completely unable to recognize the (W)hole truth of herself. And as compliments came her way, as they frequently did, Grace would slough them off, for she knew the "real truth" about herself. "I am just an ordinary cat," she would say to herself as she walked away, wondering what they could possibly see in her.

Now, this condition was quite an unusual condition for a cat. It was common knowledge that felines were noted for a great deal of self-appreciation, sometimes too much so. It was surely clear that Grace did not suffer from this "too much self-appreciation" condition. In fact, if anything, she suffered from "too little self-appreciation." Her condition was so rare in the feline world as to not have any diagnostic term. Thus, when folks around speculated over a cup of tea about whatever could have caused such a condition, they simply referred to it as "Grace's WAY."

However, the larger question was, what could one do about it, for everyone loved Grace and wished her all the best. Clearly, "Grace must be suffering," they commented to one another. "Look how hard she is working to hide from any reflections upon her nature!" Then they would shake their heads. No one had ever come up with any kind of solution, so things continued much the way they always had.

Now Grace, herself, for the most part was content with the life at hand. She had a good home. She loved her diamond sparkling necklace, and she pretty much had the freedom to come and go as she pleased.

However...secretly in her heart of hearts, she would occasionally admit to herself that she wished that she could see what others saw in her. Sometimes she would pray that a miracle would happen where she would be able to know herself and see herself the way everyone else seemed to see her.

Quietly, she thought to herself, "There's a big gap between what I feel and what they see of me. They don't match at all." She doubted that this would ever change, so she simply went about her business and resisted dwelling on this "condition" as she called it. Secretly, she felt a bit sad about this, being resigned to living with this inner-outer confusion, as she sometimes named it.

Until one day...the (W)hole situation changed.

A new man arrived in town. He was truly "the cat's meow," if you will pardon the expression, and Grace noticed him right away from her windowsill throne. She noticed how sleek and fluid his movements were, and her heart skipped a couple of beats and purrs. But she thought to herself, "He'll never notice me," and went back to licking her paws in the sunlight of the mid-morning. It was her favorite time of the day.

Unbeknownst to her, he had, in fact, noticed her…noticed her right away…and he began to make plans for how he would meet her. Well, his plans worked, and soon they were a "cat-item" in all the gossip columns of the local papers. Grace's activities were always noted by those around her. Of course, this too was something to which she was oblivious. All those who cared about Grace wondered how all this would turn out, especially given her "condition," you know.

Unbeknownst to those of the community, this new feline had his own mysteries. There was a secret about this new cat in town, that, so far, no one had seemed to notice. He frequently worried about it, but there was little he could do other than to hope that somehow things would work out. He surely hoped no one would notice he had a condition also!

He had a "condition" that affected his eyes. It had been discovered by his mother when he was small, and she had never been able to find a doctor who could help. He had been born with eyes that reflected back to the person looking directly into them the truth of their soul.

His eyes were "soul mirrors." Now, this may not sound like much, but most people definitely do not like to see their true soul-self reflected back to them in all its details. For most, it is quite a shock. The first to notice this was his mother, and although she was shocked by what she saw, she loved him so very much that she dared to face her own soul in exchange for the great treasure of being able to love and mother him. It was for this reason that she named him "Soul Mirror" or SM for short.

Now, as an aside, SM's mom had had to take a bit of time to digest all that was revealed to her in that very first *Soul Reflecting Glance.* It had not been easy. There had been much she had buried and hidden and ignored through most of her life. "Walk away from it, and maybe it will go away" had been her favorite strategy for dealing with life's challenges. Upon SM's birth, this no longer worked, for every time she looked into his eyes, she saw more of herself until there was no hiding at all. Now she was glad for this! She often purposely looked straight into his *Soul Reflecting Glance* to reassure herself of her own transparency—no more hiding for her!

However, Soul Mirror's experience of his "condition" was very different.

Sad to say, he had not met anyone besides his mom who had the courage or desire to face their soul…for the joy of being with him. Just to be with others, he learned to glance away, to look sideways at folks, and to never, ever look directly into the eyes of the other. He, too, was lonely. He doubted this would ever change. He accepted that this was how life was for him, that is…until he met Grace.

As he spent time with Grace, he was always careful not to look directly into her eyes. He didn't want to lose her, and he made sure that any time he was around any mirrors, he didn't look at her in the mirror's reflection, for it might just catch her eye and then "it," the condition, would drive her from him like all the other times before. He was sure!

It was difficult for SM to be so careful all the time because he knew he had fallen in love with Grace. He wanted desperately to spend forever and an eternity with her. He wanted to look directly into her gorgeous feline eyes and purr his love to her.

Grace, meanwhile, had also fallen tail-over-paws in love with SM, and this simply terrified her. She worried constantly that he would discover that she was simply an ordinary cat and would leave her for something better. And she was sure this would happen if ever he came to his senses. "What if he realizes I have this 'condition'?"

She was totally unaware that her fur glowed more than it ever had. Her grace seemed magnified to the degree that everyone in town began to wonder if she walked or floated, and her generous heart seemed to be larger than life itself. Something wonderful was happening to Grace. She felt loved and cherished. She didn't feel lonely.

But…

"What if he realizes how ordinary I really am?" she stewed to herself.

Time passed, and SM's little tricks kept her from noticing his condition, and Grace's fear seemed less and less possible, but neither had spoken of their respective "conditions." One day SM proposed. Grace was thrilled and purred her acceptance immediately. Still, not a whisker of discussion had passed between them about…well, you know what. Both were too afraid of losing the other if they each revealed their "conditions." Both were convinced that if their secrets were revealed, the other would walk away. So even unto the day of their union, both remained silent.

On their wedding day as they stood before the preacher, a great big black tom cat from across town, who frequently officiated at cat ceremonies, they declared their love and commitment to one another to the applause of the (W)hole town. And then, it happened…

Some say that the sun rose and set in the sky in that very moment. Others claim that all the shooting stars that had ever fallen rose up out of their earth's bed and flew across the sky like sparklers on the 4th of July.

Soul Mirror turned and looked directly into Grace's eyes. He hadn't really meant to do it, but he just loved her so much that, well, it was done.

In that moment Grace, for the first time ever in her life, saw her own soul.

There, before her eyes, was the magnificent soul she really was, and with it came the love and compassion that allowed her to truly know herself. For the first time in her life, Grace was at one with herself. Joy flooded her. Peace filled her heart, and the condition of inside-outness dissolved. She really knew herself for the first time. And even more than that, she loved who she saw.

And…as Soul Mirror saw joy fill her face, he, too, felt the horror of his condition melt away. His heart filled with appreciation for the condition he now calls "Soul Seeing" that brought his dear Grace such healing.

And it is said that as Grace looked into Soul Mirror's eyes and Soul Mirror looked into Grace's heart…the "conditions" suffered by all beings everywhere transformed, becoming their greatest gifts. Since then, compassion reigns over all the worlds, for as Heart's Grace witnesses itself in Soul's Mirror eyes, the (W)hole of creation fell in love with its own infinite beautiful expressions.

****

Avoidance of daring to face WHO we really are is a condition, an action, and a state of being. So often I have heard myself and others presume our unworthiness, our need to demonstrate our value, or to seek yet another "fix me" strategy so that finally we can relax and simply be ourselves without apology. This fable is a gentle reminder that really all it takes is to be SEEN for who we really are—Soul Walking—and then to be able to receive that wondrous truth entirely. What would any of us have to sacrifice to allow such an awakening? Our judgments. Do you dare to fall in love with yourself, without reason and for every reason?

The Pink Webbie Shell Home

Dedicated to all of us who have wrapped ourselves up in the wishes, hopes, fantasies, and imaginings of our child-selves so as to bear the ancient agonies of our young lives, only to forget that things change and so do we! Thank you to those who come knocking on our locked minds, our closed hearts and rigid spirits, calling us out of hiding.

Once upon a time that is and always will be happening somewhere in this world of ours, there was born a young girl child.

She was a magnificent soul and had a sparkle to her that by all rights ought to have elicited great joy in her family. However, there was a terrible famine in the land, and another mouth to feed was actually more of a burden than a joy. The land was covered in such darkness and despair that the air itself smelled of death, infection, and disease.

Now, this young girl child had come from a place of great light and love, as all souls who are born on this earth do, and so you can imagine her surprise upon entering into this expression on the earth. This expression of darkness was a great shock, a shock so great that for a moment she couldn't even breathe. If the truth be told, she didn't want to breathe.

It was just too awful. She tried for a brief time to find the light and love she was used to being immersed in, but it was not to be found. In fact, she did end up breathing, yet the pain was so intolerable that a blackness settled over her heart. She lived in a kind of darkness within as well as experiencing this dreadful darkness all around her.

Now, the great news, in this so far dismal story, was that she was born with a magical talent. This talent had been originally placed in her soul to further her great spiritual journey. However, it was not to have been used until she was farther along on her path, or so it had been planned, but plans often do run in surprising directions. Plans become spirals of surprises despite the best "soul laid" plans for our human experience.

This talent was so great that it allowed her to create all that she needed whenever she might be in need or wish of anything at all. She was a weaver of life. She was destined to be a Weaver of Souls. Her creator, the great Goddess of all girl children, had selected her to walk a path of great healing for others and so had given her this gift of creating in the form of weavership.

However, this child, who was named by her earthly family Lilith, was desperate to seek the light almost as soon as she arrived on earth. Since the darkness and famine were so very great in the land at the time of her arrival, she knew immediately that she was not truly welcomed. She did not feel any celebration for her descent to the planet. Hers was a sad entrance into the earth plane.

Without awareness as to what she was doing, she called upon her hidden talents. The power within responded by revealing her ability to weave. She wove a pink web all about her. It was meant as a protection, a cocoon of pink webbie threads that could be woven from inside out to encompass her, to buffer her from the outside world. Her heart couldn't bare the direct touch of life. She wove and wove. She wove until there was a thick encapsulating shell of thick pink threads. It was much like a cave without an entrance.

This cocoon then hardened into a shell of pearly, luminescent crystal, but this was not the limit of her weaving gifts. The insides of this pearly shell were so smooth that they resembled a many-faceted mirror that reflected back to Lilith her hopes and wishes, her fantasies and dreams—all that she so longed for. All the light and love she starved for was magically reflected back to her by these mirroring facets of the inner surface of her Pink Webbie Shell Home.

At first, she knew that what was reflected back was fantasy rather than reality. At first, she pretended that the shell didn't separate her from life. She simply accepted the shell-distance between herself and the world... until it all gradually faded from her awareness.

To her, looking at these inner walls was like looking at a great and continually changing landscape. So it came to be that inside her shell she felt as if she were really present to and with the world that existed beyond the pink capsule. In truth, just beyond the edges of her "Pink Webbie Shell Home" was the entirety of existence from which she was separated. Lilith lived in her own "pink world," safe from the famine, anguish and turmoil of the "real world." Quite simply said, Lilith was part-born.

She did not fully realize that she was the creator of her "pink world;" she only knew that the horrors of the world had faded from her view, and she could breath easier.

So Lilith, now inside of her safe special place, dreamed and hoped and imagined all the great hugs and loves and interactions that she so longed for but were not offered and would never be. How grand! Her creation seemed to be working. She convinced herself, almost, that the hugs she imagined were as good as real ones. She felt safe inside her "Pink Webbie Shell Home." Safety from the horrors was what mattered the most to Lilith.

For days and days on end, Lilith curled up inside her special place and dreamed her dreams. For the first eon or two she knew that there was "life outside the pinkness," but after a bit of time it became harder and harder for her to remember what that life outside was really like. She felt no pain at being part-born. Her special place allowed great lengths of time to pass without her notice. Gradually, she only infrequently recalled to mind that there was an outside. She lived in her inside "pink world" where that which was outside seemed far, far removed.

Occasionally, when she did venture out, it seemed so terrible, so hurtful, so frightening she would resolve never to go out again beyond her shell home. Then came the time when all she knew and all she believed in was what she, herself, created and saw reflected back to her inside her pink shell home.

Time passed. She grew up in the outer place of things. She married and had children of her own, yet, her pink-shell home remained intact. She had long forgotten that her true self lived secretly in this inner place. The outer and inner worlds were kept very far apart. It had been like this for so long that it never entered her head that there could be any other way. Besides, the separation was working…or so it seemed.

Meanwhile, in the outer world there were great changes. The drought had ended. The lands began to produce great fruits. The sun began to shine as never, ever before in all of creation. All the creatures and humans came into a harmonious dance of life. It was truly heaven on earth! It was how the earth was meant to be! It had become the space Lilith had anticipated upon her birth, only Lilith didn't know or notice any of it.

She continued to live in her encapsulated place, never dreaming that things outside of her inner world could ever be different than the horrors she had first encountered upon her arrival. In fact, she never even thought that thought, not even once.

However, everything was not running as smoothly as she liked to tell herself.

If she were honest with herself, she might grudgingly admit that events and interactions were frequently confusing. Sometimes she even felt a sense of overwhelming disorientation because of these two worlds she was straddling. The only remaining signals that she lived hung up between two worlds were vague feelings of confusion or overwhelm. She had lost her awareness of the actual difference between these two worlds: inner and outer. She remained part-born.

However, she believed that everyone else was like she was: separating their inside living from the outside playing of parts. Any confusion Lilith felt, she tended to blame on her own flaws. "It must be something wrong with me." Be that as it may, from her point of view, even this occasional confusion was still better than fully existing in that awful outer world. Of this there was no doubt within her.

Then one day she noticed that the ways she was responding, based on her inner world view, were really not working very well on the outer. For example, when things would happen on the outside, she would explain them to herself using her inner world, except they were not accurate, and then others would seem hurt or confused, puzzled or even angered by her responses.

Living got harder and harder for her, more and more confusing and frustrating. Often, she felt so misunderstood. What was worse was the anguish she felt when others claimed she had intentionally hurt them. It was quite unnerving to be feeling at odds with herself in so many ways. How unsettling!?! She felt "off," out of synch with herself.

Her inner world was meant to be peaceful. Her inner world, which was her precious creation, was somehow tripping her up. "But, but, but," she thought to herself, "I do not want to give up my special place. I do not want to starve and hurt and be miserable. In fact, I simply won't," and she resolved to do nothing about it. After all, she figured, "Why would one want to have anything to do with that awful place out there? I remember that place," a place she could only vaguely, if truth be told, remember at all anymore.

It was just too awful even to consider, and with that she closed the door on the (W)hole messy business of self-reflection. She'd determined to keep her precious true self safe and let the world think that the outer face she pretended to be was truly her. They really did seem to believe it, at least most of the time. And so time passed, but then, something changed.

She could not point to the moment in which it all completely stopped working, but more and more often, people were irritated with her or worse, she would feel irritated with them. The two worlds were simply not staying apart from one another, and if she was really, really honest, in her most quiet and secret moments, she would admit that she was scared. She felt as if her two separated worlds were colliding and crashing into each other. The Shell walls were failing somehow!! She was terrified! What was happening was not part of her plan. She was quietly, secretly panicking. What would happen if the walls of her Shell Home blew away?

Then it happened. There was a knocking on the outer shell of her special place. This had never happened before. It sounded a bit like a woodpecker, pecking away at the walls of her house. Bang. Bang. Bang. It felt pretty shocking, I can assure you of that, from later descriptions she offered. And nothing she did seemed to help make it stop. Bang. Bang. Bang. She would ignore it, but it didn't go away. She made up stories about it, but it didn't stop. Bang. Bang. Bang. She tried explaining it to herself, that it was just a fluke of nature, but it still—Bang. Bang. Bang.—didn't go away.

She told herself that someone or something was trying to wreck her precious pink-place. Bang. Bang. Bang. Everything around and inside of her was feeling fragile, shaky, and rigid. Bang. Bang. Bang. Finally, there was nothing Lilith could do but to surrender to the exploration of this new and frightening occurrence. However, she was stuck. She was unsure how to get out of her special place, for she did not remember how she had constructed it. She suddenly realized that she was trapped from inside.

This thought grew in her—Bang. Bang. Bang.

Then whispering ideas began to come to her of another place. At first, they were very quiet, these little thoughts. They seemed to be telling her to step out of her special inside place, to come out of her Pink Webbie Shell Home. These whisperings seemed to be coming from inside of her, yet, they sounded different, unlike her own voice. How odd…yet, she could not shut them out.

As these ideas rumbled around in her belly, an awful feeling began to grow in her heart. "I'm stuck in here. I'm stuck in here." Inside of her heart grew a deep desire to simply get out, get out of this prison that wasn't meant to be a prison, except that somehow it had become just that.

The feeling of being imprisoned sent shudders through her body, and the pecking—Bang. Bang. Bang.—continued. It was all starting to drive her a bit loony. Yet, did she dare to step out into the… "Wait. Wait," she thought to herself, "I don't even know what's out there anymore. It's all so unknown." And that thought sent cold, icy shivers up and down her now grown woman's body. Lilith was scared. Actually, she was terrified near to death!

Trapped inside her Pink Webbie Shell Home that she herself had created, she was terrified to step out, but at the same time, she was terrified to stay in what had now become a prison! All this churned inside her. She didn't even know how to get out from the inside of her Shell Prison, even if she wanted to. The pressure inside of her was building. "What am I going to do? What am I going to do," she thought desperately. She wanted to get out. She wanted to stay in. She was terrified to be naked of her Shell. She didn't know the way out. The agony of her part-born self became a tidal wave of tortured anguish.

"Oh, help me. Help me. Somebody please help me," she cried out with all her might. She cried out for help without knowing who she was calling to or even what she was calling for.

Then, in the stillness that followed, she heard a quiet, loving, gentle voice speak to her. "Child, woman-child, I have been waiting so long for you to call to me. I have been with you for forever. Through all the darkness and all the pain, I have been with you.

"I just couldn't reach you through this shell that you have woven. But now that you have called to me, I can reach you. I have been tapping on the door to your Pink Webbie Shell Home, trying to get your attention. Forgive me for the irritation I may have caused you. I just so wanted to reach you. I have missed you and longed to hold you in my arms. I am you, too."

Suddenly, in a moment filled with a blinding flash and a sound like a firecracker going off and then silence, there SHE was.

A warm radiant light rippled outwards from a shimmering figure of a beautiful being. The woman-being one moment seemed young, in the next old, in the next somewhere in the middle. She-Light-BEING seemed so filled with love that Lilith could not look directly at her.

Lilith spoke, "Where am I? Is this heaven?" She-Light-BEING laughed, a laugh that filled Lilith's heart with great glee and hope.

"No. No," she said in that same loving voice. "This is the outer world as it really is meant to be. You were born when this place was filled with death and despair and disease, but that is now gone, carried back to the oceans by time, the artist of change.

"You never knew it was changing because of your woven shell home that you so brilliantly called forth in your time of need, but now the outer world is full of love and light, of hugs and laughter, of all the things you dreamed of in your special Pink Webbie Shell home."

Then an amazing thing happened. She-Light-BEING came closer and closer to Lilith and looked directly into the eyes of girl-child-woman called Lilith. She gazed into her eyes with a look of loving, cherishing adoration. Lilith held her breath, and then, then in an act of great courage, she breathed in this Love-Look. She breathed it into her very core.

Her inner world and her outer world became one and the same, and she was (W)hole-born. Her full (W)hole birth allowed all the wisdom of her creative weaving talents to flow freely without restraint.

With that one blessed soul breath offered and received, Lilith stepped into her true life purpose: to weave anguish into hope, to weave despair into transformation, and to weave (w)holes into tapestries of living art.

It is said in that great in-breath-of-a-moment, Lilith emerged into this world, bringing with her the knowledge of her terror, the power of hope, and her talents of a Soul Weaver.

As for She-Light-BEING, she was, in fact, Lilith's Soul Light, which had been shut out by the Pink Webbie Shell Home's creation. When Lilith risked all in that great in-breath, she opened, received and became one with her own Soul's Light.

Lilith, woman of wisdom of the insides and the outsides, now spends her time "knocking." Bang. Bang. Bang. She bangs on the Pink Webbie Shell homes of those who have found themselves too frightened to breathe, too unloved to hope, too terrified to do more than create secret inside places in which to hide. And Lilith knocks and knocks—Bang. Bang. Bang.—until they, too, cry out asking for help without any hope of an answer.

Lilith introduces them to their Soul Self, who looks into their eyes offering them a Look-of-Naked-Love.

Those that receive their Soul's offering are freed from their imprisonment and become (W)hole-born. Those who shy away…well, we know what Lilith does. She keeps Bang, Bang, Banging and Knock, Knock, Knocking until they open to being loved for no reason and for every reason by their Soul Self. And then they, too, complete their birth into their own precious self-expressions: (W)hole-born.

And so it continues around the world, those Knocks and Bangs. Knock. Knock. Knock. Bang. Bang. Bang. They invite each of us at different times to look, to step out, and to breathe in, in one great in-breath, all the love that we have been longing for by daring to come face-to-face with our own Soul Selves.

Lilith, weaver of Souls, weaves the trembling Human Self with the Soul Self into a full (W)hole-Born Self, and in this way mid-wives the world. And all of this came about because of the look of love and adoration offered by a Soul and received by a frightened, trapped creature, called Lilith, who had forgotten who she was: Weaver of Souls.

Lilith tells her story of her Pink Webbie Shell home to you for you, hoping that you, too, will open your ears and your heart to hear the "Bang. Bang. Bang." of life. Lilith invites you to step out and into a great in-breath, to breathe in all the love, all the possibilities that you have so longed for that are your Soul's embrace.

Lilith is calling you to be (W)hole-born, allowing the shell of your hidey (w)hole to fall away and to see what happens.

Knock. Knock. Knock…

****

I have often pondered on the fact that as infants we are entirely involved in our moment's experience. Regardless of that moment—all of us (our mind, our heart, our body sensations, and our soul-self) are all ONE response. AND the world's response to us is the (W)hole World to us! We also are our own creators. We have a built-in capacity to create, to design our experiences by cutting off this, distorting that, and altering our perceptions. What wonders we are! This fable is an invitation to us all to listen for the knocking upon our certainties, to hear the whispered enticement to WAKE UP to our own power of creation, built into us all! And then to respond to the temptation to risk it all and come alive to one's (W)hole Holy (w)holie SELF—now. "Knock, knock. Who is there?" You—calling out to the (W)hole of YOU to come play.

The Gift of the Storm

Dedicated to all those of us who feel or have felt trapped by the raging storms of life happening to us, around us, and to those we love. Dedicated to all those who boldly step into the storms again and again searching for a different way. May this fable grant you peace. May this fable open the portals of calm in the face of the storms, within and without.

Once there was a village—it was an ordinary village as most folks would imagine. On the EAST side there were the great oceans. On the NORTH side of the village were great cliffs and rocky ledges and caves. On the WEST side of the village were the great plains upon which their food was grown and where their herds roamed freely. On the SOUTH side of this ordinary village were great open spaces and watery swamps and peninsulas extending deep into the oceans while still allowing for connection to the main body of land, called HOME by the people.

Folks lived their ordinary lives. They grew their food, married, gave birth, played around the fires at night, and time simply passed as it always had! All was well. Occasionally a storm would sweep across the Home Land. Folks would retreat to their lower gathering rooms, as they were called, and wait out the storm…and then it would pass on, and life would continue. All was as it should be. Fact be known, these occasional retreats were welcomed and enjoyed by all.

UNTIL one day, when all of this changed. However, it was not at first obvious. It was only later that it came to be called the first day of the HAH-BEE-TAH.

It began as a regular, normal everyday kind of day, as folks recalled much later. The sun had arisen, and then later in the middle of the day, clouds began to gather. Only these were no ordinary clouds. These were great storm clouds. Folks in the village began to prepare for the storm that was clearly coming, putting their homes in order and gathering in their lower rooms, as they've always done before.

As yet, they did not know how all would change beginning with this first storm day! They all simply thought, "It is just a storm."

And yes, this was true—save for one thing. The storm stayed for day after day after day.

It raged, it blew, it rained. It battered the Home Land. The noise of its shrieking and whipping winds rose and fell in all manner of rhythms. The rain pelted against the sides of their homes until it felt as if the onslaught would knock them down. AND still it continued.

Now at first, the folks of the village gave this no thought! It was just a storm, and they settled into their lower rooms to wait it out. And wait they did. And wait. And wait. And the storm still raged…

They began to call this storm the HAH-BEE-TAH (the Forever Storm).

AND…things began to change in their hearts as this "Forever Storm" stayed and raged on!

The folks of the village began to feel increasingly fearful. They began worrying about what the storm was now doing to their land, their crops, their buildings…and they worried about what the storm still might do to the lands next! They began to develop "Storm Eyes," an inner focus directed at this fearful, raging, beastly forever storm, or HAH-BEE-TAH!

Those that went out into the storm to attempt to tend to the flocks or to assess the damage were blown to their knees and thrown hither and yon, barely able to crawl back into their lower basement hidey (w)Holes. They quickly became wet, cold, battered, and storm tossed when they ventured outside.

Still the storm continued. The HAH-BEE-TAH was now the dictator of their lives—a ruler invoking fear, judgment, resentment and constant anxiety. "Look at what has happened already!?" "What will happen next??" "What are we to do??" These were the anguished, worried cries of the villagers from house to house. There was great debate and great dismay about what to do. There seemed to be no way to change things or stop the storm.

So they simply sunk deeper into the HAH-BEE-TAH way of life—surviving another day.

As the outer storm raged…so, too, the inner despair and chaos grew!

An inner HAH-BEE-TAH began to brew within the hearts of the villagers. Their hearts began to fill with

worry,
fear,
judgment,
resentment,
submission, and
hopeless despair

All emotions raged increasingly within the hearts of the village folks. An increasing fury tossed their hearts from the inside just as the HAH-BEE-TAH raged outside beyond their walls.

As the outer HAH-BEE-TAH raged, so too, there began to be raging storms of the Heart and Soul in each of the villagers—until they had no words—just their inner chaos and agonies.

The villagers longed for the sun. They dreamed of quiet warm breezes. They yearned to be free to move about. They began to hate each moment spent in their darkened lower gathering rooms. They began to resent the closeness and even each other! Their hidey (w)Holes—their lower basement rooms—began to become places of destruction and despair rather than protection and hope.

Soon there was no difference between the outer and the inner HAH-BEE-TAHs—all became storm tossed!

Now, back in a dark corner of one of the lower basement rooms was a small girl, named RAH-TOO. She, too, was so tired of the dark small hidey-(w)Hole room. Yes, it was dry, BUT oh, she was so very tired of it! She missed the sun, the playful games, the running and skipping in the sunlight.

She was also, quite frankly, sick of hearing the increasing numbers of despairing conversations between the adults huddled in her hidey-(w)Hole basement refuge. "What will become of us?" "How can we help ourselves?" "What kind of loss has already occurred—we do not even know that!" "What did we do to deserve this??" "What if we never see the sun again?" On and on they lamented and cried…she was sick and tired of it all.

AND besides, they never seemed to come to any clarity or answers… they just kept going around and around the same boring debate!

Now…secretly to entertain herself, she had been rummaging around in their lower gathering room and had found a small tunnel that led to the outside. For the longest of times, she had obeyed the rule to "never, ever go out in the storm!" However, one day she just couldn't bear it any longer. Quietly, so as to draw no attention to herself, she gathered together a small bundle, put on layers of her clothing, and slowly edged to the tunnel's opening.

When she was sure no one was watching, she tucked herself into the tunnel opening and began to swiggle her way down the small dark path. It was longer than she had anticipated; however, she kept going. Even as she heard the storm's voices getting louder and louder, still she kept going until then, there it was—the storm.

She could see it just a few inches from her face—a raging, ever-changing swirling wet windy wild presence. The HAH-BEE-TAH was right there before her.

She crawled forward and stepped out into the arms of the HAH- BEE-TAH!

Immediately she was swept up and tossed and turned this way and that. She was spinning and twirled around…lifted higher and farther than she could even imagine. Now…even if she had wanted to go back to the hidey (w)Hole, she could not.

She could see neither land nor sky nor ocean nor plains. She was dizzy, cold, scared and lost. The storm had tossed her beyond any place she had heard of. Finally she lost all of her awareness…all seemed black, violent. The HAH-BEE-TAH had become her universe!

Abruptly, she dropped—she dropped out of the storm's fury high up onto the cliffs of the north side of her village. She came to rest out on a ledge.

She crawled upwards and towards some caves she knew about. She crawled about on her hands and knees until she fell, exhausted, into a small hidey (w)Hole cave, and there she fell asleep.

When she awoke, the storm was still raging outside the cave…as it seemed it had for forever. Then, she heard a voice speak quietly to her from the back of the cave. "Greetings, little one." She turned around. There was MAH-Wah-TEE, a man who had not_returned to the village on that first day of HAH-BEE-TAH and was thought to have been lost in the storm.

Yet, there he was, and he had a light, no, a calm, no, a stillness that seemed to radiate outwards from him. She had never seen or felt anything like that. The cave was bright without any visible source of light. Something quite strange was happening here.

"What happened to you?" she asked. He smiled. "Come nearer the fire I have built in the back of this small cave here, and I will tell you."

She thought he would tell how he changed, but no, he settled down with a warm cup of Meadow Grass tea. He offered her a cup, but she was too curious to think of tea. And then he began his tale.

"When the storm blew up on that first day, I was up here in the rocky meadows tending to my goats. I saw clearly that I was not going to be able to get down soon enough, so I found a larger hidey (w)Hole for myself and the goats and settled in for the night. After all, it was only a storm, or so I thought." A long, far away look washed over his eyes.

Then, he smiled. She felt like smiling for the first time in days, and she had no idea why. Somehow things just felt better—more harmonious inside of her.

"So now," he said, "let's move you to the larger cave up the hill a bit and settle you in more comfortably."

As he said that she became aware of how cold she was…shivering and all…so rising, she moved towards the cave's entrance walking next to MAH-Wah-TEE. She braced herself to encounter the storm's fury… but it didn't come! In fact, she walked out and was embraced by sunshine and warmth and quiet breezes. She was shocked. What was happening? Where was the storm?

She turned to MAH-Wah-TEE with huge wondering eyes. She could see the storm a bit over there in the distance. She could still hear it with a bit of effort. However, where she stood it was sunny, warm, and gentle—without the HAH-BEE-TAH's ruling fury! How could that be? MAH-Wah-TEE smiled at her puzzled face.

"As we walk, let me finish my story, for as you can see, something more has happened up here…while the HAH-BEE-TAH has raged." MAH-Wah-TEE continued. "After I crouched in the cave for more than a week, I began to realize that this was something more than a mere storm. After two weeks had passed, I began to become more afraid. I was alone and worrying about what would happen to the goats in my care? What was happening to the villagers? Was my family safe from the storm? And then I wondered what would happen to me.

"I became filled with fear and resentment, judgment that this was a bad and dreadful, evil thing—this storm. AND still it raged on.

"However, I noticed something more. At first, I thought I was imagining things, but as the storm continued to furiously swirl around and since I had little else to do, I began to experiment!

"In essence, I noticed that as I became more fearful, thinking things like 'What would happen next?' or 'What has already happened?' the storm raged more furiously about my small hidey (w)Hole cave. As I raged at the injustice of this—lost in a storm alone—the storm blew that much harder!

As I grieved for my family, who must surely think that I was dead—the storm pelted my dark cave that much more feverishly.

"Then, I recalled my great grandmother NEEH Wah. She had revealed the mysteries of seeing. She had used the magic of curiosity without judgment…now, trapped by this storm, so would I! So I began to consider the Mysteries of Storm.

"If my inner raging, fearing, grieving, and judging seemed to feed the HAH-BEE-TAH, what would the HAH-BEE-TAH do if I fed it a diet of inner calming, soothing, trusting stillness? So, I began to practice and experiment—at first, I called it my MAH-Wah-TEE practice.

"As I did this—feeding the HAH-BEE-TAH calmness, trust, and stillness—I noticed that the storm inside of me began to ease. I was less anxious. I was more still. As I continued to do this, despite the outer HAH-BEE-TAH, an inner still point in each moment began to reveal itself to me. Still, the storms raged outside, yet, my own inner spaces began to calm.

"As I still continued this inner calming practice, it became simply all that I focused on as I went about living each day up here alone.

"And then one day, I noticed my refection in a pool of water near the entrance of my cave. There seemed like there was a light hovering about my image. I dismissed it as a mere quirk and continued my day.

"About three days later, I arose in my cave, expecting the usual darkness and the sounds of HAH-BEE-TAH's voices screeching their greeting, but this time it was different.

"All about me was warmth, calm and stillness. The storm was removed from my particular moment. I was as shocked as you are!

"Things have continued in this way since then. Where I am, there is sunshine, warmth, and gentle breezes. And where I am not, the HAH-BEE-TAH seems free to be in its fury!

"Revealed to me by this storm is the mystery of the "Here I AM"—stillness of each moment.

"This was the mystery, the gift of HAH-BEE-TAH!"

RAH–TOO burst out, "Teach me! Please teach me the gift of the HAH-BEE-TAH!"

MAH-Wah-TEE smiled. "Yes, let me tell you the mystery of storms. They feed upon our inner storms and cannot sustain themselves without that diet of worry, fear, judgment and resentments—that nourishment of 'What if's…' and 'What now's…' that churn around inside of us all.

"We feed the outer HAH-BEE-TAH as we move into the inner turmoils! We are in these inner storms when we are in resistance to the stillness of 'I AM here.'

"Yes, I came to see that it was I who was feeding the HAH-BEE-TAH. As much as I wanted it gone, I was the nourishment and the daily meals of this monster."

MAH-Wah TEE paused. "I did not want to see this at first. It was easier to be victim to the HAH-BEE-TAH than to admit my own responsibility for it! However, once I could let myself know this, I came to know that my inner raging was my resisting the presence of the storm around me.

"Now I know that when we drop all our resistance to the outer storms and allow them to be as they are, we can sink into the 'Here I AM.' This is found in each moment. I have come to think of it as The Great Hum, the Great Hum of I AM, I AM, I AM, I AM …. hhhuuummmmm.

"Not ahead of the moment. Not behind the moment. Not fearing the next moment. Not judging the past moment.

"So, first, the inner HAH-BEE-TAH calms. As we cease to feed the inner storms, the outer storms also have no more meals of worry, judgment, fear, blame, shame, and anxiety. Then, this light life seems to be the result!

"Exactly how all it works is a mystery still and is likely to remain so!"

And so it began that MAH Wah TEE taught RAH-TOO the practice of The Great Hum.

And here is the GREAT HUM practice:

What one must do is ask only one question—a true wisdom question: "Where am I?" Listen for the answer from deep within: "HERE I AM."

Over and over ask and listen, ask and listen…until you are walking The Great Hum. I AM I AM I AM I AM… hhhhuuuuuuummmmmmmmmmmmmm

It is this that apparently expresses itself in the sunshine, the warm breezes, the calm stillness, the ease and tenderness—all amidst the HAH-BEE-TAH.

RAH-TOO was an adept pupil and quickly was walking in sunshine whether she was near MAH-Wah-TEE or on her own. The HAH-BEE-TAH was no longer the ruler of her world! What freedom! What courage it had taken to admit that "No, she was not victim but co-creator of the dreadful storm."

As they sat one day looking over the village that was still caught in the HAH-BEE TAH's growing fury, RAH-TOO asked, "WHY have you not told the others?"

MAH-Wah-TEE nodded sadly. "I tried," he said, "but when I knocked on their doors and cried out that I could help, they refused to let me in. They said, 'It is a monster of the storm come to trick us,' or they said, 'It is our imagination that such sounds are words.' They could not believe that one can walk in peace in the middle of this storm. It is just wishful thinking.

"And so, I returned here to the rocky mountain cave, living in the sunshine of The Great Hum until you arrived, dumped here by the storm."

They sat in silence for a long time. The HAH-BEE-TAH still raged around the villagers, and finally RAH-TOO could stand it no longer.

After great discussion with MAH-Wah-TEE, they determined that RAH-TOO would return to her hidey (w)Hole basement lower level room and say nothing. Perhaps only a natural curiosity could break through the inner HAH-BEE-TAH of the villagers.

And, so it was…

RAH-TOO traveled down to the village and back through the tunnel, back to her hidey (w)Hole basement room and sat quietly in the back corner. Those around were none the wiser of her absence. They had been too caught up in their own HAH-BEE-TAHs to have noticed her absence or her return.

Then one day, despite RAH-TOO's quietness, a small child noticed that the back corner of the room seemed to be filled with more light than any other place. The child crawled over to be near this bit of hope. And then another and another of the young curious ones noticed and moved over to be near RAH-TOO, whose light was steadily growing and pulsating and inviting.

RAH-TOO had continued The Great Hum practice even after she had returned to the dark hidey (w)Hole.

On the day that is now called "the First of the Last Days of the HAH-BEE-TAH," a small child called out, "Look. LOOK!! There is a light in the dark corner! Look. Look. Feel the calm, the stillness, the peace near RAH-TOO! Come look!"

The Elders in the hidey (w)Hole "pooh-poohed" the young child and turned again to their serious discussions. They were, after all, the Elders. This was a "serious situation," and as elders, they must be the ones to figure out this forever storm!

So at first, only the young ones responded to the call, but soon all were gathered around in their now open curiosity.

Finally, they were open…no longer so storm tossed as to be unable to hear or see or feel!

So it began in this one dark hidey (w)Hole of RAH-TOO's. RAH-TOO was able to teach them the practice of The Great Hum: Ask "Where am I?" Listen "Here I am." Ask and listen, ask and listen until it is I AM I AM I AM I AM…HHUMMMMMMMM.

And it was true for all—the peace of this inner call and answer.

First, it stills the inner HAH-BEE-TAH until the inner resistances are no more, and then it ceases to feed the outer storms until…finally, nearly all of the village, save the Elders, were walking The Great Hum—A Stillness of moment—I AM I AM I AM, regardless of the outer conditions.

Finally, the elders in RAH-TOO's hidey (w)Hole relinquished their tight minds and fearful hearts and began to learn The Great Hum practice as well. They were sick of the HAH-BEE-TAH and were ready to do anything to be free!

Then, the children of RAH-TOO's hidey (w)Hole crept out to other lower level basements to teach the Hum Practice…until all in the village were engaged in The Great Hum.

All were curious to see what would happen…for as yet, the HAH-BEE-TAH still raged around the village. One day, some of the villagers began to sense that the outer storm was subsiding! One by one, all the villagers began to come out of their hidey (w)Holes. The outer HAH-BEE-TAH, having nothing to feed upon, soon left to move on to another village—to offer its gift again.

MAH-Wah-TEE was reunited with his family, who later moved to the great caves above the village for all time.

RAH-TOO became "First Youngster" of the village, a new position created after the HAB-BEE-TAH, for it had been determined that without the natural curiosity of the children, all would have been lost…the villagers lost and storm-tossed for all eternity!

And so it is now and has been that rather than only Elders leading the village folks, the town now has Youngsters consulting the Elders, cautioning them to remain open, curious, and humming along.

And from that time to this very moment, all of this land called Home is cradled by the practice of The Great Hum. And if you listen carefully, you can hear the Hum of all the hearts sighing and singing together, "I AM I AM I AM I AM…HHUMMMMMMM."

Yes, still storms come and still Storms go, but never has there again been a storm that stays, for there is nothing for it to feed upon.

And so it is…how to be Peace amidst the storms.

Where are you?

I AM HERE!

****

There is no doubt that the first reaction for many of us when life gets tough is to actively batten down the hatches, hide in our (w)Holes, and wait for it to pass over or "go away." There are others of us who dissect and analyze, seeking to identify the cause so we can "fix it." And there are still others who despair, collapsing into passivity, and then there are those who rage in impotent outrage at the experience of feeling victim to Life's (W)holy Mystery. And finally, there are those who blame either themselves or the other so as to have an explanation in the hope this will alter the moment. What we all have in common in the face of a moment of "Life Chaos" is we look towards someone or something for rescue. How wildly human of us! As babies we depended upon that "rescue" from a dirty diaper or a hungry belly. And what is more is that we, as humans, tend to contract when "IT" hurts. When the storms rage, we look OUTwards and we CONTRACT.

This fable is an invitation to each of us to dare to stay open—choosing curiosity rather than conviction, choosing risk rather than the familiar, and choosing from inside out rather than remaining outer-driven. Where are you hiding out? What would you risk, if you dared? How might your (W)hole life be different if you were "humming" your way through each moment?

The Story of Wah-NEE

Dedicated to those of us who walk wide-eyed in the world after fate has demanded that we tear off our blinders in order to live. Dedicated to all of us who are opening our eyes to the new lives we are being called to walk into with open eyes, naked perceptions and bold hearts.

Once upon a time a long time ago and is still true today, there was a village. It was high upon a mountain, and it was known for its vision and its boldness, for its aliveness and its potent presence. It was like a beacon for all the lands around, but it was not always this way. The story of its birth is whispered with awe and trembling around the campfires. And sometimes the tale of its emergence from the darkness preceding it is told in the darkest part of night to remind us of hope in clear sight. It is the journey of Nee-WAH and how she came to be called with such a wide-open name. Even in saying her name out loud, one's mouth opens wide.

Once, moons of time before the village had moved to the top of the mountain, it sat at the bottom of the mountain. All the people of the village were farmers. They were a community of what they thought of as ordinary folk, save for one thing that we might consider unusual. Honestly, they gave no thought to this element of their form. They were all born with "scales," flaps of skin shaped like discs descending three quarters of the way down in front of their eyes. There was a narrow slit through which they saw others and their world. This was not considered unusual. Everyone's eyes had these scales that descended three quarters of the way down. They knew one another by the appearance of the feet that they could see through the slits. Obviously, feet were very important. How they looked, what they wore, and how they moved—feet were one's initial introduction to others of the tribe.

The members of the clan moved through their day, and they farmed, and they married, and they gave birth to others, all of whom had the same scales three quarters of the way down their eyes. And then one day something changed. The land seemed "off" somehow. It was a subtle shift but a shift nonetheless.

The farmers began to notice that there was a smell in the air that wasn't quite right, and those that would cook noticed that there was a subtle taste in the water that was not OK. Now, the elders of the town pooh-poohed those that gave voice to their concerns, and to be frank, it was because the elders had no idea of what it meant, so they just chose to ignore it. But the farming folk knew that something harmful was creeping into their lands and water and food stuff. There were whispered conversations in their homes. There were huddled clumps of folks guessing in trembly voices what it might be. The truth was that something was amiss, and no one knew what it was.

Time passed, and those that dared look began to notice that there were brown edges around some of the plants, and there were fewer birds singing. Clearly, the people admitted to themselves there was a blight of some sort upon the land. They could see evidence of it through the slits beneath their scales, these same vision-slits which allowed them to behold the dear, precious feet of those they loved. More and more evidence accumulated until the blight upon the land was spoken of as the "browning and the dying." That was what they named it. Everywhere they looked, the green things of their world were becoming brown and then dying. "The Browning and the Dying" spread until there was nothing left untouched! Still no one knew what it was or what to do.

In their fear, the village elders began to create rules: Rules of pretend and denial, Rules of blindness and deafness, Rules of muteness and threat. No one was to speak of "The Browning and the Dying," and if you did, you would be slain or imprisoned, for truly it was not a problem, or so they declared. And yet, the people and the children and all those that were out and about on the land, they knew this was a grave threat. But what to do, still no one knew. The elders' fear grew like a cancer in their elder gatherings. They were more afraid and more afraid, for they, too, if they admitted it, were seeing the "Browning and the Dying." But they did not know what to do, and they were the elders, the leaders of the village. They were supposed to know. In their shame of not knowing, they hid ever more passionately behind the veil of rules. They created more rules, more reasons to not speak of IT, more threats if you did. And their fear grew to such an extent that it came to be that when the newborns were born, their scales were sewn completely shut so that they could not see what everyone else could see. This was done by the decree of the Trembling Trembly Terrified Elders for "the sake of the welfare of the village."

And so the blight grew. This portion of the tale is often whispered, for fear of stirring the "Trembling Times" (as they were called later) all up again. The Trembly Terrors became so all encompassing that no one could sleep, and no one could work, and no one could think. The village folks simply succumbed to the Trembles. And yet "The Browning and the Dying" was still progressing.

In the village, there was a young girl. Her name was Wah-NEE. Wah-NEE had played in all of the lands. Not only had she been born here, but she had spent all her growing-up time out and about on the lands. She knew all that the space beneath her scales would allow her to see. She knew the smallest of bugs and the little area near the creek. She knew what it was like to smell the freshly cut hay and to hold the little grains near enough so she could look beneath her scales at their shape. Her heart was breaking at the destruction of her home by "The Browning and the Dying," and none of the big people were doing anything at all, nor did she know what to do. But she did know one thing: She knew she must do something. She must do something.

And then in the middle of the night it occurred to her. "Ah, I will go to the top of our mountain, beneath whose shelter we have always lived. Maybe, if I am high up, if I tilt my head back, perhaps I will see something beneath my scales that will show me what this is all about." But to do this risked death, for it had been declared by the elders that anyone who went to investigate the "Browning and the Dying" would be shunned and killed if discovered in this poisonous act of curiosity. She had to choose. Would she dare on behalf of her people and her land and her precious bugs and little bits of river that she had played by, or would she acquiesce? She decided that she simply could not acquiesce.

So she gathered supplies, which was quite difficult to do, and in the dead of night she crept out. In the darkness, she was blind because her vision was limited to what she could see beneath the slits of these scales.

At night without the bright sun to shed extra light on that which was at "feet level," darkness was all she could see. All that she could do was move forward, feeling for the incline of the mountain. Touch sensations were all that guided her, her knees and elbows scrapping along the pebbled earth, as she blindly extended her arms to choose her next move.

And she crawled, and she fell, and she cut her hands, her feet, and her knees. She tried to walk in a slow shamble but would stumble, falling to her hands and knees. Rising again, Wah-NEE kept creeping upward and upward and upward, not even knowing what she was climbing towards or if it would do anything for her blessed and beloved village. She did not know, and still she climbed and fell. And no one saw her tears. No one felt the pain of her skinned knees and hands and elbows and feet. And no one saw the bloody tracks of her passage up the mountain.

And it is said that finally she arrived just before dawn and fell in a heap at the crest of the mountain and slept. When the sun rose and she raised her head enough to see through the slits beneath the scales, she saw great spaces stretching from the pinnacle upon which she sat. Then she heard a voice. This voice said to her, "I have been waiting. I am glad you came." She whipped her head around, not really even expecting to find anybody up upon this high place. She tilted her head back so she could get the best view possible, and there before her was a small being with very wide eyes and no scales hanging from the eyebrow ridge!!! She had never seen any manner of creature like this, and she jumped back. She said, "Who are you?" "Ah, I am Abba-EMah," the creature said.

Abba-EMah said, "Up until now, I have been the one who has held the vision and the witnessing on behalf of all the lands, but now it is time for this to change. YOU are the one I have been waiting for." Wah-NEE was completely confused and did not understand. She stuttered, "What, what do you mean?" She settled herself down and tilted her head back quite carefully. She did not want to miss any part of this encounter.

Abba-EMah explained that all that was now occurring had been set into motion eons before this moment. It had been decided that there would come a time when something would occur that would call forth, even demand, an evolution within the people. At first it would be seen as a great danger and a great threat. And it would be a small one who would begin the transformation.

Wah-NEE had never heard of this and did not understand. She asked again, "What do you mean?" And then Abba-EMah told her something she never thought she would hear!

Abba-EMah told Wah-NEE that she was here to begin an evolutionary step of her people, and it required that she tear away the scales from her eyes. "This will allow you to see boldly and clearly and cleanly all that is before you. All the land depends upon it." Wah-NEE was shocked and backed away from Abba-EMah. "I cannot imagine. This has never been allowed. I have never heard of this. In fact, I have been told that if you tear away the scales, you will die, and it will be agony in the process."

And Abba-EMah said, "Yes, that is what you have been told. And now you must decide in your heart what you will choose, for if this radical transformation does not occur, the lands will die and so will all your people." And Wah-NEE said, "Give me a moment." She dropped deeply into her heart and determined that life without the land and her people would be nothing. It would be meaningless. So if it meant that she had to die, if it meant that she had to rip away these scales and suffer great agony, so be it. Wah-NEE chose. She would find out if there was great agony in this choice. She would do it.

She took a deep breath. She turned to Abba-EMah and said, "How do I do this?" Abba-EMah smiled a gentle smile and said, "Grab a hold of the lower edges of the scales and simply lift." This sounded very frightening. Wah-NEE was sure that she would be causing herself great agony. She took a deep breath and grabbed a hold of the lower edges of both of her eye-scales. She lifted up, and suddenly, they were in her hands!

There had been no agony. Barely any sensation at all had accompanied the tearing away. She squinted because she did not know how to be in the world with such clear vision. Even squinting was new to her. It had never been needed before. She held up the eye-scales, and there they were, between her fingers. Wah-NEE carefully turned her gaze towards all that lay before her from the top of the mountain. She saw a world she had never seen before.

"Now you are ready to begin to learn what you need to learn to take back to your people," Abba-EMah said. "When you look," said Abba-EMah, "upon something that is of the 'Browning and the Dying,' when you really, really look and allow your vision to penetrate beneath the surface to see what is really there, you will see great rivers of life. But it must be witnessed and seen and recognized for it to be sustained. Witnessing life's flow is what nourishes its continuation. Your people could not witness effectively with the scales covering their eyes. It was for this reason that I have been 'witness on your behalf' until now. Now the time has come for you to be your own witnesses. And now we will practice."

And so from the top of the mountain Abba-EMah and Wah-NEE looked across, and Wah-NEE began to see. "Ah, when I look at that bush showing the 'Browning and the Dying' and I allow myself to see beneath that, there is life flowing in golden swirling currents. I can see it." And as she practiced this witnessing, this seeing beneath the appearance, "the Greening and the Living" began to flow again within the bush. The bush seemed to straighten up and glow with the flood of new life moving through its leaves and stems. "This is not so hard. This I can do." So Wah-NEE practiced and played with this wondrous gift called Witnessing.

One evening as the sun was setting and Wah-NEE was truly enjoying what she saw with her wide open eyes, she let her heart drift to her family and friends still locked in fear down in the village.

"Abba-EMah, now you must come with me to the village and tell all of the people how to offer this witnessing gift to the lands," said Wah-NEE. Abba-EMah gently shook her head and said, "I cannot. That is for you to do." "Why?" Wah-NEE challenged her teacher. "Because," said Abba-EMah, "I am up here. I am holding all of the land from complete death. I cannot leave. If I step aside for even one moment, all will be lost."

Wah-NEE said, "What can I do? I'm scared. They're going to kill me when I go back, even though I've found the most wondrous of all things—a way to bring life back to the things that are brown and dying." Abba-EMah said, "You will know what to do when the time comes, but you must go now. Time is running out. Either your people will learn to see beneath the browning and witness the true life of what is or all will perish. Now is the time!"

Wah-NEE took a deep breath, and she chose in her heart, "Whatever it takes, I will take this back to them. Even if I must die in the process, I will go to my people." She did not realize how different she looked. Her eyes were wide. They were free of eye-scales. Having spent much time with Abba-EMah, she had become accustomed to her new vision and manner of seeing. Truly, she loved it. She could see things she had never seen before. And she could see the life flowing inside all the things around. It was quite extraordinary. Wah-NEE could see with a bold, bright, clear vision, never imagined in all her young life. "They will be so happy when they learn about this. It will be great!"

She purposely set aside her trepidation for having broken all the Elder-Rules.

She ran down the mountain, skipping in glee, and every bush that she looked at she could see the greening and living coming back. She could not wait to get to the village. "What would happen if everyone in all the lands learned this wonder of witnessing?"

She arrived at the edge of the village. There is a sentry standing guard. The sentry demanded, "Who are you?" Wah-NEE said, "I am Wah-NEE."

"That cannot be. You do not have scales on your eyes. And besides,' added the sentry, "I know her, and she has been lost in the wilderness for days. No one has seen her. We have all given her up for dead." However, the sentry's concern was not for the "lost Wah-NEE" but for the strange being lacking eye-scales who stood before him. He rang the alarm bells.

The villagers gathered at the sound of the alarm. The stood around Wah-NEE, but made sure to keep their distance from this strange one with wide eyes.

As Wah-NEE told her story, some of the smaller children crept closer, but the bulk of the villagers kept a good space between them and her. She had kept her eye-scales to show to them so they did not think she was simply from another tribe or created a great myth. The eye-scales were secreted away in her pocket.

She said, "I'm here to tell you, all of you must take off your scales." The villagers shrieked and protested. "We can't." "We can't. We'll die." "This is against the law." "We'll be thrown into prison." "We'll be slain and shunned." Everyone in the village went into great uproar, and they fled to their homes, save for the youngest children. They stayed, and Wah-NEE said, "Wanna try?"

And they did. The children reached up, and they simply lifted their scales off. Now, many of the small children did not have eye-scales and could see far more than those that were older. This unsettled some of the older children, and so they, too, sat with Wah-NEE to gain courage. And then they, too, removed their scales. Soon parents and aunts and uncles, grandmothers and grandfathers were choosing to remove their scales. This radical choice spread throughout the village until finally everyone was walking around wide-eyed in their vision, save for the elders. They were standing across the town square with their arms crossed and their heads tilted back so they could see all these wide-eyed beings. They still refused to dare that last step.

Standing in the back of the crowd of elders was the eldest of elders. This particular elder was so wizened up and churned up that he could barely tip his head back far enough to be able to see through the slit. Creak, creak, creak, this elder moved herself to the center of the town. Then, in front of them all, she stopped before Wah-NEE and said, "I do not know what to do about the 'browning and dying.' You have come to us with something. I have nothing to offer. Thus, I cannot say no, and yet, I am quite afraid."

And Wah-NEE said, "Trust me. It's meant to be. I will be here with you." Thus the world changed when one of the youngest of the tribe invited the eldest of the village to become wide-eyed!

The elder reached up and she lifted off her eye-scales without even an iota of pain, her scales caught between her two fingers of each hand. Squinting and then wide-eyed, she turned to her other elder companions and spoke, "Now. Now is the time. This is what I was told so long ago. I was told there would come a moment when all the world would change, and we would wake up. And I know THIS is the time! I know what to do."

Later it was revealed that this elder of elders had been instructed, as a very young child, all about the time of change. What had not been revealed was the "how" of it, only that once it was clearly known, the village was to go on a "walk-about" of renewal.

And so it was for a year, the entire village went on a wandering-wondering-witnessing-walk-about, moving throughout the lands. The witness would stand before a person or a bush or a tree or a body of water which was touched with the "Browning and Dying." Then, with their Wide-EYED vision they looked beneath the surface to the true life flowing there. In this manner there was great celebrating and renewing of the life that still flowed there. And as it was witnessed, it rose to the surface. "The Greening" would awaken. All that needed to happen was for life to be honored, for though it still existed, its value had been forgotten.

All of the people—children and elders alike—moved throughout the lands, and then at the end of the year gathered together again. Now, the lands were green and alive. The people had taken off the eye-shields believed to be permanent for all time, and in doing so, their way of seeing became a tool of healing. No longer did anyone simply look at the surface of another, but rather offered True Sight, which healed, transformed, renewed.

Wah-NEE changed her name to Nee-WAH. She did this because she wanted her name to have an opening feel and sound at the end of it. Nee-WAH. She insisted everyone say it with a wide open mouth that she could look at with her very big clear bold eyes.

The village was moved up to the pinnacle mountain. Abba-EMah greeted them all, "Welcome to your final destiny. This is what your people have been called to do for all time. It is now done."

And so it is that the blight of "the Browning and the Dying" was considered the best gift of all, for it brought great sight. It called forth from all of the villagers the courage to take off the eye-shields. It moved them to a new location of far greater sight. And the entire town and all those people who lived within its borders became known as the holders of clear vision with the power of Witnessing Truth beneath all appearance.

****

I would invite each of you to take this story into your hearts, into your souls. And in those times when you are with people who still have the shields covering their eyes, see beneath that for the life that flows. When you look at the lands that in some way seem broken, it is not to deny what is there but to see beneath it so that life knows you still hold the truth, and it will come forth by your authority: The Authority of TRUTH WITNESS.

Where and how and upon what we place our focus is of great importance. As one places one's gaze upon anyone, including one's self, our focus calls forth its own reflection. What we seek to see or believe that we are seeing is the very framework that determines our sight. Sometimes we see with hard, harsh eyes, sometimes with gentle, embracing eyes, and sometimes with indifferent eyes. How our heart's eyes focus leads us into experiences of a particular and marching sort. To dare to take up the responsibility of choosing to see and of deciding how we will focus and upon what is a leap of unrecognized proportions. It is a leap into the wild truth that what we see, what we focus upon is our "real world." What are you choosing your world to be?

Ceques of the Heart

Dedicated to those of us who have hardened our hearts against the agonies of life. Dedicated to those of us who have inadvertently stumbled back home to our selves, only to find a village embracing us in welcome. Dedicated to those of us who thought a hardened heart would save us from heartbreak, only to realize that when our hearts break open, we awake to life itself.

Once upon a time, in a time that was a long time ago and is still true today, there was a woman who was known for her soft heart. This was not always the case. It was said that for many years—perhaps even eons of time—the only words ever spoken about this woman were in reference to her hard-heartedness. The children, the old people and even those of the middle time of life—all of them steered clear of "the woman." It was said that with a glance she could harden even the softest of flower petals.

How this all came to be was a mystery. It is whispered that "the woman" was to be viewed as an example of what can occur to a person who has broken under the weight of the horrors of life itself. "*It could even happen to you and you and me and us.*" Around the fires and on the long walks from the town to the fair even unto other villages, there would be occasional huddled inquiries as to the state of the heart of this one or that. All secretly feared that they would become like "the woman!" All feared her and focused only on her hard-heartedness for so long that she was simply known only as "the woman."

In point of fact, "the woman" did have a name. Unknown to the people of the village, she had been baptized Alzibet. Each day she would rise and go about the business of life—eating a meal, shopping for supplies in the nearby farmer's market and tending to her pets, a snake and a rat. Although they were an odd pair of companions, these two creatures suited her perfectly. All who lived with her in her small third-floor flat were by nature contained and a bit hardened, just like her.

After each day's activities were completed, Alzibet would sit in her hand-me-down chair and look out over the village. There was not much to her view, save for a large, very old oak tree. The tree's branches soared skyward, and its roots dug deep nearly to the center of the earth. The tree and Alzibet, "the woman," would sit in silent observation of each other and the village during the afternoon hours when the sun would slide from its height down to the rim of the sky, only to slip into the unknown until its next emergence. Each day, this silent encounter of tree and woman would mark the beginning of the afternoon for villagers walking by.

For many years this continued: The silent companionship of two hardened beings consisting only of face-to-bark reflections. And then something began to happen.

It was subtle at first. Alzibet was sitting as tradition would have it, in her broken-down chair, when a whispery voice touched her ears. Startled, she sat up, abruptly alert, yet unable to discern any words. Then it faded away. Writing it all off as a common occurrence of elder ears, she settled back into her chair. Again and again as the days unfolded upon one another, Alzibet would hear this whispery shuffling voice whose words and meaning were unintelligible. As water drips from leaves after a spring rain—a drop, a drip and another drop—within Alzibet there was a dripping of days that watered a curiosity within her.

This in itself was surprising, as even curiosity requires a bit of open-heartedness to sprout in a human's heart. And as everyone knew, Alzibet was "the woman" of the hardened heart. Nothing, it was said, could grow in such dried up soil!

It was a day in mid-February that the first clear measure of meaning within the whispery sounds was revealed. As she told this tale later, it seemed that abruptly an alignment between her ears and the sounds occurred. In truth, it had been the slow drip drop of days passing that allowed this alignment to occur. Curiosity is like that, rooting itself ever so slowly into even the most hardened.

The whispered words she first heard were, "*If only I were a great tree… whose roots dug deep and whose branches soared sky-ward. (sigh) If only…If only …*"

Alzibet realized that it was the tree itself who was whispering—the Great Oak Tree opposite her balcony! It was the inner voice of the tree! As this realization drifted deeper into her awareness, the meaning of the words struck her with a greater shock than even the hearing of the tree.

As her curiosity took root, Alzibet wondered to herself, *How could it be that this huge tree before her eyes would be hoping to be a great tree??? Didn't it see itself? How could it not know the truth of its huge presence?*

No answers came. The only words she heard were the whispering, echoing cries of the tree repeated over and over again.

If only…If only I were a great tree whose branches knew how to soar and whose roots dug deep in ever-expanding rings. If only…If only…

And then the sun would slide past the edge of the earth's crust, and darkness would lay once again upon the village.

Alzibet's mind was agitated.
Alzibet's heart was disturbed.
Alzibet's body felt trembly and tender somehow.
Alzibet's curiosity was awakened.

How had it come to be that the tree was so confused about itself? It made no sense. It was this very nonsense that Alzibet could not shake off! It was so obvious to her that the tree was a GREAT TREE!

She mulled on this for days. She could find no sense to the tree's whispered longings. Gradually an insistent subtle curiosity arose within her. This curiosity could not be refused, and it formed itself into a larger inquiry, beyond how the tree came to not know itself.

This greater fascination was with another question: *How might she show the tree its true nature? Was it even possible?*

In later years, as she told of her remembering, she would pause here and laugh with gentle self-appreciation. The magic of her fascination was a gift only recognized after it had opened the locked places of her heart. Only after the fact was Alzibet able to view the potent alchemy of curiosity, which had been the key to her unveiling. Only after the heart-miracles did she realize the immeasurable worth of persistent questioning. Her hardness was revealed as merely a disguise. And what an unwrapping it was! However, this is ahead of the telling of this tale.

From the point at which her curiosity took root, all her days changed. This change was not conscious as much as primal. She had to know. Could she reach the tree with the truth of itself?

She rose with the sun, and she moved rapidly through her chores so as to take her seat on her balcony across from The Great Tree. Soon it was that even when she was not on her small perch or even outside, she could hear the whispering pleas of the tree. It was always the same plea.

And every moment that did not require her attention was filled with this one wondering question: *How might she remind the tree of its true nature?*

Over the course of many days she made various experiments. For a time, she talked at and with the tree. In spoken words, she described the tree to the tree. She spoke of all its bark and branches and shapes. She spoke of all its secret shadowy places and its great size. Nothing apparent happened.

Next, she considered that perhaps an image—a drawing of the tree—shown to it might somehow reach into its essence and remind it. That next afternoon, she began to draw, in charcoal, images of the tree. First, she drew its entire shape as she saw it from the balcony. Next, she began a series of sketches of its branches and roots, its bark and its shadows. Finally, she lay down upon the ground and looked up through the branches. She sketched all the shapes of its soaring limbs with the sky as the backdrop.

Her charcoal mirror complete, she set all the images before the tree, hanging them from the rail of her balcony each afternoon, where the sun would light them directly. Then taking her seat, she would listen for any change within the whispered longings.

If only I were...If only I were a great tree whose branches soared skyward and whose roots dug deep into the dirt...If only...

As long as she sat there, day after day...there was no apparent change in the tree.

Now…unnoticed by "the woman," her behaviors were so radical and so "out of character" that the entire village had begun to observe Alizbet. This had become a community-wide query. The folks in the village had noticed that she no longer moved sluggishly through her day but seemed to walk with a purpose and fervor. She no longer seemed to have a blank dead-look in her eyes. For some reason, she seemed less threatening to the villagers when she spoke what little she spoke to them.

One day, while sitting on her balcony, another thought occurred to Alzibet. *Perhaps the tree would respond if she was in physical contact with it? After all, she could hear its cries…maybe it could feel her touch or sense her replies!*

She rose immediately and descended from her balcony. She walked across the village and began to touch the tree. She lay against it. She stroked the bark. Days passed with her touching every part of the tree which she could reach. As she touched the tree, she mentally sent images of the tree to the tree. "The woman" embraced the tree with a passionate curiosity.

Nothing changed.

Then, she considered that perhaps if she walked nearby the tree, it would feel her presence and her invitation to know the truth of itself through its roots. Perhaps the vibrations of her footsteps would be transmitted through the earth to the very roots of the tree, then, maybe...

In a sort of spiraling meditative walk, she began to move around and around the tree. She did not know that what she was doing was, in fact, an ancient art. She was laying down Ceques—"presence imprints."

These Ceques or "imprints of holy presence passing by," can only be laid upon the earth and empowered by one with an open-loving naked heart. Her curiosity and love for the tree had awoken in her the heart of her heart—her wisdom grace presence—her Soul! With each step she took around the tree, Ceques, webs of loving presence, were woven about the tree. She fell into a "Ceque Trance" in which she forgot herself and forgot the tree. Everything became the spiraling weaving walking-dance. Around and around and around she moved, ever weaving herself to the tree and the tree to her own soul.

She whispered and chanted and hummed over and over primordial messages birthed from her heart. So ancient were these messages that she did not comprehend their meaning, yet allowed their flow through her heart and voice. Trance-walking, she trusted in something beyond her knowing, yet of her primal wisdoms.

And as she breathed these primordial whisperings, she walked, she spiraled, she moved around and about the tree—weaving ever more layers of Ceques, while lost in an interior cocoon of forgotten wisdom. Unbeknownst to her, speaking in languages of the ancient ones, she called to the tree in the language of Soul.

These language sounds linked a Soul to the Souls of all beings:

SeHA, SoEL, nee AHpa, OOKaay, NEEya, TePaaHH, MeeWahnah. Dear Tree, wake up! You have branches that soar to the sky, and you have roots sunk deep in the heart of the earth! Wake up, Wake up—you are who you have always cried to be! Wake up! Wake Up!

And then she would begin the whispered chant again!

SeHA, SoEL, nee AHpa, OOKaay, NEEya, TePaaHH, MeeWahnah. Dear Tree, wake up! You have branches that soar to the sky, and your roots sink deep into the heart of the earth! Wake up! It is time—now is the time!

The villagers had never seen such a thing! "The woman" of the hardened heart was acting in a radical, most peculiar and unexpected manner. She appeared to be caring for the tree. She appeared to be in a great passion on behalf of the tree. She was in a state of open-heartedness. They knew they stood as witnesses to a miracle of sorts. They all watched to see what would occur.

After days and days of her Ceque spiraling, weaving walk through storms and heat waves, spring rains and winter blizzards, something happened.

She stopped.

She stopped her whispering chants and her spiral circle dance about the tree.

She could go on no longer.

"The woman," having given it her all, lay down against the tree. "The woman" closed her eyes. She rested.

Some of those of the village with heart-eyes to see stared at the tree which was now encased in a cocoon of light fibers, each radiant of colors and shimmering with life.

She had heard nothing more from the tree. Nothing had changed, or so she thought with her still closed eyes. She had done all she could think to do. In this moment, she gave up. She felt her heart break open in grief for the tree, for the souls of all who were lost in confusion. Holding her head in her hands, she wept. It had all been for nothing.

Finally, it was time to go. The sun had set long ago, and the evening air was growing cold. Her tears had finally run dry. Her heart felt like a shattered lump of brittle ice in the middle of her body.

Without conscious thought, she rose up from the ground. She happened to lean her hands—wet with her tears—up against the bark of the tree as she stood.

How is it that you could love such a one as me? I am nothing. You confuse me.

This thought pierced to her core! She was hearing the tree directly! The tree has begun whispering. The dialogue had begun: the tree and "the woman" were communing.

How did you come to forget the truth of your magnificence? asked Alzibet.

I know not. What I recall is this. Once there was a man, when I was a small sprout with only a few leaves. He was a man of cruelty and smallness of heart.

He went from village to village bartering. Not only was he small minded, but he reveled in adding to the misery of others. I thought of him as "bad," as so much less than myself. I thought I was "good" and would do no harm. I thought to myself, "The world would be better without him!" I had hoped he would pass by quickly. He did. Then, it happened that he passed nearby this very spot once again. It was hot that day. He took off his cloak and sought a place to hang it. I remember crying out, "No, no, do not touch me! No, I am not like you! No stay away!!"

The tree continued its story while "the woman" stood hand to bark and listened.

That day when he hung his cloak upon my branch, the world changed for me. Up until that time I had loved my scrawny, twiggy self and knew that one day I would be a great tree. When his cloak touched my bark, the world became darker, scarier and less possible. I can recall nothing else since then. (sigh)

Alzibet thought, while keeping her wet hands against the bark of the tree, *Oh, I have great news for you! During all that intervening time, you kept on growing! You are magnificent, with great soaring branches and deep abiding roots! You provide shade and comfort for many. I have sought all manner of ways to communicate this to you, but nothing happened until now!*

I can feel your touch! said the tree. *I feel a light movement flowing into me—a flow of light sensations—a warm pulsing flow! Something is happening to me!!?!*

Tell me what is happening, said Alzibet.

Then there was a large sound like a sigh…the tree trembled and shook. The earth around the tree rippled with waves of movement. The branches swirled in the sky. The bark shivered under her wet hands.

I remember, waved the branches. *I remember,* trembled the bark beneath her hands. *I remember me,* shimmered all the leaves and tiny creases of the bark skin. *I remember all the years and all the forgotten moments! Yes, I am a Great Tree with soaring branches and deep roots. Yes, this is who I am! I remember! I grew despite the forgetting!*

The tree danced in place. The tree shivered in joy. The tree came alive to itself.

"The woman," Alzibet, slumped against the tree—she had done it! She had helped the tree to remember! However, that was not all that had happened. Alizbet had remembered too!

She remembered the death of her husband and children. She remembered the horror of the wars and the starvation that had taken so many from the land. She remembered her determination to never ever feel that horrible pain of being left alone! She remembered her rage at the armies and the general who had ordered her husband into battle. She remembered her anger at her husband, who left her alone in the world. She remembered how she had judged herself, as a fool, for loving at all.

She remembered hardening her heart to life itself. She remembered the day she locked love out of her life! She remembered her righteous outrage and brutal judgments.

She had remembered too! She had not realized that she had pushed it all aside.

She thought to the tree, *I remember too! Thank you! You have helped me remember, too! It was so long ago, and I have been so hard of heart for so long I had forgotten my choice! The tears I wept for you were also for me! I had given up on ever caring again. Life was just too risky! It was too hard. It hurt so much sometimes. But life has gone on as I sat shut in by my judgments and shut out of love by my fears. Now, I have tricked myself into awakening—into remembering love!*

The tree answered, *Together now we shall be who we are! I am Great Tree offering shade and beauty, strength and rootedness for all to see! You are Woman of the Wisdom-Heart, the Woman of Ceques—who knows that those who have forgotten are brought alive only when they are loved as they are, wept over and tended to without any need for them to wake up. This is the mystery of whole-heartedness—now rooted in my branches, bark, roots, and leaves. This is the mystery now settling into your fibers and bones, cells and senses. Judgment hardens hearts against all that is true. It is with "imprints of presence" offered freely and without pressure that reach into the heart calcified by pain-avoidance.*

The woman answered, *Yes, I remember all of it.*

It is said by Alizibet, herself, that the tree was her greatest and truest friend. The tree had shared its naked, nonsensical anguish and in doing so brought Alizibet back from the dead.

And so it is from then until this very day, she sits against The Great Tree each afternoon speaking to anyone wanting to recall the Holy Truth of themselves. Through her continued communion with The Great Tree, the wisdom of the ancients flows out her mouth and from her big heart—wrapping Ceques around and within those who choose to listen. Those who choose to hear, remember who they truly are. Those who choose to walk away, remember on another day.

All the villagers were transformed on the day Alizibet and the tree remembered. Each came alive in their own way, softening in their own hard-hearted corners and dark crevasses.

Sometimes there are many lined up waiting to speak to her, and sometimes there are days when no one comes at all—in either case—at the end of the day, she rises and weaves Ceques around The Great Tree. And The Tree sighs in gratitude for the woman who dared to open her heart and love again.

The Tree whispers to you, *Will you choose to remember yourself today?*

****

Curiosity is an odd creature. Have you noticed that it may take you to places and spaces that are quite unexpected? Once that whispery voice is allowed in, no, invited in to wander around in one's innards, curiosity roots quickly. Requiring little soil and only a bit of water, curiosity can cause great cities of thought and thick walls of frozen cold rage to tumble into nothing but a small mound of dust. What opens the door to this potent presence? My answer: a wormy, squirmy wish to be more of who we are, to feel passion flow in our veins unimpeded. What is your answer?

MarNEEya and GherTiid: Blessings of Anguish Revealed

Dedicated to our (W)holeness, which is disguised as brokenness. Dedicated to us all—cripples in one form or another. Dedicated to those who tend the "crippled parts" and to those "broken bits and pieces" in us all, who lean heavily upon the others. Dedicated to the power hidden in the weaknesses of being a "human being."

She fell onto her knees; the weight of the burdens overpowered her determination to stand. Her hand wrapped around her face, she despaired of ever being able to open her heart again. She despaired of ever being able to blindly trust herself again...it had been so long, so very, very long that she had held steady in the face of all the dreaded moments. But she would not allow the tears to flow, for then she was sure they would never cease. No, the weeping was for others.

Would it all ever end? Everyone was turning to her to make the impossible decisions, to shoulder the responsibility for choices that had no outcome that would satisfy the souls involved. *Who should get the one cup of water, the baby or the mother who cared for the baby? Who should they feed today, the weakest of the clan or the ones strong enough to care for the village?* The impossible choices were everywhere...and they all looked to her to make them. Each choice was only possible from an open heart and clear wisdom; yet, would she be able to risk that again? Could she risk it again, "the terror of error" that arose like acid into the back of her throat?

It is here where this tale begins, the tale of MarNEEya and her daughter, GherTiid.

It all began with that one infant, a girl—the one they had placed in her arms after hours of pushing, the one who had cried immediately without the traditional slap on the bottom. "It was all her fault. If it wasn't for her, I would not be faced with all of this. But I loved her so…and I nearly lost her altogether."

Her mind's eye flashed back to the moment it all began.

The small one's eyes had been big and round with the surprises of being born. Her arms were fat, and her small tiny fingers had wrapped around MarNEEya's one finger with a bold determination to live.

There would be little chance of that now. She had been born with a broken body. The mid-wife had shaken her head and slowly prepared burial clothing. TARIC, the baby's father, stood in the shadows of the room—a witness to both the birth and now the pending death of his firstborn. As is the clan tradition still, it was she who labored who held the power of choice. TARIC waited in his stillness. She must decide.

MarNEEya, the mother, weeping quietly into the sweat-drenched pillows of her delivery bed, had already fallen in love with her baby over the months they had shared a body. Now…now it was all about death, not life. She had seen the baby's form. It was clear even to her…death was the only way.

However, this way was not to be.

Right at that moment, the Shamanesse of the Mountain Village across the river parted the curtains of the birthing hut and walked in without even a say so. Her name was Shee-YA. Stern of presence, beautiful of face, and powerful of body, Shee-YA commanded the room. "You will stop this death preparation at once! This child is destined to lead, and lead she shall!"

"But, but, but," sputtered the mid-wife, "Don't you see her broken, crooked body. It is best that she be made comfortable—the easier to die gently."

"Nonsense," said Shee-YA. "Give her to me."

MarNEEya looked up. She was full of hope and despair all at the same time. She had no idea of how to tend to the broken baby's body, and yet, it was her child. "Maybe there was hope," thought MarNEEya. "Maybe

Shee-YA, who was said to know just about everything, maybe she knows a way to save my baby."

MarNEEya nodded.

Shee-YA scooped up the baby, who let out a lusty yell. Shee-YA offered her a goatskin bottle filled with healthy nursing milk, and her cries were silenced as she hungrily drank. "She leaves with me," said Shee-YA. "I will tend to her and then return her. She will live! However, you must know, mother MarNEEya, this little one will go through much pain and suffering, and you will travel this path parallel to her. This is also true for you, father TARIC. You, too, will walk deeply into the well of anguish. This babe's journey will forge in her a great strength of spirit and a firm leader's spine, which will allow her to meet the challenges of leader. Both of you will be put through great moments of turmoil in which you may feel your heart breaking into pieces repeatedly. Mother MarNEEya, you will be forged into a Woman of Heart-Soul depth. None of you, mother, father, and babe, none of you will leave this parallel path unscathed.

"Mother MarNEEya, the time is now! You must choose. Will you stand on behalf of her? Or will you collapse before the unknown anguish before you?"

MarNEEya stood up from her prone position, despite her obvious exhaustion from birthing. She glanced at TARIC in the shadows, who nodded his deference to her authority to chose. A shroud of silence descended upon the birthing hut.

"Yes, I will stand. I do not know how. I do not know what will be asked of me. Yes, I will stand for my baby and her destiny."

Shee-YA nodded, turned and left with the baby.

MarNEEya fell to the bed moaning and thought, "What have I agreed to? Maybe it really would have been best to allow the baby to die, her body so broken!? And yet…" There were no more words within or without her. Her vow was made. Shee-YA would brook no backing down. The new mother sighed and fell into an exhausted sleep.

Shee-YA, as she carried the infant, hardened in preparation for what was to come. She had dealt with one other baby broken as this one was and knew it would be a long and arduous path, filled with many moments of heart-wrenching child-cries. The only way that Shee-YA knew to enable the baby to grow, despite the original form of the child, was to purposefully break and caste the bones at certain very specific ages. Shee-YA was fully aware that it was she alone who had both the know-how and the heart courage to embark on such a path.

"How can I not?" she pondered. "I awoke the moment she entered the world with a clear vision of her leadership. I will not deny my vision's wisdom. The tides have now turned and will require great stamina from MarNEEya, the mother, and from…" She paused. "What shall I name this little one who will face such vertical summit climbs?" Shee-YA grew silent for a moment. "Ah, her name shall be GherTiid, *the broken made (W)hole, the one who turns the tides of the ground herself on behalf of the ruined ones.* Yes, GherTiid it will be."

And so it was that Shee-YA took GherTiid to her hut and set about the long, slow process of breaking the bones of little GherTiid's body to allow them to grow as straight and as true as was possible. Each time was an initiatory breaking, for these were not just rites of body but initiations of heart and spirit. GherTiid would then be bound in tight linen strips so that her body was held stationary during the healing process, thus forcing her spirit to wander the ethereal realms. This initiation was said by the Sages to be the most grueling, with the initiatory rites being the most arduous, yet also, the most alchemically transformative.

After each initiatory breaking, Shee-YA would return GherTiid to MarNEEya with clear and careful instructions as to the care of the girl child until such time as Shee-YA would again appear at the door to take GherTiid on yet another initiatory journey.

MarNEEya came to hate the sight of Shee-YA. She knew the pain that would soon be inflicted again upon her precious child. Seeds of resentment, regret, fear, and outrage all took root in her mother's heart.

Yet, MarNEEya loved Shee-YA for her strength of heart which allowed her to engage in such a long-ranging, pain-causing initiatory journey of her dear GherTiid. Without Shee-YA, the precious daughter of her own body would have been long buried in the ground.

And so it was from each time of Shee-YA's appearance and immediate departure with GherTiid, MarNEEya would go into a deep grief. She would sit, moaning in despair, eating little, and sleeping less until once again Shee-YA would appear with GherTiid, bound in yet another set of healing linens and with eyes wide and dark ringed from her own ordeal. Mother and daughter were each delving deep into the wisdoms and grace found only in experience of pain inflicted for the sake of life's greater expression. The daughter was the one who must bare the pain of being body-broken for the sake of a living (W)holeness. The mother must be the one who bares the pain of being heart-broken for the sake of a (w)Holy cause and vision.

It is not possible to say who suffered more, MarNEEya or GherTiid. It is safe to say, however, that both suffered in ways that reached far beyond the edges of words. MarNEEya, whose heart was broken time and again, was unable to do anything more for her child other than to simply be there for her, holding her close as she cried.

MarNEEya had had to harden inside herself, in some secret place, to be able to bear the foreknowledge of even more times of brokenness. While she did all she could to open her heart's arms to her child each time she was returned by Shee-YA, her heart was pushed and pulled between being open and loving and at the same time dreading the cost of such openness. She hid her heart's anguish from GherTiid. She never spoke openly of her secret resentment of how her daughter's presence burdened her heart. She never spoke of her terror at the sight of seeing Shee-YA's face each time she came for GherTiid. And she never spoke of the relief that her daughter still lived! Over and over MarNEEya held steady, breaking open into wisdom and grace ever more deeply.

GherTiid, whose body was broken time and again and who was unable to resist the potent determination of Shee-YA, hated her sometimes. GherTiid came to know what it was to be imprisoned by her body and what it was to be released to soar in the realms of Shaman Wisdoms. She did not speak of her hatred of Shee-YA. Nor did she speak of her rage at her mother's apparent disregard for her body's pain. There was no choice. Shee-YA had made this clear. GherTiid could be no other than who she was—*The broken made (W)hole.*

All those in the village knew that GherTiid's path was an apprentice path of fiery hell—unsurpassed by any other chosen one. It was not an option, once one was chosen. All members of the village watched the mother and daughter. An apprentice's mother was considered a sage in her own right, so once Shee-YA chose GherTiid, MarNEEya, too, became a wisdom source for the people.

As time passed, MarNEEya showed such courage of heart that the people of the village named her their leader. She, they knew, understood both the turmoil of the breaking of a heart and what it takes to be true to the greater path. They knew that she walked in compassion and yet, could harden her heart to endure the wiser steps to a larger vision. All felt assured with her as leader. They knew that no one's pain would be denied, and yet, the pain would not override the clear visions. MarNEEya agreed, as is correct for a village member who is chosen, to abide by the call to lead. She shouldered the cloak, made of the threads and beads and bones of all those who had been leader before her. The cloak was a heavy one. Her heart was broken again and again, and each time she chose to open her heart to the impossible decisions all leaders are called to make. The tribe of the village had chosen wisely.

Meanwhile, GherTiid was kept at Shee-YA's for longer and longer periods of time. There were great stretches of days in which GherTiid was immobilized by the rigors of Shee-YA's initiatory rites of breaking, molding and stretching. GherTiid came to know the depths of hell and the glories of a simple step. All the blood that was shed by GherTiid was caught and stored in a plain jar kept on an upper shelf in Shee-YA's hut. At each "breaking," her blood always spilled forth. This blood was called Broken Life Blood, for it flowed from the point of the break, and its life force became magnified thrice over through the alchemy of the touch of Shee-YA's hands and the sounds of the apprentice's screams in the presence of the Great Mysteries.

GherTiid was becoming Shamanesse from the inside out.

As all this was transpiring, the village itself was in jeopardy. It seemed that the land that they lived upon was dying. The cause of the land's starvation was unknown.

The food was diminishing, the earth was offering less and less produce, the waters were drying up, and the people were dying in greater and greater numbers as every month passed. Everyone turned to MarNEEya for guidance. It was she that made the impossible decisions. It was she who moaned alone after these choices tore her heart into shreds of bloody compassion and strands of assured failure. They all trusted her, yet she feared to trust any of her choices, for she didn't know any more than they did! Still she chose. Someone must. She rose again morning after morning to meet the next impossible questions until she found herself in that moment, falling to her knees—the anguish beyond what she could bear.

She was responsible, yet, without the powers to renew the land's life. She was leader, yet, without the god's power to restore the river waters. She was accountable for each decision made, yet, blind to the outcome. She appeared assured as she quivered inside with the horror's terrors. She trusted, yet without hope, that they would all live another day.

MarNEEya finally crumbled to the ground…and was lost in darkness. "The impossibles" had finally crushed her spirit.

Up in Shee-YA's cave, a sound like the cry of the Earth's Soul was heard. Shee-YA knew it was now GherTiid's time. Shee-YA and GherTiid rose and walked down to the center of the tribe's huts where MarNEEya had fallen. No words were spoken as they walked, Shee-YA with the straight spine as "Shamannesse of the breaking hands," and GherTiid with the hunched over spine and rocking gait of the "Broken Made (W)hole." Her spine was not straight. Her body was still not like others, yet GherTiid, the one who was to die, lived. "The One who was Broken" was (W)hole in mind and spirit far beyond most with unbroken bodies. GherTiid moved with the authority of "Heart's wisdom and grace" melded into her Soul. This was the moment so long ago foretold.

They arrived at the center, where they found MerNEEya's crumbled body shuddering with broken sobs, crushed into abject despair. "I am done," she said.

Then…in that moment…GherTiid, who alone truly knew what her mother's leadership had cost her, reached down and lifted up her head so their eyes could meet as they had in that first born moment. GherTiid spoke, "Mother, leader of our people, you are no longer alone. It is now together that we will be able to save the tribe. I bring to you my part of the only potion that can heal our land. It is only the two of us, naked and true, that can enliven the ground of our Beings.

"Are you able to set aside all that remains of your secret resentments of our mirrored journeys, all the regrets and fears and shames, all the hardness of heart you forged to bare the agony of being my mother, as Shee-YA broke my body and taught my spirit? Are you able to set this all aside for our peoples' sake?"

MarNEEya looked back into the true eyes of Shamanesse called GherTiid. "Yes," she said, "if you are able to release all the ways I could not protect you from the breaking? If you, too, can release all your hidden resentments and longings for a life different than what has come to us. Can you soften your heart to me knowing I could have said 'no,' and the "breaking pain" would have stopped? I chose what hurt you. I chose knowing you would feel the agony of breaking bones. I chose a living daughter rather than a buried dead one. I chose to harden my heart so you would live. Can you set all this aside for the sake of our people?"

GherTiid knew well to what her mother was referring—her great secret hatred of the one who had borne her and not granted her immediate death-release. She had hated her mother while at the same time loved her for her gift of life. Now the secret was hidden no more. This secret had never been spoken aloud to Shee-YA, who knew it nonetheless. This secret had never been acknowledged between MarNEEya and GherTiid. They had each, at times, hated the other.

The gaze that passed between the two of them carried with it the freedom only truth can offer. In that moment they were both set free. From this point forward, only truth could be spoken between them, even if what was shared would break heart or body. The truth would be faced directly. There would be no secrets that could be justified anymore. The freedom was absolute.

TARIC, ever the silent witness, stood once again in the shadows—yet this time in wonder. Miracles were happening for real. Hearts were granted release from the eternal prisons of the hate-secrets' bondage! He felt showers of spirit's presence dancing along his body's entirety.

GherTiid rose to her full bent-height and said, "Now is the time! We must awaken the land and its people. I bring the alchemy of my brokenness. I bring the authority of my wisdom and the blessing of the mystery of Grace itself. You, mother, carry in your tears that which will activate this liquid called Broken Life Blood. Come!"

So it was that GherTiid walked with MarNEEya to the rivers' edge near the village center. Taking the plain pot in which the Broken Life Blood had been kept and filled through her repeated initiatory breakings, she said to MarNEEya, "Weep. Weep now. Weep for your people. Weep for the impossible choices. Weep for the land and all its broken places. Weep; hold back your tears no more!"

TARIC stood at MarNEEya's shoulder, offering his love and gratitude in silent presence.

MarNEEya took the pot from GherTiid's outstretched hands. She looked once into the eyes of her daughter born with a broken body and knew she was looking into the true eyes of Shamanesse. She wept…the dam that had built up inside of her had burst. Her tears were a waterfall of shame, pain, blame, hatred, and grief.

As her tears fell into the plain pot filled with Broken Life Blood, GherTiid's own heart gift, the pot filled to nearly overflowing…and then… TARIC allowed his own passions to arise within and a single tear rolled down his rough cheek and fell, in slow motion, into the pot of Broken Life Blood.

That was it!

The pot became too much to hold…filled with the heart substance of all. MarNEEya dropped the pot.

It shattered into many pieces, and from where it broke, a fountain of ever-flowing water burst forth from the earth. Wherever this water moved, it left behind new life, renewed life with abundance beyond anything words might frame.

And so it was that all the people came one by one to the fountain, named the Fountain of Living Waters, and drank. Those born with straight bodies were made (W)hole again, saved from starvation and dehydration. Those born of broken bodies, when washed in this water, were renewed in spirit and granted access to their potent and particular wisdoms. When they drank of this water, the last vestiges of hatred and resentment for their broken bodies was replaced with a depth of compassion for all beings who are broken in some way, obvious or not. The lands were watered from large cisterns filled with the Living Water and hauled out to the fields.

The corn grew tall, the peas and wheat, the broccoli and the eggplant—all flourished once again.

And it is said, as this tale is told around the fires, that it was the Blood of the Broken Daughter and the Secret Tears of a Mother's Heart, when mixed and stirred together, gave all the peoples life again.

GherTiid, Shamanesse of Broken-Truth's Wisdom, and MarNEEya, Leader by Broken-Heart's Grace, saved the people by their mutual naked embrace. TARIC's steady presence continued to serve as a bedrock for the tribe, for MarNEEya, and for Shamanesse GherTiid.

From that time until this current moment, together they have ruled, knowing that truth without heart is cold, and love without strength of will is weak. The Fountain of Living Waters still flows in the center of the village, and Shee-YA returned to her mountain-side hut to await the next call of The Great Mysteries.

GherTiid lived in gratitude for her broken body and its blood that had saved her people. GherTiid lived in great appreciation for the arduous apprenticeship she had undertaken, for it had truly led her to a (W)holeness beyond the body. MarNEEya lived in gratitude for her daughter's broken bones and bleeding flesh, for they had been the doorway for new life for all the peoples and had led to the blossoming of her heart compassion. MarNEEya lived in gratitude for her own tears' potency, for these had freed her people from an inevitable death.

So it is said, the Mother of the Broken girl child, the Father of the Broken-of-Body, and the Daughter of the Broken-hearted leader saved the day and the peoples through their own naked embrace. The Broken made (W)hole as life's waters in all forms were allowed to flow.

****

Originally written for a group of folks experiencing life from within crippled and deformed bodies, this fable has expanded to embrace us all. For the (W)hole Truth is that we are all broken in some way or another. Whether in body, mind, heart or spirit, it is this very woundedness that shapes our choices, our lives, and our unique expressions. It is our "crippleness" which marks us human.

The greatest form of "crippleness" is that which binds and restrains our hearts and souls. Broken or twisted bodies present great challenges, yet it is that which is within our hearts and minds which determines our expanse or boundedness. The shackles on minds and hearts are made of rigid links of our secret hatreds, shames, doubts, blames, and imagined failings and are then forged together with a commitment to judgment. It is judgment that seals our fate, turning the key in the lock. However, it is not without great riches, our path of The Broken Ones. Ultimately, it is our participation in our self-perception as "broken" that can set free our heart's greatest wisdoms—wisdoms that restore life to itself.

Who better to reach out a hand that heals? Who better to reach out to touch a despairing soul than one who has embraced one's brokenness only to reveal the Holy (W)holeness within? My invitation? When will you choose to bring into the light of NOW those secrets, heart-hidden, which shackle you in life? When will you speak them aloud, shattering the chains binding your Soul so that you, too, stand revealed as (W)holeness walking? WHEN?

The Awakening of a NOMAD

Dedicated to those of us who have felt like "rootless" orphans in the world and in our lives. Dedicated to those of us who have fought against our own natures, only to lose the fight, falling into our own embrace finally. Dedicated to those who ripen into themselves, kicking and screaming along the way, who upon finally arriving home, take their first deep breath.

Once upon a time that was so very long ago it has nearly been forgotten, there was born a little girl. Her name was E-TAH. As long as she could remember, the tribe had been on the move. She would say that there were villages in which they had lived that she could only vaguely recall, clumps of fuzzy faces in her memory. Other hut gathering places were just blank spots in her heart's-history. It was a never-ending cycle: they would settle in and then they would move on. She would make life-roots, as she liked to think of them, in the village wherever they happened to be, and she would make friends. She would play and explore her new village and learn new customs and traditions from her new friends. And then, for some mysterious and unclear reason, her mother and father and sometimes others in the village, but not all of them, would pack up and move on. She would have to say "good-bye" to the village and all her friends. And then she would get to the next new place, where they would stop, for no apparent reason, and the entire process would begin again: meeting new people, beginning new schools, and learning all about the new village.

On these moves, occasionally some folks that she knew would make the same move, but this happened rarely. So ultimately, the only consistent people in her life were her mother, her father, her grandmother, and her brothers and sisters. But even her family seemed kind of distant to her. It was only her grandmother who she had any real tender heart-connection with. Everyone else just seemed too busy to spend time with her or to play games with her or frankly even notice her. Whatever she did was always fine with them. They allowed all!

When she was little, E-TAH really didn't mind all this moving around too much, except for when she had to leave all her friends. She would cry herself to sleep for a couple nights, usually in the arms of her grandmother. When they arrived at the next village, a stopping point decided in some mysterious way that she could never quite comprehend, she would cry a bit to herself about feeling like a stranger once again in a strange land. She would get to know all new people and make new friends, over and over again. Sometimes it felt like such pressure. Sometimes it felt fun. But then after a while it would feel like home. She would settle in, coming to know the ways of how THIS particular cluster of huts, this group of elders and these playmates functioned and flowed into making a life together. Then after a time, for some mysterious reason, they would pack up once again.

As she got a little older, she began to feel a shame—shame when she would cry as she left the old village, shame when she would cry when she had arrived in her new village. What was wrong with her? The big ones around her seemed to laugh and to joke and to greet one another, even strangers, as if they'd always known one another for forever. She did not feel any sense of the celebration that they seemed to demonstrate. She felt she was flawed to her core, that something was very wrong with her. She came to believe that her very essence was poisoned in some dreadful way, and this was the biggest shame of all.

Her shame cut her off from the others. Knowledge of her "obvious" essential "badness" caused E-TAH to hang her head in despair and to pull away more and more from the others in the village. Her secret shame grew within her, while her self-disgust and frustration took deep roots in her heart. She never spoke of any of this to anyone. It was too horrible to speak out loud, and perhaps if she did, it might increase her differentness. E-TAH silenced her secrets, imprisoning them deep within her heart, in a cell made of bars of shame and the cold cement of despair. She couldn't tell a soul, not even her dear grandmother. She was alone in her secret solitary confinement.

The settling, moving, re-settling pattern continued over and over again. As she got a little bit older, she began to sense when "IT" was going to happen again. She would then see the signs: her mother and her father would begin to look about and gather things into the moving-on bins. They would slowly begin to pack-up and prepare the sacks that they would put on the donkeys and on their own backs. E-TAH could see and feel IT coming. They would be on the move again soon. Her interiors would knot up, and her mind would fight and rebel "Oh, no. Not again!"

Over time, E-TAH's imprisoned shame-secret became frustration, outrage, and rebellion. "I don't want to move again," she would scream out inside her secret prison-cell. "No more. I don't want to say 'good-bye' anymore or say 'hello' anymore. I'm tired of having to learn it all again." And inside she raged and fumed and stewed and fretted. ALL were muted screams in her heart. The outside kept changing, and it all felt so hard.

The shame held her silent. In truth, it required her silence. She didn't reveal her inner imprisonment. She thought for sure if she shared her shame and her anger or even her sadness, they would all laugh at her and mock her and set her aside, perhaps even leave her behind the next time it was moving-on time. The terror of being shunned was greater than her shame. She had heard once of a woman dying of the Shunning Curse! She didn't hint at her secret feelings out of a primal terror of being shunned. She clutched her feelings tight in her guts to assure that they not leak into an eruption, which might cause death by shunning.

And so it continued, and she grew a bit older. She became resigned, rather than rebellious. She began to settle for less, rather than scream her frustration. She acquiesced, rather than resisted when the gathering up began. This was how it was to be on the move. She submitted, not by choice but from the profound fear of what might happen if she gave freedom to all the emotions that churned inside of her. No one seemed to notice her struggle.

Resigned to saying "good-bye," resigned to saying "hello," her life was one woven with threads of quiet shame-filled resignation. Eventually, she didn't open herself up to the "NEW" friends when she met them. "What was the point?" she wondered. "I'll only be leaving again anyway." She resigned herself to it all. She knew the "good-byes" would soon follow. She hardly cried at all anymore when it was deemed time to pack up because she hadn't let much touch her heart. Resignation and disengagement from the journeys of moving over and over again became the atmosphere of her heart. It never occurred to her to do anything but just simply move again and again. Each day seemed a bit dustier and drier and emptier of any juice or spark. Often, she thought of herself as plodding through each moment with feet weighed down with her own personal shackles of shame-filled defeat. She felt little joy and laughed very little.

She grew a little bit older. She went through any number of moves, for they were always on the move, E-TAH and her family. And still she didn't know why. The resignation became a rotting moldy resentment: resentment of the disruption of her life, resentment that someone else was picking her up and moving her at their whim, resentment that she could never settle into one place and stay, resentment that she had to keep saying "good-bye" to her friends. Still, she would pack up and hoist the bundles upon her back and travel on with her family as they left one village for another. "We have no roots, no home," she moaned to herself. "Will there ever be a consistent place to be?"

Now, it had become clear to E-TAH that her grandmother was recognized in many of the villages as they moved about from one village to another and yet another. She was recognized as the old wise crone woman, as some named her, one of great wisdom and graceful presence. Often, after they had been in a village for only a short period of time, E-TAH noticed that people would begin to seek out her grandmother. Some would come crying. Some would come in joy. Some would come scowling and stomping. Each one, different and yet the same, would huddle with her grandmother, squatting by the fire pit inside whatever small hut they lived in at the time. The rest of the family was shooed out to allow for private exchange. Even when she tried to sneak closer to the hut's walls to listen in on what was being said, grandmother would stop the conversation. Somehow, grandmother always knew when E-TAH was crouched just beyond the hut's confines.

Then on a day of bright sun and clear bold blue sky, E-TAH again saw the first signs. They were packing things up. They were gathering the bundles, again! In a moment she just knew she would burst with rage, with sorrow, with resentment, and with sadness. And deep underneath this chaotic morass of emotions, the shame of her own secret flaw pierced her heart to its core. E-TAH could not make peace with any of it AND could not make sense of life as she knew it no matter how hard she tried. Everything was being disrupted again, inside and out.

And each time they prepared to move on, there would be this one and that one crying or screaming or yelling, "Have a good time." "I will miss you." "We hate for you to be leaving." "Hope we meet again." "Are you sure now is the time to leave?" "I will mourn your departure." "Great journey to you." There were always celebrations, with wide-ranging reactions, in the village that they were leaving and in the village in which they were settling. It wasn't easy. It wasn't neat. It was messy. It was chaotic. Crying and laughing, tears and screams, partying and grieving: all of this rose up in each community as a moving day approached. The villagers became all stirred up from inside and outside. "Again." E-TAH thought. "We will go through all the passionate outpouring of emotions again. For WHAT??!!"

This time she didn't want to go through it again, didn't feel she could stand to go through it again. Truth be told, it was the absolute nonsense that really twisted her guts into knots. There was no reason to uproot themselves again. None whatsoever!!! E-TAH felt sickened by the shame she felt for all of these reactions. As she looked around, no one else seemed to feel as she did. E-TAH saw no hope for herself.

She walked away from the village to be by herself. She sat down, facing away from the village because she could not bear to watch the chaos and nonsense. For the first time ever in her life, she did not help in the gathering up of their belongings and the packing of the sacks and bins. She didn't help construct the straps that would allow them to carry or transport their home-stuff to another place. She simply sat there. E-TAH, apparently invisible to all and the only one in pain, sighed. She hated that none of it made sense. It had been this way for as long as she could remember, this moving around from place to place, and yet, she still didn't know why they could never stay.

And then she noticed it. She felt it first—a presence coming up from behind her—but she didn't care. She resented all that was happening, and she did not want to engage in a conversation with anyone, even in the littlest bit. E-AH imaged a wall around her, a wall that blocked it all out! She wanted to scream, "Stay away from me!!!"

And then she felt a hand on her shoulder. It was a knotted hand, the knuckles gnarled, the fingers all bent at odd impossible angles. The strong, twisted hands, old beyond anything she could imagine were attached to the one person who might be able to hear her turmoil. She recognized them right away. And she smiled a smile that did not touch her face. The carved flesh-hands belonged to her grandmother.

The old crone woman sat down directly in front of E-TAH. E-TAH could not look away or turn away, for there was this old crone woman filling up her eyes. She was wrinkled in a way that old, old parchment is wrinkled. She was hunched over by all the miles that she'd walked carrying her sacks. Grandmother's face had these creases by her eyes that when she smiled seemed to stretch her face even wider and make her eyes bigger. Grandmother looked at E-TAH. There's no place to hide when an old crone woman looks at you. One cannot hide inside or out. E-TAH knew this.

She was so mortified, so humiliated, so terrified.

E-TAH took a deep breath and hoped that perhaps old crone-woman-grandmother would get up and leave, but of course, she didn't. And finally, her grandmother reached out and with a gnarled fist knocked a little bit on E-TAH's knee where she had been resting her chin. And the old crone woman spoke.

"Speak to me. Speak to me, child, for you are poisoned from inside, and this can go on no more."

All it took was just that one request, one never extended to her before. E-TAH's tears spilled out. All her words tumbled across and over themselves, and all of her anguish and shame and resentment and resignation erupted like a geyser bursting forth from the bowels of the earth.

"I am so ashamed, grandmother. I'm ashamed that I resent all this moving around. I'm ashamed that I feel so confused about my life. I'm ashamed that I've felt sad over and over and over again. I don't like to leave the roots I have put down. I like having my familiar friends and places and playgrounds. I don't like to have to go meet new people over and over again. I'm mad, mad, mad. I hate this. I resent all of this—the packing, the schlepping, the hoisting, the carrying, the walking, the unpacking, the unsettledness of it all—I hate it all. I tried to resign myself to it, but I just can't. No one else seems bothered by this at all! I'm ashamed because something is dreadfully wrong with me." E-TAH's agony, like molten lava, ran down the edges of her words, shaping her tears, burning her to the core.

And the old crone woman received it in a silence so spacious that there was room for it all and more.

Silence.

Space.

Room to breathe.

What was left beneath this volcanic burst of truth were the questions that E-TAH had never dared to ask, formed so long ago by the little girl: "How come, how come we keep moving?" "How come we're moving again?" "How come everything has to keep changing?" E-TAH stuttered and spewed her most hidden of all wonderings.

And the old crone woman looked at her and inquired, "What do you wish would happen next?" Grandmother had not replied to her questions. It gave E-TAH pause.

E-TAH said, "Well, what I wish is that we would all get to stay at ONE village. We would all be welcomed there, and I would be able to settle in and STAY! I'd keep my friends for a really, really long time. In fact we'd stay so long that I'd never, ever have to give them up. And it would be all the same and stay the same. I would be able to rest then, relax then. We wouldn't always be on the move, wandering from place to place without our own home! I wouldn't always be wondering what will happen next or when would the move happen, again. I wouldn't be so confused. I want to feel rooted."

The old crone woman looked at her and smiled. Reaching out and putting one knobbly hand on either side of E-TAH's face, grandmother said, "Sweet one, you've come to the time of knowing. It is a time that everyone in the village comes to. But no one can come to it without first having the room and space for all the feelings, questions, reactions, and experiences to swirl and spiral and dance within their minds and hearts.

"No one in the village has tried to make you happy. No one in the village has tried to take your mad away. No one has tried to convince you to be resigned or not resigned, to resent or not resent. No one has judged you, nor fixed you, nor required anything of you. We of this village and of all those villages before have gifted you with all the spaciousness to be all of who you are. We have offered you an embrace without restraint or condition.

"And now it has brought you to this question: WHO are you? Now is the time for its answer to be revealed. YOU are ready to know. You have proved yourself willing to listen, and you are now able to open your heart from the inside out."

E-TAH didn't seem to quite understand, but it was reassuring to know that others had come to this same dreadful place. And she said, "Please, help me understand. I don't understand."

Grandmother said, "Rise."

They rose and stood together facing one another. The crone woman reached out. She put one hand on E-TAH's heart and another hand on her forehead, where her third eye wisdom resided. With a hand on E-TAH's forehead and a hand on her heart, the crone woman spoke truth to E-TAH.

"Sweet one, this is a sacred initiatory moment. It is a time of coming into the truth of yourself, for up until this time, you have believed that it is the outer which would create your rootedness. You have been wrestling with the outer, against that which is beyond the edges of your own skin. Unknowingly, you have been attempting to conquer your inside self, but you did not know this. You have delved into the depths of your being. You have named the secret truths in your heart-space. You have made efforts to bury yourself alive...and yet, still you live. You have fertilized your soul with an authentic anguish that can only be offered by the creature-self to the Soul-Self. The soil of your being is now ripe for these seeds of truth.

"I see that you are truly ready to know the answers to your questions, and it is simple.

"By your nature and the nature of your people and the nature of your soul's journey, you will never arrive at any one place. You will never finish this movement. A Soul journeys through all time, space, and vibration for the shear joy of the experiences and the sensations, which it gathers up along the way. We call this 'NOMADing.' You are a nomad, and as a nomad, it is your nature to be on the move.

"However, you have been a child-nomad up until this very moment. It is for a child to wrestle with their nature, to resist it, to feel it, to explore it, to have all manner of reaction to it until they bring themselves to this point. It is correct for a child to have all the space to wonder within and without themselves, without restraints, or judgments or pressures to be anything different than they are in that moment."

E-TAH said, "What is nomad? Tell me more." And Grandmother, still with her hands upon E-TAH's head and heart, smiled and said to her, "Nomad is when there is nothing that you need to do. Nomad is when there is no place to go. There is no need to hurry. There is nothing that you need to accomplish. You do not 'have to.' You can take it easy and enjoy what IS until it is time to choose again, to move on again. The truth of nomad is the truth of every soul on this planet.

"Every soul is here to simply be on the move within. What occurs beyond the skin of a Soul is only to serve all inner movements. Nomad is to be at home in the moment, to be in an inner state of "***No-need-for-Other-than-the-Magnificence-of-All-that-is-Directly-experienced.***"

"This is for you to choose. No one will impose this state of Freedom of Being upon you. The truth is, no one can.

"This initiation is a moment of choice. It is for you to choose to become **consciously nomad**. What this means is that your roots become inner. It means that your roots descend into the depths of your very essence. All outer elements can change; in fact, the outer will always be shifting. Therefore, it is in your inner rootedness where your permanence lies."

Suddenly, it was as if the shackles fell away. The doors of E-TAH's inner self-created prison swung wide open, and a cascade of light poured through her being. Ah, it made sense. Nonsense no longer flogged her mind and heart. All those of her family and the others in past villages who were ever on-the-move and packing and moving again, they all knew of inner roots. She had thought that it was all about the outer. Suddenly she laughed right out loud.

"Let us pack! Let us go onto the next village and see, for I wish to explore inner rootedness." And she turned around and boldly walked into the village with her shoulders high. She could feel the shame falling away, and she called out to the villagers, "Come. Gather. Gather, for I now know I am nomad, one of inner roots. I now step into each moment in peace, for there is no place that I can go or any place in which I can stay which offers me anything beyond what I already have within myself. I do not need to be anywhere. I do not need to hurry. I do not need to stay. I do not need to await. I do not need to go. I can simply be and enjoy. In honor of this, I name myself AH-tea, the one of inner roots."

And with that, the villagers ceased their preparation for the next moving-on and created a great celebration. They all sat around, encircling AH-tea in great laughter and joy, for the villagers knew that any time anyone came to this understanding, the entire nature and depth of their village transformed, deepening even more. All had been birthed anew, as E-TAH, now called AH-tea, came into her Nomad-ness by choice and celebration.

And it is said that from this point forward, AH-tea herself ripened into an old crone woman, taking the place of her grandmother, who had initiated her into Nomad Wisdoms. AH-tea, taking up the mantle of Initiatrix of her Clan, was often found squatting in small out-of-the-way huts, conferring and offering "con-soul" to those lost in the confusions of inner and outer rootedness until they, too, came to peace with being NOMAD.

No way to be, No place to go, Nothing to do, All welcomed as correct in its own time.

And so it has been across all times and eons passed that each member of all the villages of the globe would come to a moment when they discovered that it's all about inner rootedness. And this was so only after they'd wrestled with all that was around them, discovering the rich wild terrains of the interface between the inner and the outer. Their initiation into Nomading was offered only after they had delved to the depths of their anguish, touched the wisdoms offered by shame's imprisonment, and suffered the turmoil of the question: WHO am I?

And so it is until now and will be for forever and always has been.

****

Wisdom and understanding come in response to our readiness to receive it. There is no way to hurry ripening souls. There is no way to push into fruition that which is still maturing within us. Truly, there is no reason to push or strain, for all are ripening, each in their own time, unveiling our perfection to ourselves.

Yet, when that moment arrives, when the frustration of "restrained-awareness" breaks through into the unknown void with naked curiosity—then the mystery of US responds. This fable is an invitation to be tender with ourselves as we ripen into the more of WHO we are: (W)hole Holy Expressions of Love-Light moving, ever moving through the dimension called "Life." Arriving at a particular place or condition or state is not the point! Thriving in our continuous pulsations and expressions of us, this is the (W)hole Point. Will you choose to embrace your essential nature?

Shame's Wisdom

Dedicated to all of us who have felt "different," set-apart for no reason, only to discover later, much later, that it was this very imagined "flaw" which birthed our true and holy wisdoms. Dedicated to the Mystic of us all. Dedicated to the "different ones" who long to belong, and when they are embraced, reveal themselves to be far more than they ever imagined themselves—leaders for us all.

Her village had been entirely destroyed. In fact, it was said later that all of the villages in the area had suffered similar destruction. The adults had been slain or taken away, and the children for some unknown reason had been left. Those from distant villages had heard of this and sent their elders—women, men, and older children—to each of the villages to bring back the orphaned children. It had been, let us say, an effort across all the lands, for no one village could absorb all of the abandoned children, and no one knew what had happened to the adults. They had simply disappeared. So…the abandoned children had to be housed and homed.

Now as it happens, one of the villages that replied to the call for help was formally called The High Place and informally, just High Place. High Place was unusual in that it was a place one might call a monastery, but it was not. It was a place where men had retreated to go deep into their hearts and to find the spaces within them that had been forgotten. High Place was not a religious community; it was simply a place that honored men for their uniqueness. After a time, High Place became known as a retreat place for the men. And, yes, even High Place had responded to the need for a place for the left over, left behind, forgotten children of this destruction.

And as it was, by the time those of High Place had arrived at the central gathering for the abandoned children, there were only boys left, save for one very young girl. Her name was Tee Cah. And because all the other villages that had responded to the need had already absorbed their fill, Grandfather of High Place agreed to take Tee Cah. After all, she was just a very young girl. It would be fine, for they would raise her in the same manner in which they raised all the youngsters that were to be taken to High Place.

Now what was unusual about this is that High Place had no children living in their male community until this time. This was the first time ever that "children tending" had arisen as a need. And so at first, Grandfather and all those of High Place were a bit disoriented. How does one tend to children? Their schedules were rearranged. Their meeting style and their eating style were also adjusted to accommodate the wide range of ages and nutritional needs. There were men within High Place who courageously took over this new responsibility for the young ones, and they discovered new and wondrously surprising talents. There was one who found that he was quite adept at instruction in letters and numbers and in the written words. There was another who found a great and surprising talent at feeding and nourishing the young bodies with healthy foods. And there was another who'd surprised himself with a talent for teaching all the children the skills of the hunt. Archery, running, riding the animals, and all of the many physical stamina challenges became the specialty of another member of High Place. And also within this same talent he discovered the ability to teach the young ones to enjoy and develop the strength of their young bodies, making it great play as well as deep and strong skill development.

Then there were all the talents and skills of commerce, accounting, communication, and commerce management between the various villages; this, too, was taught by another of High Place. Quickly, those of High Place stepped up to meet the challenge of ensuring all the children would have the very best of education they could offer. And so it was for a time High Place, having made this adjustment absorbing the children, continued on while Grandfather continued in the position that he had always held. Grandfather was the one that all in High Place came to when they were in need of wisdom. Grandfather was the oldest of the men who lived at High Place. He was all this and nothing more than this.

Meanwhile, Tee Cah, the young girl, was raised along with all the other young boys. She was treated no differently. She was just one of the children. She studied with them. She ran with them. She rode with them.

She learned archery with them. She ate with them. She slept with them. And so it was. And no one gave this any thought whatsoever.

And all was well. In fact, High Place had come alive in a way that it had not been since it was first established. New life had come as a blessed surprise to the men of High Place. All flourished. And all of the children grew.

Time passed for all those of the community, until one day it began to become apparent to Tee Cah that she was different. She noticed that her body shape was slightly different. It had not really struck her before that she was in any way different from the other children until this one day when they were swimming and playing in the pool. One of their teachers had allowed them to cool off in this deep clear pool on the edges of High Place, after a great deal of running and jumping and competing with one another. And she was struck with some concern. Even though other times she had noticed her body was a bit different, she had not felt any concern. She had simply let it pass by her, pass over her. But it wouldn't pass by her awareness, not this time.

She began to worry about it, stew about it. What made her different? "How come she was different? What did this difference even mean? Was it an illness? Was it indicative of a flaw in her body?" These fear-filled worried thoughts went around and around in her mind, troubling her heart most deeply.

Remember, there were no women at High Place, and no women ever came to High Place. So Tee Cah had no context in which to understand nor other bodies with which to compare herself nor a relational context in which to make sense of the significance of this difference. And, beyond all this, she did not even know that she lacked these resources. She knew only this: She was definitely different. She could hide it with less and less ease as time passed. All this began to concern her greatly.

She did not speak of this to anyone, for inside her fear-filled concern began to grow this knot of shame, shame for something that she did not understand, shame in a way that she felt she must keep it hidden. Perhaps if she did not speak of it and she did not show or make it evident to another, perhaps this difference would somehow go away. And yet as time passed, it became increasingly clear to her that the difference was growing. Her shape was becoming even more distinctly different than her best friend's, and the shame within her grew. And still she did not speak to anyone of how different she felt until finally one day, one of her best friends turned to her and began to make fun of her.

"What an odd shape you are developing," he said, for neither he nor Tee Cah had seen a woman. None of the children knew or remembered what a woman was. They knew the word "man," but they did not know what "wo-man" meant or signified. Tee Cah knew what her friend was saying was true; and yet, she did not understand what it was that was setting her apart. What was happening? What was her body doing? And finally in this public shaming moment, Tee Cah knew she could not remain silent anymore. She hung her head in shame and turned to the only one she thought she could bear to speak to about this. Her secret shame was no longer secret. She could pretend and hope no longer. Yes, somehow, Tee Cah was different. She felt afraid.

She went to Grandfather's hut. She knocked and entered as was the custom. Tee Cah said, "Grandfather, Grandfather, may I spend some time with you?" And he said, "But of course, Tee Cah, sit here." And they sat with bowls of warm soup that Grandfather had made and blessed with his loving presence. But Tee Cah could not drink or eat of it, for the shame was so great it filled her guts with bolts of iron. There was no space for food. The shameful worries filled her belly with an angst and an anguish that up to this moment had held her mute.

Now, Tee Cah's words spilled out of her. "Grandfather, I do not understand. My body is shaped differently than all of my friends. I do not seem to appear as anyone else in High Place. I am sure there is something terribly wrong with me. What is happening to me? What am I becoming?" And she wept bitter tears and hung her head, afraid to look at Grandfather, afraid that Grandfather would say, "Yes, you deserve to be scorned. You are diseased, and you must be shunned by the village and sent away to die." Tee Cah held her breath. She waited. She had run out of words.

There was a long, long pause. Grandfather did know what "woman" meant, for he had known women. And he had mulled in his heart for a great many years, knowing this moment would come, and had never come to clarity about what to do. In her shame, Tee Cah sat with her head bowed. In his own uncertainty and shame, he felt tears run down his face, for he felt so ill-prepared for this moment. Grandfather had failed Tee Cah when all he had wanted to do was provide her with family in the place of the family she had lost.

And they sat in their shared shame. Each one's shame solitary, their mutuality of anguish unrevealed.

And then in that space of shared shame, a decision, a knowing arose in Grandfather, and he said, "Tee Cah, I know now what we must do, and it will not be easy for you. We must send you to this village that I know of. It is filled only with those like you. It is a place for those called 'women,' for you are becoming woman. You will not know what this means until you go to this village. It is a place where others like you gather to be in community. Often there is drumming and chanting and much celebration in the form of ritual and song. It is a place called Inner Place. Yes, we will send you to Inner Place. And you will spend a number of seasons there, and out of that time you will come to know what next is correct for you to do."

Tee Cah had never heard of Inner Place, and she was deeply shocked that she would be sent away, and yet, what else could she do? She was so filled with shame at her differentness. She felt so lost. She felt so alone because she was the only one like this. And so she submitted, without understanding, to Grandfather's decision. She was taken to Inner Place.

High Place settled in without Tee Cah. Everything felt a bit "off" to everyone. Tee Cah had been an alive and wild child. She had laughed boldly, and she had played with all of her being. Her passion at play and at learning was unmatched by all the other children living at High Place. There was a missing note, as it were, in all the sounds of High Place. Her friends did not understand what had happened to her, and yet, they knew that it was not theirs to question Grandfather's decision. And if truth be told, they knew that Tee Cah was different from them, but they silenced their own questions.

Time passed. What happened during the months that Tee Cah was at Inner Place is for another tale. Of significance to this telling is Tee Cah's return to High Place and what transpired thereafter.

Many, many months passed before Tee Cah returned. Tee Cah looked entirely different than when she left. As she walked into High Place and went to Grandfather's hut, Tee Cah strode with an authority and grace rarely seen in Any Place, as the world was called back then. She knocked,

"Grandfather, Grandfather, it is Tee Cah. I have returned, and I now know myself as woman. I can hold my head high. I have returned with all the wisdom taught to me at Inner Place. I wish to share with all of you at High Place the deep wisdom of Inner Place. I come so there may be peace within and without for all at High Place."

Grandfather was shocked, for he had not anticipated ever seeing Tee Cah in his lifetime again. He was most glad, for truth be told, Tee Cah had a special place in Grandfather's heart and had from the moment he first saw her. It was the reason Grandfather had made an exception to have Tee Cah come to High Place. And here she has returned, knowing herself as woman, a title of power and presence. She had named herself, in particular, "Woman of Shame's Wisdom."

Grandfather invited her to take up residence in High Place, and she agreed.

Tee Cah stayed for quite a time, offering the wisdom that comes from having walked in the footsteps of shame and having followed the footsteps of shame into dark places, having gone deep within and then by her own choice, emerging once again into Light Places. She, Tee Cah, was not afraid of the dark nor was she afraid of the light. Only in this truth could she return to High Place. Many came to her hut to sit in "con-soul" with her.

Time passed, and their world, called Any Place, had changed, all because of Tee Cah. Now, men and women journeyed to High Place and to Inner Place. Man and woman were no longer separated as they had been before. And the root of the destruction done to Tee Cah's original village was revealed by those of Inner Place to those of High Place.

The reason that Tee Cah's village was destroyed was that all had been out of balance. There had come to be a great division between the High Places and the Inner Places of each person of the land, causing great violence to burst forth across the lands. For a time, some men had become rage-filled because of this imbalance and acted to destroy, kill, and cripple others in their flight from their own inner terrors. They had lost their own way to their inner places.

And for a time some of the women had cowered and hidden themselves, having forgotten the way to their own high place within their own beings and within the whole of creation. Neither one nor the other was able to be true to their essential nature. A corrective measure had been taken by the land's caretakers. They had allowed High Place and Inner Place to drift apart for a time so as to create a calm and steadiness in each. Then and only then could the reunion occur. Tee Cah, in her naked shame, was the agent of this re-union.

It was Tee Cah's willingness to travel from High Place to Inner Place, where strangers called women lived, which allowed for the re-union to unfold. Tee Cah, though frightened and filled with shame, had woven together these two places within her being. High Place and Inner Place had become One within her, a place she called My Place.

All was well. And then there was the greatest moment of all. A moment tender and rich with wisdom when Grandfather knocked on Tee Cah's hut and asked if he might come and sit with her and receive some of her wisdom. Tee Cah was shocked. What could she offer Grandfather that he did not already know? He came and sat in her hut, and she offered him soup that she had made with love, but he could not eat it. His belly was filled with knots of fear and bolts of worry. There was no room for nourishment of the body. Grandfather came to her filled with a shame that he had dared not name, even to himself, until Tee Cah had returned and settled into High Place.

Although everyone in the village turned to him for wisdom and everyone thought that he was fully certain in all moments, his secret was that this was not so. He was not certain. His secret shame was that he often did not know. And he had had no one to tell this to until Tee Cah returned in her own wisdom and could sit opposite him in her own inner authority. Only when could he set aside the High Place, in which he was often placed by others seeking his "con-soul," could he reveal this burden.

Tee Cah sat for a time, humbled by his inquiry. Shame was exchanged, humility was exchanged, and a sacred silence was woven between High Place and Inner Place.

And Tee Cah spoke these words, "Shame's embrace is what heals. It is always your shame revealed that opens the doors to wisdom and peace. Dear Grandfather, it is your knowing what you did not know that birthed the wisdoms. Dear Grandfather, it is your shame and your ability to touch this place within you that embraces all who enter your doors. Rise up and be at peace."

And there was a pause. Grandfather looked up at Tee Cah, and Tee Cah looked at Grandfather. In that exchange between their eyes and their hearts and their knowing, the (W)hole world was made (W)hole again, One across all the lands: High Place and Inner Place known to one another as parts of Our Place.

And men and women, both, now walking, talking, sharing, teaching, eating together in great circles of community—OUR PLACE was in balance.

And so it is from now until the end of time, that this story occurs within us, around us, through us and around about the (W)hole globe.

****

Shame is different than blame. Blame is a judgment directed towards the "outer." Shame is far more treacherous. Shame is a judgment directed towards the "inner." Shame points to the felt conviction that one's essence, the core of a person, is inherently "wrong" or "flawed." Shame can kill. Shame separates us from others and from ourselves. Shame for our humanity, shame for our "lack" of perfectness, shame for our shapes—shame may touch any and all arenas of a person's life. Shame thrives in the darkness, where secrets live. Shame melts away in the face of naked, loving, truthful embrace. Shame-filled experiences can be the midwives of authentic compassion—the Healing Wisdom of "embrace-without-reason."

May this fable be an invitation to your secret-shames to come out of hiding and thus birth your own Wise Compassionate Self. May this fable remind us all that Shame Kills while Naked Relevations heard without judgment heal from inside out. The (W)hole Truth: None of us are flawed. None of us are "bad beings." We are Souls remembering we are ONE Being. The path home is through transparent nakedness—here is the freedom from Shame—here is the threshold to peace—here is the portal to Love's Presence as us.

Come out of hiding, if you dare.

Wanikiya—Light Mountain That Was

Dedicated to those who look where everyone tells them not to. Dedicated to those who dare to step into their own authority as the outer "bosses" and "sources" fall away. Dedicated to those who come when the call goes out to choose a NEW path of (W)hole Life.

(Wanikiya = "life giver" in Lakota. Source: *"Calling the Sacred"* cd by Denean)

The day began as all the days began in the village. The people would walk to Wanikiya Light Mountain and open their Heart Spaces through rituals and song and dance. Wanikiya Presence would touch each of their inner centers of life with Light Presence, thus renewing their inner Light for another day. The Light-Life-Self of each villager required this re-freshment daily. This Inner Light-Self was called MEE-Kah.

The MEE-Kah of each of the villagers, old and young, was refreshed each day at the Wanikiya Circling.

It was common knowledge that the MEE-Kah requiring this "refreshing" was normal and no cause for alarm. During the dark time of each day's cycle...the MEE-Kah of each villager dimmed to near extinction and required the touch of Wanikiya Light to once again enflame the full heart space. This daily "dimming" was of no concern either, for it had been so for ages of time and would, they all imagined, continue for forever.

The gift of Wanikiya Mountain made this "enflamement" possible.

It had been given to the people so long ago that the True Source had been lost in time and the question of its presence was never raised. It just was. No one could now recall how it was given. Wanikiya Light was the vital hub of all of their existence. All depended upon Wanikiya Light and the mountain in which it lived.

"Our Great Wanikya," as it was sometimes called, was located at the center of their village. It sat upon a huge pointed mountain, which had fairly symmetrical sides, although one side had a pile of boulders that prevented the villagers from being able to walk all the way around its entirety. On the very top was Wanikiya Flaming Light. This Light seemed to be much like a small version of the sun, save that it sat at the top of Wanikiya Mountain. Like the sun, it was constant and continuous and without variation in intensity, at least as far as anyone could tell. The primary difference was in its shape: It appeared more pointed rather than round. Beyond its implied shape, it never dimmed and it never changed. It simply was Wanikiya.

All knew that without Wanikiya, the villagers would be extinguished since their MEE-Kah would have no Enflamement Source for their daily re-freshment.

It was one of the Elders of the clan that initially noticed the change! At first, those she mentioned it to laughed and explained it away as "aging eyes" or "the vivid imagination of the old ones." Later, this Elder, who was named LEE-BO, was honored for her wise sensitivity and her precognitive knowing of the most terrifying of all events—the dimming of Wanikiya.

This had never happened before. It was horrifying to even consider the idea of what might happen if Wanikiya shifted at all.

So after dismissing LEE-BO's concerns as exaggerated and "elder eyes," the villagers settled back into their usual routines. LEE-BO quieted herself and settled into presence with her own knowing—she waited. LEE-BO did not, however, discount her own knowing.

About a week later one of the other Elders, GEN-II, thought she, too, noticed a change in Wanikiya. It seemed dimmer, slighter, and to be wavering a bit. GEN-II spoke to LEE-BO, and they both admitted between themselves that there was something happening; however, for the sake of peace in the village, each held their own council. Neither invoked the greater Con-Soul, or gathering of the Elders of the village. (*NOTE: Con-soul is a word coined by Rev. Ahtea and Rev. Anne in 6-2009 to refer to the coming together of Wisdom and Grace on behalf of those seeking Soul guidance and comfort.)*

Daily the clan still gathered for the morning's re-freshment, and daily the re-freshment occurred. Wanikiya Presence continued to offer the daily enflamement that sustained all.

THEN a month later, a young girl rose early to go to the daily gathering. Upon arriving at the village center, she found that Wanikiya had become but a hint of its size and brightness! There was no doubt now! Wanikiya was diminishing rapidly.

She ran, yelling and crying out: "Come. Come—something is happening to our SOURCE, our Great Wanikiya! Wake up and come!"

AND so the villagers did!

LEE-BO and GEN-II were not surprised. However, they were quite grave—they had yet to come to any conclusions or resolutions about what the dimming of Wanikiya light meant for the clan much less what might be done in response!

The day of Awakening, as it was called later, had arrived!

Now prior to this day, something else had been occurring within the clan.

A group of pre-adults, or as they were called by the clan, Le-NU, had been secretly exploring around Wanikiya. They had heard what LEE-BO had said along with the rest of the villagers; however, they had taken it more to heart. So together they had decided to investigate the mountain upon which Wanikiya sat. AND to be honest, it gave them an adventure of their own: They imagined they would uncover the mysteries of the possible dimming of their Life-Source and be heroes one and all.

The Le-NU began to explore all the nooks and crannies around the base of the mountain. They walked it, they sat upon the edges, they moved brush, they poked and prodded every bit of the mountain that was reachable. They explored without restraint. None of the rest of the village gave much thought to the Le-NU's oddities. They were by nature a bit strange! It was known to all that as one passed through the Le-NU time of life, to expect a bit of the bizarre.

However, to their surprise, Le-NU had, in fact, inadvertently uncovered a secret about Wanikiya and the mountain!

The mountain had a tunnel that led to the center of the mount upon which Wanikiya sat! This tunnel hadn't been known about due to a pile of rocks, which had disguised the opening. One of the Le-NU had been climbing on these rocks and they had shifted, revealing the opening.

As Le-NUs in general were a bit "full of their nearing adulthood," they determined to keep quiet about the tunnel. Instead they actively explored it and kept the secret to themselves. They had all, as a group, entered the tunnel, and found at the inner heart of the mountain a flame that seemed to be perpetual. It was not overly huge, and it didn't seem to be sourced from any place. However, no matter what time of day or night the Le-NU came to the inner heart space of Wanikiya—the flame was alight. They had concluded that it somehow fed the outer light on the top of the mountain. The connection was not obvious but somehow implied.

The Le-NU had learned other things about this flame:

Touching it didn't hurt.
Touching it didn't feel hot or cold.
Touching it didn't feel like anything at all.
The flame did not burn paper or other materials.
The flame was not solid or liquid.

They had learned all this by being curious, in a wild daring sort of way: A very typical Le-NU way of living. They were known to be the first to enter the newest of places and the boldest in a blind sort of way. That was a Le-NU way of being. Still, despite all their Le-NUness, they had no idea of the importance of this flame!

One night, they had again gathered in the inner heart space of the sacred mound, inside of which sat this constant flame. Le-NUs had taken to doing this more and more, since the tunnel had been revealed. The space felt very embracing and thus easy to return to over and over again. One of them had spoken of it this way, "Who wouldn't want to feel embraced from the inside out?" And they all agreed this was how they felt in proximity to the perpetual flame.

Their leader, Mow-TAY, stood to speak. She placed her hand upon her heart, and as she stretched her arm outward and upwards, Mow-TAY inadvertently placed her hand in the flame. As this occurred, she simultaneously happened to be speaking, beginning with her own name:

"Mow-TAY, I AM." She was doing this in preparation for a speech to the Le-NU about their up-coming "adult-made" rituals. Later, Mow-TAY admitted she was pretending to already be "Adult-Made," at least as she imagined what that would be.

Instantly, a current of flame ran from the flame itself, from her hand which was in the flame, to her other hand, which rested upon her heart! Then her heart space seemed to glow and be re-freshed beyond anything anyone there had ever seen before! All Le-NU present were brought to mute silence.

Mow-TAY stepped back. With her hand removed from the flame and her other hand dropped at her side—it was clear something more transforming and permanent had happened. Her own heart space was glowing and radiating. It was magnified beyond measure! Her eyes were calm and clear, yet, they, too, seemed to have become more piercing, more penetrating in their gaze. Her breathing was steady and firm, and yet it seemed to be flowing from the very center of the atmospheres. Her heart space—her MEE-Kah—was filled to overflowing with an embracing loving calmness. She knew all was well! She did not know what it all signified.

Of course, they all wanted to do "it" too. What a Le-NU kind of response, yes? It took some time but finally they deduced the key variables by attempting to imitate Mow-TAY.

One by one they stepped up, placed one hand upon their heart and one in the flame and spoke their names. The same thing occurred to all of them: A transmission of light from the flame to their MEE-Kah. Each Le-NU felt the all-inclusive rippling transformation of their very essence. All Le-NU present began to feel themselves becoming a calm, loving presence, and a gentle emanation of radiant light pulsed from each of their MEE-Kah. None had seen this before. None had felt such peace before.

What did this mean?
What of Wanikiya Light?
Had they violated some sacred law?

They determined to keep this secret between the Le-NU. Of course, you know that Le-NU love keeping secrets.

Using extra layers of clothing to cover the light emanating from each of their MEE-Kahs, the Le-NU exited the tunnel and continued in their usual daily routines, even unto gathering each morning with the clan at the base of Wanikiya. Their secret was that their MEE-Kahs didn't seem to require re-freshment as did the other villagers.

The Le-NU continued in much this fashion, particularly enjoying the great and powerful secret they held fast. Months had passed. None had leaked this private knowing to the rest of the village. The Le-NUs were very proud of themselves and honored Mow-TAY with the wise leadership, which had supported their hidden alchemy.

On the Day of Awakening, upon seeing the absolute and undeniable dimming of Wanikiya and in the heat of the horror at the now clear evidence that the Source for the village was so greatly diminished, the Le-NU knew that their secret must be revealed.

Mow-TAY was the one to do this; however, she was not present.

The Le-Nu gathered as a group amongst the villagers and called aloud:

Mow-TAY
Le-NU
Le-NU
Gow-TAY

Mow-TAY
Le-NU
Le-NU
Gow-TAY

Mow-TAY
Le-NU
Le-NU
Gow-TAY

Upon hearing their call—Mow-TAY rushed to join them—knowing only that something quite grave had occurred for them to share what the Le-NU called "The chant to the hidden flame," which they sang in the heart of Wanikya.

LEE-BO and GEN-II waited. They both could feel the power and potency of this call. The hairs on their heads and necks stood on end. Their hearts raced, while their breathing paused in anticipation.

Mow-TAY came to the center of the gathering. She stood before all the villagers with the other Le-NU around her. She spoke, telling them all the story of what the Le-NU had done and what they had learned. The entire clan held its breath to see what the Elders would say, for nothing of its kind had ever occurred.

GEN-II, after hearing the story, walked to Mow-TAY and embraced her. Turning to the village as a whole, GEN-II said, "It is clear what we must all do! It is a day of great change and awakening! Each of us must enter the heart of Wanikiya and receive the '*re-freshment from within.*'"

There was great discussion, trembling, and turmoil in the clan! Fear, curiosity, wonder, and terror were all expressed. How could it be otherwise, in the face of the Source-of-ALL dimming and diminishing right before their eyes? Now, Wanikiya was barely a flicker of a light. The din of conversations, weeping, and wailing, the noisy shouting and debating converged into a great wave of deafening noise. The Village was drowning in terror-sounds.

The Le-NU quietly began to chant:

Mow-TAY
Le-NU
Le-NU
Gow-TAY

Mow-TAY
Le-NU
Le-NU
Gow-TAY

Over and over and over they chanted, letting the light of their MEE-Kah show by setting aside their garments previously hiding their radiance. The MEE-Kah light and peace gently reached out and touched the villagers one by one, until there was a growing spacious possibility of a pause. Until, finally, the chant deeply penetrated the chaos and panic of the village.

All became silent!

The pause said it all. No more discussion was needed.

Led by GEN-II, LEE-BO, and the Le-NU, the villagers entered the tunnel to receive the re-freshment from within. The Le-NU chanted quietly the entire time as the villagers one by one entered the now revealed tunnel to the inner flames of Wanikiya.

No one knows exactly when Wanikiya dimmed to nothing.
Only that it did.

No one knows exactly when the Flame in the heart of Wanikiya Mountain ceased to burn.
Only that it did.

No one knows what led to the GREAT Awakening.
Only that it did happen.

AND from that point on, all children born were born with their MEE-Kah requiring only ONE re-freshment—the re-freshment of their parent's hands resting upon their hearts and their name chanted three times, followed by the chant that saved the Life of the Village, the chant that had called Mow-TAY to Wanikiya, the chant that had preceded the Le-NU revelations.

One new part had been added to the Chant: Hae-NU, Hae-NU, Hae-NU. This meant: Forever, forever, forever.

So it was that the Chant came to mean: Spirit-Light and I are ONE. Forever, forever, forever.

And so it has been for all time.

Mow-TAY
Le-NU
Le-NU
Gow-TAY

Hae-NU, Hae-NU, Hae-NU
Mow-TAY
Le-NU
Le-NU

Gow-TAY

Hae-NU, Hae-NU, Hae-NU
Mow-TAY
Le-NU

Le-NU
Gow-TAY
Hae-NU, Hae-NU, Hae-NU

****

Each of us in our own way creates "traditions" or "routines" that easily become our source upon which we rely. Unwittingly we have then placed our life's flow beyond the edges of our own being, thus become more "less-than" in each moment. Shaking us to the core when the outer dims, demonstrating its own demise, in that moment we are brought back to our senses. WE are our own experts, our own authorities, and our (W)hole Holy Source. We are Souls walking, infinite Holy Beings wrapped up in skin bags, awakening as Creator-Selves. When the "traditions" fall away and we are brought to that moment when we only have ourselves to turn to—it is then that we re-encounter ourselves as Light Being.

Hot Stuff

Dedicated to all of us who have felt lost, alone, and full of despair. Dedicated to all of us who still kept on going, one flicker of hope at a time. Dedicated to all of us who have dared to listen to others rather than to the "scary-blaming-judging" voices inside us, when we were too blinded by terror to hear our own (W)hole Truth.

Once in a time that is perhaps difficult to imagine yet truly did exist, a flame's flicker got lost. One wouldn't necessarily think much of this, but this loss caused the (W)hole world to change. And it all started because of a slippery flicker.

Now it happened this way: In the world at this time, physical birth required inputting a flame of life into each potential being before it could be born. Prior to this "job" of in-flamement, all the flames of creation were free to wander in their original free-floating flickery forms until such time as they temporarily sacrificed their freedom to give life.

Upon the death of the body of that creature, the flame would return to its independent state until it could again chose to participate in (W)hole Life Expressions. Flames loved to be free, and so it was truly an act of sacrifice to share their life flame for the sake of borning a physical being. And flames loved to give life, and so it was a joy to offer in-flamement. Flames played between these two ways of being. Anyway, to get back to the story…

These flame-forms looked like what we might call campfire flames. One group of flickers were required to join together to make up one flame. All the flames were then linked to other flames by the inner fires, which wrapped around the center of the earth and were then woven into one great web of life by the tendrils of inner heat radiating from the earth's core.

Once, a flame had said that it looked like threads of liquid light woven throughout the earth's being.

A flame would become a soul of what we call a critter or person by entering the body at the time of birth to empower them with the passions and fires of life. This was called in-flamement, which has already been mentioned earlier.

Well, there was this one flame who wandered very far afield in its search for learning. As it danced in its joy of life, it danced so wildly that a piece of itself, a flicker to be precise, became separated from this (W)hole flame. This flame was called Hot Stuff by its flame-friends. Hot Stuff was so alive and full of fire and passion that no one could compare to her, thus the reason for her name, Hot Stuff. Even more to the point, her heart was just as warm and inviting as a hearth fire in the middle of winter. She had never lost a piece of flame before. Hot Stuff had always been a (W)hole flame, all flickers in place. Hot Stuff felt awful. She wasn't herself, and she knew it.

Hot Stuff noticed right away a sense of incompletion. Truth be told, it was more like a weakening.

She felt as if her fire-flame-self was trying to sustain its flame though a bucket of water had just been dumped in their midst. Hot Stuff felt smoky and sputtering and damp-cramped.

What had happened? Hot Stuff had no idea other than she knew that a part of her, a very crucial part of her, was missing. She did not know where to begin in search for a lost flicker. Hot Stuff had heard of this happening occasionally, but had never learned how the flicker was found or how it was joined again to make the flame (W)hole once more. Her situation was becoming urgent. Hot Stuff was, in fact, fading rapidly, becoming weaker and less vital by the second.

Without this particular flicker, she was no longer (W)hole and no longer able to in-flame a body with full life. "A flame without all its flickers is nothing!" she smoked to herself.

Hot Stuff was getting weaker and weaker, glowing only occasionally, as one might imagine the coals of a fire on its last embers of life, its glow only due to its past passions. She felt herself disappearing.

A star floated past Hot Stuff and called out, "Hey, do you know you are fading?" With some concern the star stopped and hovered nearby waiting for a response.

With a weak voice, the embers of Hot Stuff responded, "I have lost my core flicker. Now I am fading. My ember self feels so lonely and cold. It is as if the world is big and confusing. When I was (W)hole, I danced in wild abandon and I played with the stars and the sun and the fires of the earth's core. Then I could…," but her words faded away because Hot Stuff knew that that was then and this was now. There seemed no way it would be possible for her ever to feel fire-full again. It just hurt too much to talk about it.

The star floated on, not really sure of what to make out of this.

Time passed.

The flicker was also having a bit of a rough time. It was lost and confused, flickering and flittering from one thing to another, trying to find that which was made of its own material. You see, a flicker knows its home by the feel of things, the feel of hominess—a "You are like me and I am like you-ness." The lost flicker wandered the (W)hole wide world of soul-flames, questing and seeking and trying and learning and studying all so it might find home-ness, to touch same-ness, to find itself. At this point, it was becoming a bit panicky. Home-ness was still missing.

You might have noticed this lost flicker. The clue would have been a flash of light bouncing off a tree leaf or swinging off the edge of a wave that is about to collapse on the beach, for, as unusual as this was, this lost flicker had wandered even into the earth world as you and I know it.

It was so hungry, so desperate, so frail in its flickery self that the flicker was seeking everywhere for its own flame. Perhaps the trees had it or the mountains or the stars. Maybe a creature had stolen it, or maybe it was dampened out of existence!!?? So this flicker went flickering and flitting from one thing and then another seeking its (W)hole flame-self. It was feeling so lost, it had nearly forgotten its name.

A mole waddled past a green leaf just as "Sparkles-with-Life," the name of this particular flicker, landed on the leaf.

The mole knew something about this, as word had spread that there was a lost flicker and to keep an eye out. This particular mole was a very curious sort of creature and thoroughly enjoyed knowing all sorts of things. In this case he knew that a flicker was lost, the flame was fading, and that it was becoming sort of urgent to resolve the difficulty. He also happened to know the shortest way home for any flicker.

So he called out, "Hey, you there, you little flicker of a flame. Hey you, little Sparkles-with-Life, come on over here a minute. I think I might be able to help."

Sparkles-with-Life leaped quickly to the nearest shiny surface next to the mole's nose and flitted without moving (this is a learned skill for flickers) and cried out, "Really? Oh please help me. I want to go home. I want to be (W)hole with my flame-self again. I want to fill a body with the fires of life. I want myself (W)holly back." And then Sparkles-with-Life began to cry. As you might imagine, tears put quite a damper on flickers.

Then the mole said, "First, you must evaporate those tears of yours before you extinguish yourself. (Sigh) There is one way I know for you to return home, but it will take great courage and stamina. It will take curiosity and determination and a big earth mound of passion. Do you think you can muster all that up from your tiny flicker self?"

Sparkles-with-Life paused. This seemed a very tall order for a very fragile feeling flicker. But the wish to get home, to be safe and sound, snuggled up in the warm passions of the big raging fiery flame of her (W)hole self was a compelling hunger.

She answered, "Yes, I will do it, as best as I know. Tell me where and how I must proceed. I cannot bear to be less than (W)hole."

The mole pointed towards the earth. "That is the way home. You must dig in the earth. You must dig a tunnel deep into the underground of things. You may meet horrible creature-things of all sorts, feel feelings that are nearly wet enough to extinguish you, and still you must go on. You may sometimes even wish to give up. You may hope that someone else will save you, but still you must push forward, alone.

"To dig is to be curious, smelling and sensing your way straight to the fires at Earth-core. Then, once you have arrived there, seek the thread of your (W)hole self, and it will lead you to your particular flame. You must do this quickly, for I sense that your flame is dying for lack of you. Hurry."

With this, the mole, who rarely speaks at all, was so exhausted that he waddled off for a very long nap. The mole, named Nudgy, was shocked at himself for all the words which had spilled out of him, yet pleased he had known the way to Sparkles-with-Life's home. Secretly, Nudgy had a very big heart, which he tried to hide from most beings. However, he just couldn't bear to think of that cute little flicker lost forever, nor could he abide by the loss of the great flame he'd heard was called Hot Stuff. He smiled to himself as his eyelids tucked his eyes to sleep.

Sparkles–with-Life wasted no time and began the dark journey, scared but determined.

The light began to grow dim and still the flicker dug.

Then creatures of all sorts began to appear, making sounds and telling the flicker things that were surprising, frightening, and sometimes even annoying—because what the mole had not said was that all the things one learned on this journey were about one's self. "This digging into the underworlds was surely not meant for the weak of flame," thought Sparkles-with-Life.

"Sometimes you want to take up ALL the flame space, don't you?" whispered a horrible truth teller, who had showed up on her left.

"Remember when you took the embers right out of the flame's tendrils? That was mean!" whispered another.

"So you want to be part of a creature's birth! So you want to participate in a soul-flame journey into a body! Who do you think you are?" This time the horrible truth teller, whose name tag said 'Yuckie,' screamed and then rushed away.

Sparkles-with-Life only hoped that that Yuckie screamer would stay away for a long time, for it had just named one of the great secret doubts which lingered deep within Sparkles-with-Life. "Maybe I got lost because I am not good enough to stay!??"

"This is hard. I wonder if anyone else ever had to dig around in the darkness?" wondered Sparkles-with-Life, as yet another creature came over and began whispering to her about a bad habit she still had not resolved.

Then Sparkles-with-Life remembered that the mole said the key to this journey was curiosity. So each time one of these difficult encounters occurred, she would say, "Oh, how interesting," and try to consider how the hidden truth in the whispered horrors might make her burn hotter and brighter when she was returned to her (W)hole flame self.

She kept on and on—there seemed to be no other choice. Finally, there she was at the core. She could smell the scent of home. She followed the liquid fiery path, and suddenly there, right above her she knew she had found home—her (W)hole Self.

She paused.

This was a big thing to return home. There was much Sparkles-with-Life would return home with that she had not had before this adventure. She made a list in her head:

> There is wisdom found only through naked curiosity.
> The dark places and the journey to wisdom require the power of persistence.
> The Horrible Truth Tellers who scream and whisper along on the way offer gifts, like presents wrapped in ugly wrapping paper.
> Success isn't in how big your flame or flicker is, but how clean and true you burn in each moment.

Finally, there was the courage one needed to face the unknown. Sparkles-with-Life had had to trust only in her own self, to listen and to learn about her real self. There had been no room for shame or blame. To arrive here, to come home had taken all the courage she could muster! That mole had been right!

Most importantly, she, as a simple flicker, had become more alive and more vital than she could ever have imagined before her journey. She wondered what that would be like for her flame when she merged into (W)holeness.

Instead of sitting there and wondering, she jumped up into the hearth of her home flame and moved up through the fiery roots of Hot Stuff's flame lineage, its roots found only deep in the Earth-core.

With a whoosh and a rush of smoke, a huge, magnificent fire of life, an en-livened passionate flame leaped to the skies. Hot Stuff just moments before had barely been a bit of glowing coals. Now, she was a flame of such heat and power and presence that all the other flames in the land stopped. They cheered and celebrated the aliveness and passion emanating from this huge flame, now (W)hole, again.

And it is said that with the return of Sparkles-with-Life, Hot Stuff was so transformed that a new name was given to her.

From the time when Sparkles-with-Life returned home to now, for all eternity, Hot Stuff was renamed Passion's Fire. And the very process of in-flamement was changed, for the power and life that this one flicker brought back from her journey made the need for an entire soul-flame unnecessary for a birth of a being.

So all borning-beings from that time forth were given but one flicker from Passion's Fire, for that was all it took to inflame a body with life.

And all the other flames, rather than having to sacrifice their independent freedom to enter the body of creatures being born were simply asked to choose one particular person or creature to dance over and around, making sure that that being's particular flicker was never lost.

And it is said that when one is lacking passion, all one needs to do is call out to Passion's Fire. The flicker named Sparkles-with-Life will be dispatched in a moment to take you on a journey into the dark realms so as to bring you home. And all it will take is a bit of courage, some wild curiosity, and the deepest of hungers to come home to your own (W)hole self.

And so it has been for all time since that fateful day when a flicker was lost and then found its way home.

****

Life often seems to be all about losing our way, only to discover Life is really all about finding ourselves over and over again. The twists and turns, the dark moments of dimming life force all converge into one invitation: Will we choose to open up—even in our terror—to an entirely new viewpoint, new feeling, or new action, or will we close up, hide in the darkness of our (w)holes, waiting and hoping it will "all go away?" Here it is so naked—The Choice. We all get to choose over and over and over again. There is no wrong choice, just many different options with many different results.

Yes, your experiences and my experiences and our experiences matter to us all! They are the (W)hole Point, for from them grows the authority to reach out to another who is wandering lost and far from home and say, "I know the WAY."

The Dragon in the Box

Dedicated to the Wondrous Creatures we all are—independent of our current shape or feel. Dedicated to our precious "boxes" which have served for so long and now are crumbling into dust, so we may remember who we really are! This fable is dedicated to all of us who have thought ourselves so small, when in truth we are wondrous beyond all imaginings.

Once upon a time, in a time of long ago and today, there was a great and glorious dragon who was squished in a very small box.

Now, in order for this to have been possible, his soul had to have been removed and placed outside of the confines of this box. The reason his soul needed to be removed was because his soul contained all the knowledge of his grandeur, and it would simply not have been possible to place him in this box if he had known who he really was. Dragon Wisdom is gathered over eons of time and is quite extensive. It is housed in the Soul-place within them.

Now, it has been said that a very evil but resourceful magician had done this to him, while others said that it was his parents who had done this after his mother gave birth to him and found not a child but a dragon child placed in her arms. The truth is no one really knew why or how a dragon had been placed inside this huge box—it was as it was.

But in any event, once a long time ago and is still true today, there was a great and glorious dragon who was squished into a very small box. His soul was left just outside the walls of the box, and so it had been for eons and eons of time.

Now, at first the dragon had bashed and pushed and pounded at the walls of the box, but after the first 5,000 years or so, he had resolved that this would do no good and had settled into a life squished in this box, a box that seemed to get littler and littler as he grew larger and larger until his very creature self filled every nook and cranny of the box. However, being very creative, even without his soul, he actually got to the point where he forgot that there was such a thing as life outside of the box and in some small way came to feel some sort of peace with his existence. Dragons are quite skilled at adapting to their places and spaces. It is for this reason that they have existed since time began. Anyway…

He settled into his boxed-in existence, so to speak, until one day a quite extraordinary thing occurred. The walls of the box quietly, silently dissolved into a pile of dust. Time had simply worked its magic. The box was gone. It was just a pile of dust all around his boxed-in-shape.

The amazing thing was that the dragon didn't move. He hadn't moved for so long, he had actually forgotten it was even a possibility. In fact, his soul lay just beyond his reach, and it sparkled and called to him in every way imaginable, but it didn't seem to illicit anything from the dragon creature. The dragon had forgotten his own soul even existed. He couldn't hear what he didn't believe in. This went on for some time…until it was clear that the solitary soul would be unable to awaken the dragon's attention.

So, his soul called out to the angels in heaven and all the great helpers from above. "Do something. Do something!" called the soul.

Many days passed and still the dragon stayed in the shape that the box had insisted upon even though the box was now just scattered dust on the winds. His soul could only wait and hope that one day it would get close enough to him to merge back with its creature and thus, restore full soul knowledge to the dragon. Then about a week before another eon had passed or perhaps two eons, the most beautiful, mischievous mosquito began fluttering around the dragon's head.

Now, unbeknownst to him, this was no ordinary mosquito but one of the angels from heaven transformed into a beautiful, magnificent waker-upper critter. This angel mosquito was named Harriet. Well, to make a long story short and a short story very long, Harriet landed on the dragon's nose and bit him really, really hard. That is a waker-upper for you!! She had assessed that his nose would be a point of sensitivity and thus, had approached this direction.

Well, the dragon leaped up. There was suddenly great shock in him. He was in a shape other than a box! He was standing bigger than box size. He had no awareness of any tiny bite on his nose—he wasn't at all aware of his own powerful presence. And this dragon was magnificent beyond many of his own kind. His wings had a span of hundred feet each, and they were transparent, gossamer with the strength of steel. They were designed to carry him high and far, as far as he wished to go, over land and sea, through clouds, in fact, around the world if he chose.

His belly was filled with great fires, designed to burn his foes to cinders, to roar his power and passion to the furthest corners of the earth and sky, to melt any frozen places that he encountered. His heart was as deep as the wells of purest water and was designed to love with a passion more potent than the greatest magic in all the lands.

But sadly, none of this was available to him without his soul.

He shook himself a bit and then simply lay back down again. He knew how to be in a box, even without the box being there anymore, and so he did what he knew how to do. His soul was like a giant gem of the purest crystal diamond, glittering and shimmering and calling to him, "Pick me up. I need to come home to you. You need me to come home to you. I and you are one. I dare you to pick me up. I dare you to embrace me, to know yourself as (W)hole."

But you see, the dragon had gone back to sleep in his box-shaped way, for only with his soul inside of him would he remember who he really was, not some disappointment or embarrassment to his human parents, not some boxed-in creature who was meant to be nothing. With his soul inside of him, he would remember he was a great, magnificent expression, a magnificent creature with a mission that was crucial to the world.

Harriet knew this, so she flitted around once more. She was quite persistent, this mosquito, and so being somewhat of a prankster, even as an angel, she landed this time at the very end of his tail. She opened her mouth very, very wide and bit him as hard as she has ever taken a bite out of anybody. "Zowie," yelled the dragon as he leaped about five feet forward from his original position. He landed by accident, though Harriet would claim in later years that it was all her planning, right next to his soul and then brushed up against his soul with the smallest edge of one of his great claws.

That's all it took. His soul melted into him. It entered every cell and fiber of his being. It filled him with the knowledge of himself and reformed itself in the very heart of his heart and has remained there ever since. In that instant of self knowing, he lifted his head up high. He rose on his great haunches and let burst forth from his belly his flames of passion and power. As the flames filled the skies with fire and roaring vitality, he spread his expansive wings and lifted off the earth and soared into the skies, going higher and higher beyond all sight, it is said.

He was glorying in his magnificent self, the magnificent expression of himself. He called this expressed inner wisdom "Being me" in his later years, when he shared his own story with those newly awakened. And finally after eons of time, he remembered how all this had come to pass. The puzzle of his birth was revealed to him. This knowing had been held within his soul until that moment of "soul Re-Union," and now he knew who he was.

He had been sent by heaven to be a prince child in a dragon family. However, on the way to be delivered, the wisest ones in the heavens asked if there was a soul who would take on the task of helping those who soul selves had become separated from their creature selves. This dragon soul had quickly offered to help.

What he had not known at the time was that first, he, himself, must lose his soul and then reclaim it before he could begin his true calling.

It had been close, Harriet pointed out many times over the years. It had been a close call, and, of course, Harriet got credit for moving the process along, that pesky little waker-upper critter, for who knows how many more eons of time the dragon would have remained unaware that the box had dissolved and become dust on the winds of time?

Be that as it may, the true glory finally belongs to the dragon, for it is said that this great dragon who lived squished in a box now spends his days soaring around the world, seeking out those who had lost touch with their souls. It is a great and grand mission for a life, would you not say?

And it is said, too, that when he finds such a separation, he dives into his great heart and from there sends a wave of curious, courageous passion so enticing that it fills the lost souls with hope and carries them to their boxed-in creatures.

And with this same wave of energy, the creatures and the souls are reunited and filled with the power of their own soul knowledge. And thus awakened, they soar on into their own destinies, and thus, the world is just that much more alive.

And this, all because of a dragon, who was boxed in for eons of times and then one day was bitten by an angel, reclaimed his soul, embraced himself, and now carries hope to all the worlds. And this has been true for all time and is still true today.

And this story is told with an invitation that you, too, look around and notice the box has dissolved, and it is now time to soar. Be you. Be you. How big can you be? Soar now.

****

The experience of being "boxed-in" gifts each of us the authority to know what being small feels like and what allowing our soul to flow into our being feels like. Without boxes, we wouldn't know freedom. The boxes of "should's," "ought to's," and "have to's" squeeze in upon our huge and magnificent selves until one day, if we are lucky, a waker-upper critter comes along. This may be an event, a person, a challenge, or an inner anguish. Regardless of its form, the message to each of us is a simple one: The boxes have no substance, save by our choice to abide by their restrictions. And with this comes a most profound invitation to allow our glorious Soul Self to wake up, rise up, and soar into its own remembrance.

The Gift of the Gazorah's Gaze

Dedicated to all of us who admit to being our own "jailors" and still dare to chance the encounters which reveal the doors to freedom. Dedicated to all that was once considered lethal and is now unveiled as the source of Life. Dedicated to those who choose to gaze directly at Life and thus come alive.

Once upon a time there was simply ONE great tribe which covered all the Globe. And then a creature came to the land. This creature was a crawling-upon-the-ground type of creature. It had large piercing eyes. It killed its prey through its direct gaze. Its killing-gaze pierced into the eyes and heart and soul of the one looking at it, poisoning their spirit instantly. Although it lay low to the ground and had few reasons to attack, it often killed simply for the sake of killing. For this creature, killing was not just about feeding itself. It killed simply because.

The tribe was in grave danger from this crawling-upon-the-ground creature. Many had died from its gaze. They would simply be walking along, and there would be a movement in the brush. Their eyes would catch the movement, and they would look. Then and there, they would be caught in the gaze of the Gazorah, as it was called, and they died on the spot.

In fact, so many had died that the tribe's Shamanesses gathered. After great long council, they determined that the only way to save the tribe from pending extinction was by triggering an evolutionary leap within the physical forms of the peoples. This had never been done before. However, the ancient knowledge for such a change was still known by the eldest elder. Written in primary language on a parchment near to crumbling, the words of instruction barely visible, the eldest elder directed the preparations for the initiatory ritual. No one was clear what exactly would happen, only that the needed shift would occur. The great ceremonial ritual was set and enacted. Time has stolen the secrets of this alchemy, so no one now can say what had actually occurred during this ceremony of transformation, save for one element. Pivotal to the process was the direct wisdom-gaze-medicine of the eldest of elders. The changes began immediately. Every one participated, and every one was affected by the ritual, young and old alike.

In only one-half of a generation, the one tribe had divided. Now, there were two tribes. One tribe was called the BAC-TOE Tribe; the other was called the WAH-SEED Tribe. These two tribes had abruptly evolved in this way: Their necks had became rigid and fused, causing their heads to be tilted slightly so that their chins were protruding and elevated, thus better to avoid unplanned direct gaze encounters with the Gazorah. The two tribes had also evolved uniquely in their pattern of movements across the earth's surface.

The BAC-TOE tribe's movements, the way that they moved through the forest, had shifted to a backing-into pattern. They walked backwards as opposed to walking forwards. They now had a way of backing into the moment. The effect was to block inadvertent, unplanned direct gaze moments with the Gazorah, since their backs were what came to the moment first.

The WAH-SEED tribe's movements had also shifted. Rather than moving in the old forward way motion, which had allowed one to be most easily caught-up in the Gazorah's gaze, this tribe of people began to move in a sideways manner. With their rigid necks and their new sideways motion pattern, incidental lethal direct-gaze-moments with the Gazorah were inhibited.

With this combination of rigid necks and these newly evolved ways of motion across the earth, the Shamanesses had successfully thwarted the Gazorah's lethal attacks. And since the Gazorah were no longer able to easily kill the people, it was deemed a great success over the generations. Some still died, but they were far fewer and with far less ease for the Gazorah. The tribe was saved despite the significant cost of the division. There was no animosity between either tribe, and neither tribe was considered better than the other. It simply meant that the tribe, as a (W)hole, divided and altered in these ways, was far less susceptible to inadvertent lethal Gazorah gazes.

Legend has it that the Gazorah, no longer a living terror, retreated to the underworlds from which it had emerged. Birthed from the unknown, it surrendered into the embrace of mystery's darkness.

Generations passed, and now only those with the "new" evolutionary transformations existed, save for two—one old elder in each tribe. These two old elders still walked forward and each had a neck that flexed and rotated without restriction. Many forgot the time before the Gazorah, although there were, of course, the scary stories told at tribal fires. But they became more myth-like legends than truth. For now, all was well, and all were safe.

And then…a new situation arose.

The infants suddenly began to die in both tribes. Many were born—conceiving was not a problem for either tribe. However, after a few weeks, the infants' eyes would search. How natural this was! The infants' eyes would search for what was called the Life Gaze, the direct eye-to-eye gaze that affirms the value of life of the infant. In the BAC-TOE tribe, they would say the Life Gaze granted permission to back into the moments of one's life, and in the WAH-SEED tribe, they would say the Life Gaze granted permission to sidle into the moments of one's life. But either way, the Life Gaze was the first and most crucial of all elements for the new-born. Without the Life Gaze, the new-born withered and died. It was that simple.

Now, by tradition, this Life Gaze was first offered by the mother and then most significantly and repeatedly, by the tribal elders, who tended to the infants. However, because of the evolutionary leap instituted to save the tribe from the Gazorah, the capacity to Life Gaze had become less and less available, less and less natural to offer over the generations until, as it is written, only one of each tribe had the capacity to tip their heads down, capture and hold the gaze of an infant held in their arms and offer the Life Gaze. Only the two remaining elders were able to naturally and comfortably assume the physical position for Life Gazing.

Each full moon season, the two tribes would gather and witness the two oldest elders walk directly towards one another and offer the Life Gaze on behalf of each tribe to the other. All who had witnessed this blessed encounter felt their hearts open in renewal of their original unity. These two elders were very, very old people, left over from before the time of the Gazorah. At any moment they could die! What would occur if the Life Gaze was lost with them? The tribe's existence was in jeopardy again, ironically due to the very manner in which the tribe had saved itself from the prior Gazorah threat.

Although once again the tribes were in danger of extinction, this was a different type of threat. The threat was not from an outer source but from an inner danger: a danger coming from within the tribes and due to their physical forms. The Life Gaze could be lost if something wasn't done. The tribes would simply die off. A temporary solution was attempted.

The two tribes working together created a Life Gaze nourishment circle for the infants: each BAC-TOE tribe member was paired with a WAH-SEED tribe member and an infant. With backwards and sideways movements and with a taller and shorter tribe member paired together, it was minimally possible for an infant to be placed in a direct Life Gaze position for enough time to sustain its life. However, with the number of infants, all requiring daily Life Gazing, something more had to happen. This maneuvering and adjusting and shuffling to come into the correct alignment for Life Gazing took much time and placed great strain upon the physical structures of both tribes. All were exhausted at the end of each day from their alignment efforts.

But then a radical, radical decision was made. Through an ancient healing process the two old elders would seek wisdom through a sustained Life Gaze. They were the only two who recalled this process, called KLAS. It was their last resort. The two old elders agreed that even if they died in the attempt, so be it. Regardless of the risk, it was their only hope, and it must be done. What they hoped for was that KLAS would reveal to them how to save the people. What they feared most of all was that nothing would occur.

Leaving the two tribes and retreating to the sacred grove where the great change ritual had been done generations before, the two old elders walked with determination and trepidation into the circle of stones at the grove's center. After building a small fire for warmth, they sat across from one another. They settled into the quiet of the grove's green grasses. The over-hanging rustling branches ceased their twitching. All of existence held its breath. They looked up and into the eyes of the other. Breathing slowly and deeply, they did not look away.

Worlds began to pulsate. The life breath of all began flowing, swirling and spiraling around and about them. And the power began to grow.

No words were spoken.

Later it was said by some that they sat for a year. Others said they sat for just days, and yet others said it was but a moment's time.

All members of the BAC-TOE and the WAH-SEED tribes had set aside all of their tasks and had gathered at their central meeting place. Stiff-necked or not, backwards-walking or sideways-walking, they slowly moved their way together to watch and wait. Urgency painted the air around them all. Many of the infants had been lost, and more were on the edge of death. Time mattered.

The BAC-TOE tribe members backed themselves across the central meeting area until they were all the way across the circle, their eyes facing the center of the gathering. The WAH-SEED tribe members had sidled across the space in such a way that the two groups were able to partially see each other, while also being carefully positioned at right angles to each other, forming an intersection of sorts. They waited. The tribes were at a crossroads and had, per the instructions of the old elders, mirrored this in their orientation to one another.

Meanwhile, at the sacred grove the two elders still sat in direct Life Gaze. They sustained KLAS. They gazed into the depths of the other's being, resisting nothing that arose or was revealed. They assigned no words or values or judgments to what they saw and still they gazed. KLAS had never been dared with such determination or perseverance. It is said by two elder witnesses that at times it appeared as if the two old elders became one being. Pulsing emissions and vibrational waves flowed from the point at which their two gazes met. KLAS energy rippled around the globe.

Meanwhile, at the BAC-TOE and WAH-SEED tribal intersection, something stirred.

Some of the tribe members later said that they could feel the power beginning to radiate outward from a glancing gaze caught between one and another. Some said that they felt a rush of heat flooding their hips and knees. Some reported a trembling sensation in the back of their heads where their necks connected to their spines. Some said they began to feel an aching in their chests, and their eyes began to water while their necks throbbed with a hot tension. Everyone had their own story, their own experience. What is absolutely true is that the (W)hole world changed that day. What can safely be said is that every member of the two tribes experienced something.

What is agreed upon by all is that there was a quickening of the energy at the center point where the tribes intersected. This quickening began at the point where the central BAC-TOE elder and the central WAH-SEED elder stood. There was an unrecognizable stillness and then a wave of heat washed over the entire clan. All noticed the winds began to churn and spiral first round the two central elders—just those two! And then it picked up and began to spin around the next BAC-TOE and WAH-SEED tribe members, who were positioned next to the two elders.

And so it went, the winds and heat and light weaving two together two at a time until all of the members of the two tribes were involved in this energy of spiraling wind weaving. A warmth emanated from the ground, and it entered through the feet of all present, moving upward, upward until the spine of each was so hot as to be nearly unbearable. And still it spiraled upward until it reached the necks of all the stiff-necked.

And then each began to notice a sweet scent in the air. Some described it as the smell of new dew. Others described it as the first smell of morning or the last smell of the sun before it sets. Others claimed that it was the smell of a first born. There was a taste in their mouths, a sea salt tang of the original waters of life, clean after a storm. There were warm breeze fingers gently caressing the cheeks of all present and freshening breezes that cleaned the vision so all was clearly seen. And finally, there was a sound.

At first it was simply that, "a sound," and then it grew. The source has never been named. Some have taken to calling it a "Soul Sounding." It grew until distinct notes could be heard. It grew until these notes melded into a melody that seemed to be different for each listener. It grew until it surrounded all gathered. It grew until the melody became music, and the music vibrated through their spinal cords and ear drums, through their necks and feet, through their eyeballs and fingertips, until it vibrated in time with their heartbeats. Each person there became the music until each knew themselves as ONE being, joined with all the others in a symphony of life itself.

Without consideration, without restriction, without hesitation all of them began to turn their heads this way and that, seeking the source of the music. Without noticing what was occurring, they began to turn and move around, only a few giving notice to what this might signify. Too much was occurring. Then some and then more and more began to dance and weave and spin and swirl amongst the others—no longer were they two tribes but ONE dancing being.

Gently the tribal beings were lifted up, rising above the ground, the music itself their cushion, their embrace and their own orchestra. It, the "Soul Sound," surrounded them completely. It was beneath them, around them, in them, and above them. An unknown amount of time passed.

Gradually, all became still. And then all began to awaken, finding themselves laying upon the earth, sprawled all about, each tribe mixed with the other: a tangled web of beings. Some were afraid. Some were excited. Some were terrified. Some were hopeful. Some were entranced. Others quivered in hunched up balls, while still others rose and danced in a weaving wavy sort of way. All knew something had happened. And indeed, it had.

As each rose, they found that they could all look completely about. They could walk in all directions and with their necks no longer stiff, they could gaze in all directions. They were free to move in whatever manner they wished. They had been freed from the restrictions instituted to save them from the Gazorah. They were free from those outdated survival restrictions gifted to them by their own creator-selves. They had now been gifted freedom. They were free! Completely Free! Free to move and gaze and encounter without restraint.

It took time for all this to be digested. At first, there were some that needed great comforting and assurances before they could allow themselves to settle into this new freedom. Others moved directly into great celebrations, while still others took a time of inner meditation to digest their newly born way of being. The infants were no longer in danger. Life Gazing nourishment was now readily available for all. The tribe was no longer threatened, and the original ONENESS had been restored. That which had set them apart from one another was no longer useful, though always and for forever BAC-TOE and WAH-SEED lineages were celebrated as their precious explorations into the experiences of restriction and their conscious birth into freedom.

From that day forth, each new day began with KLAS, the practice of sustained direct eye-gazing. No longer restricted to only the elders, all participated in this tribal custom. Each day also ended with Life Gazing. The tribe was re-named: The Naked Gaze Tribe.

And at any time that anyone of the ONE tribe of The Naked Gaze was in "an unbalance" or began to notice that they could only move the old BAC-TOE or WAH-SEED way, or their neck began to stiffen in avoidance of another, someone would offer them a moment of open-hearted KLAS, and their freedom would be re-established and once again they would be able to choose Naked Direct Gazing, aligned to their true natures.

What had been discovered about the effect of sustained direct-Life-Gazing was that there was a secret hidden within it. The secret was that there was nothing that was meant to be kept secret! There was no reason to hide anything from another or oneself because all were ONE.

The gift of the Gazorah and the grace-wisdom of the old elders converged into these simple living truths:

There is no safety in blindness.
There is no life sustenance found in separateness.
There is no continuance without risk.
There is no alignment without truth.
There is no aliveness without transparency.
There is no birth without nakedness.
There is no conscious (W)holeness without conscious brokenness.

And finally, all life depends upon itself ever evolving into what is called for in the next moment.

And thus, being "Love-Life-Gazed upon," without restraint, became the nourishment for all.

And without reason or need to hide or be separate, all lived in freedom to be, to move and to live in ways that had never been gazed upon before.

The old elders never did return from the sacred grove. Some say that their presence is what enlivens every KLAS, for something more is always present when any two tribal members gaze directly into one another's eyes—some ONE beyond the known.

The Naked Gaze Tribe is revered for forever, for revealing that a direct look of love, free of all restraint and restriction, changes the (W)hole World, again and again.

****

Often that which has saved our lives at one time later becomes our soul's prison. This is not cause for shame, but rather for celebration. It offers evidence of our great potency. We are creators and thus able to re-create ourselves, no longer prisoners but pioneers, no longer less-than but rather (W)hole and Holy, no longer bound by the past, but rather alive in the moment. How do we step across a soul-prison's threshold? How do the life-saving restrictions we ourselves have created become the doorway to (W)hole Living? In a naked encounter with oneself, opening to the mystery, the doors swing wide as one awaits without cause, purpose, or goal. Mystery's Presence can't be held hostage to our fear of direct gaze, rather it is risking it all that our mysterious being awakens to its own wondrous (W)holeness.

The Stroll of the HoorTeeTah

Dedicated to those who have become so adept at hiding that others don't even notice their absence. Dedicated to the maneuvers we all engage in to keep secret our "badest" secrets in fear that we will be found out and reviled for it. Dedicated to all those who have been called "the bull in the china shop," "the one who always puts their foot in it," or "the ones who seem to step right into the shit." Dedicated to the revealers of truth—purposely or accidently or invisibly. Thank you.

This is a story of HoorTeeTah. HoorTeeTah is a being of transparent presence, and it all began this way. Once there was a village. It was a village or a city much like any other village or city that one lived in. All was going along as it always is. Then one day this being, HoorTeeTah, a being of transparent presence, walked through the center of this town.

Now, strange things began to happen, unexpected things. As the HoorTeeTah walked through the center of town, it passed by the presiding villager. Now, this presiding villager had a title in town, and the title for that role was YahHoot. The YahHoot was presiding over a meeting. The name of this particular YahHoot was Eetoot. So this was YahHoot-Eetoot presiding over the village, and they were having a meeting.

Now as the meeting was progressing, the HoorTeeTah walked past YahHoot-Eetoot. Secretly, unbeknownst to anybody in the town, this particular YahHoot presiding over the town had a secret, and the secret was that when he was falling asleep at night, he would suck his thumb. And when he was anxious, he found it most comforting, but it was something he had never, ever, ever let anyone know about. And then it happened. As the HoorTeeTah passed by him, there was this compelling effect, and suddenly before them all, before all of the village, there was Eetoot sucking his thumb because he had been anxious in the middle of this meeting.

He had thought later he would suck his thumb, but the effect of this transparent being was the secret was revealed right then and there! So there he was sucking his thumb in front of everyone.

There were snickers and laughs as this suddenly occurred, for it had never occurred before, and this secret had not been known by anybody. The laughter died away as the HoorTeeTah walked passed Hannah, the town baker, who was right next to the leader of this meeting. She had, as she usually did, her basket of carrots. Her basket of carrots was what she carried with her in public all the time because she was always, always, always on a diet. She would often say, "Oh, I've tried so hard to diet and so hard to lose weight, and look at all these carrots I must eat."

But she had a secret, and as the HoorTeeTah walked passed Hannah, suddenly without giving it a thought, she found herself reaching into her pocket and pulling out a handful of chocolate. She consumed it right in front of everybody. And what was her secret? Her secret was that each night she would go home and consume at least a pound of chocolate in secret. She always had a stash of chocolate hidden on her being. However, she had this joy of complaining, and she liked to look good, as the one that was the victim who always had to eat the carrots.

Suddenly, this secret was revealed because the HoorTeeTah had walked passed. There were more chuckles and laughter, except not quite so loud this time as when the YahHoot-Eetoot's secret was exposed. Then, the HoorTeeTah continued to stroll, oblivious to what was occurring, past the pastor of the village. Now, the pastor was somewhat horrified by the two secrets that had been revealed unplanned. He had known neither of them, so he was a little upset, as it were, that he hadn't been "in" on the secrets. And he had a secret. The pastor loved to walk naked at night and loathed the sensation of clothing on his body. Only his wife knew this secret. As soon as he walked in the door of his home, he would take off all his clothes. This was no problem for either he or his wife, for they lived alone.

As the HoorTeeTah walked by him, he found himself stripping off all his clothes. The town villagers who were watching this would start to laugh, but then they would hold back their laughter a bit. They were worried what would happen when the HoorTeeTah walked past them.

As it was, the HoorTeeTah continued its stroll and walked past the oldest member of this village. Her name was Sheila. She was very staid and proper in her old age and had a very pursed face, as it were. Inside, she was chuckling secretly at everyone. Clearly the HoorTeeTah would never have an effect on her. After all, she was the eldest. Now, her secret was that whenever she could, in the darkest of nights, she would wildly begin to dance. With her swinging breasts and her lose skin, she would stomp her feet and swing and sway herself all over the room. She looked quite a sight, but she loved to dance. She had told no one. It would be simply "beneath her station." You can guess what happened next. The HoorTeeTah passed by Sheila, and suddenly, without any thought at all, she found herself dancing wildly in the middle of the town square, stomping and singing and making all sorts of noise.

Well that was it. The HoorTeeTah, obviously, became shunned by all—not because of appearance or smell or attitude or style of dress. It became shunned because of its presence. Others were brought face to face with their secrets—whatever they were—in the most amazing and magical ways. And so it was that the HoorTeeTah ultimately was escorted to a distant cabin, far removed from the village, by the five youngest children of the village. They had been given this order by Sheila, the eldest member who had finally stopped dancing. She had chosen these five children because they seemed to be unaffected by the HoorTeeTah. They didn't seem to have any secrets because they were simply who they were.

Daily, the children brought the HoorTeeTah food and drink and anything else it needed to ensure that the HoorTeeTah did not come near anyone else in the village. And so it was that the villagers' secrets were again maintained for a time.

Now, as with any village, people come and people go and various things happen. Over the course of a few months, some strange things happened—things that had not occurred before in the village. Items began to go missing. The baker's favorite big bowl was suddenly gone. The blacksmith's knives and this one sword he had been working on for quite some time had gone missing. The textbook that a young child had been reading was suddenly not on the bench where he had left it.

Stealing had never been a concern in this village before. No one could determine what was occurring, and none of the lost things were being found. Much discussion occurred, and, of course, the village presiding YahHoot, YahHoot-Eetoot, was called to task. "How come you have not solved this? You are, after all, the presiding villager?" YahHoot-Eetoot paced and paced, sucking his thumb night after night. (He never did admit to everyone that the secret continued. He just didn't do it in public anymore, which was easier to do now that the HoorTeeTah was at the far end of the village.) So as he paced and sucked his thumb, he went around and around all sorts of ideas of how he might discover and solve the mystery of these missing items. After many nights of pacing and thumb-sucking, he had it! His solution would require great courage of all of the villagers, but he could think of nothing else.

He called all of the villagers together and explained his idea. There was great silence at the end of his idea presentation. The villagers knew that his idea would call for great courage from all of them to do this. However, they did not want to keep losing their things, and they did not understand how or why it was happening. It made them all feel unsafe and uncomfortable that things were disappearing and not being found. And so, the villagers agreed.

The day came when the entire village was brought together. All those in the village were required to attend, and the constable was sent out to round everyone up who was in the vicinity of the village. The five children went and brought the HoorTeeTah to the gathered villagers. For a time, as you can imagine, there was chaos. This one was stripping his clothes off. That one was sucking his thumb. And here was Hannah eating all of her chocolate in great public displays. One by one the villagers' secrets were coming out. I'm sure you can imagine your own most secret thing. How uncomfortable would it be for you to expose that secret?

And yet, the villagers held through to their decision. After all the chaos had calmed and all the secrets had been revealed, the thieves were also revealed. Next to one who had not been long in the village lay the baker's bowl on the ground. Next to another, there were the blacksmith's knives and sword. Next to a third was the textbook of the young child. And so it was that those three were set apart from the village, sent on their journey to some other place. The YahHoot-Eetoot felt very proud of himself that he was able to solve this mystery and end the villagers' discomfort. In fact, he was so pleased with himself that although sucking his thumb felt very good, his anxiety had died down so much that he was able to stand there not sucking his thumb.

It was determined that the HoorTeeTah would be recognized as a significant and important member of their village and would be brought into their midst on a regular basis. And so the village came to be in a state of great peace and harmony, for no more was there hiding. And since all of their secrets had been revealed—all of them—there was compassion, an understanding that did not require anything other than just the decision to accept that was extended to everyone in the village.

And so it came to be that the day the HoorTeeTah first walked through their village, revealing Hannah's love of chocolate, the pastor's hatred of clothing, the YahHoot-Eetoot sucking his thumb when he was anxious, and Sheila's love of dance—that day became known as the day the village was born again.

****

There isn't one of us who hasn't or doesn't have a secret that if "found out," would, we imagine, ruin our image—our projected self. Isn't it also true that as these secrets are revealed, a surprising relief washes over us? Of course, it takes huge energy to contain and veil our real selves. It takes huge energy to force fit ourselves into a particular pre-designed, pre-assigned shape. What if there was a Being who revealed by its very presence all your secrets? What if there came a time when no one could hide what was inside? What if there comes a time when we are by nature telepathic and all is revealed without restraint? What would you find revealed? This fable is an invitation to imagine a world without fear of being exactly how and who you are.

Olli's Echo

Dedicated to all those who "walk first into the mysteries." Dedicated to all those who trusted and roped themselves to those "First Ones." Dedicated to the mysteries of life which call us to engage and dance with them in the daily moments of life's simple complexities.

Once upon a time in a time that was a long time ago and is still true today, all the lands were enclosed by what we might think of now as a great barrier or a container. Although at the time it was not considered such. It was considered simply the edge of the world. Now this barrier had at times been attempted to be climbed, but it could never be climbed because it was always farther than the climber could go. No one had ever seen over it, and no one knew if there was anything on the other side of it or what it was to even look upon the lands from such a height. It was simply the edge of the world as it was known, and they called it The Eternist, and it was taken for granted.

All the villages were scattered about the land, and there was one particular village that was filled with many elders—not all elders, but many of the elders would settle in this particular village after they had done many of the walk-abouts that elders were called to do in the process of ripening into an elder. And it was snug up against the Eternist simply for the reason that it was little bit farther removed from those noisier places on the land. Elders enjoy quiet.

And in this particular village there was a place, an organization as it were, called TEE-AH, and those that were members of TEE-AH were held as the wisdom keepers even amongst the elders. Now, it had been noted that the Eternist was not a smooth surface. It had been explored by many of the elders, and what had been recorded was that it had various indents and scratches and marks of all sorts and, of course, the youngsters of the tribe had made marks on it and made indents and scratches in honor of what particular moment had occurred to them, but none of these seemed to faze the Eternist. It simply continued to be what it was.

Now, at one point on the surface of the Eternist there was what one had come to call a zigzag that went somewhat vertically from ground toward the sky. No one knew how tall it was. And then at some point at the top of it, it had been noted by someone with a spy scope that there was a horizontal zigzag going across, and then there was another vertical that seemed to descend from the end of that horizontal zigzag. And no one knew what it meant, and it had been named Landmark and was taken for granted. In fact, this landmark then, because it had been taken so for granted, had had its own mythology and finally had been named the ZIGZAGZIP, simply because that was fun to say.

One day Olli, a member of the Wisdom Village and also an elder within the TEE-AH was walking near the Eternist gathering herbs and flowers and also gathering great deeps of breaths of sunshine, for in the last three years, there had been less and less sunlight, more and more rain, and fewer flowers. This day was a grand treat. The sun was shining in all its magnificence. The green of the grass and the colors of the flowers were rich, and Olli, as a elder, could wander to her heart's content throughout the day and even into the evening if she so chose. Her wanderings had taken her from her hut closer and closer in a spiraling manner to the Eternist, really without purpose but simply closer and closer. And then she found herself even closer to the ZIGZAGZIP as her baskets became heavier and fuller until there, near a path, she set down her baskets, and she sat down on a rock. She closed her eyes and felt the warmth of the sun as she breathed deeply and felt the warm air rush into her older but still functioning body. Enjoying that, she softly opened her eyes to enjoy her eyes and let them sweep over the entire landscape.

But wait, wait. That couldn't be. What has happened? She rose. She walked closer and closer to what she saw. She reached out a hand to touch, but there was nothing there. She sat, not by choice so much but by shock. The ZIGZAGZIP had become a gaping wide void, a black void. There was no sound emanating from it. There was no smell. There was no movement. There was apparently nothing that had caused or been left that had changed this. There were no boulders. Nothing had fallen. There was no evidence at all of what had caused this. There was simply a space of nothing.

An ancient wisdom mystery took hold of her mind, but then was gone in a flicker. Olli paid no mind really. She was stunned, shocked. This has never been written about, never known in all that she had ever studied in all of the TEE-AH wisdoms. Now what was true was that Olli held a particular position in TEE-AH. She had the position of Mee-Ya-HAH. This was a most sacred and bold position. It meant literally "she who walks first into the void." Yes, Olli was the Mee-Ya-HAH of the TEE-AH. This was her formal title, Mee-Ya-HAH TEE-AH, and she had held it for quite some time, but she had frankly never encountered a literal void. She had walked first into many mysteries, and she had walked first into many emotions and places that had frightened her or others, but she had never stood across a space, from a void as black as this.

She sat. She breathed across this huge black emptiness in the Eternist, and she knew what she must do. She knew it instantly, for it had arisen up in her belly and into her heart and flickered and moved throughout the entirety of her being. It was her duty as well, a chosen duty, of the Mee-Ya-HAH of TEE-AH. But still, she had never, ever been confronted with something that required such a bold heart. And yet, she knew.

She decided. She stood up. She left her baskets as they were, merely forgotten. She dusted herself off, and she took a step, another step, another step toward the void in the Eternist, for Mee-Ya-HAH Olli was bound by oath to walk first into these mysteries, and so it was. She held true to her promise, to her vow, to her choice, to her aligned life. She stepped into the Eternist's void.

She had prepared lifetimes for this. She has prepared and prepared in this lifetime to do this. And so she did. There was nothing save the smooth surface she was walking. There were no smells, no sounds, no breeze, no tastes in the air, no colors—nothing, simply black empty void. Olli, the Mee-Ya-HAH of the TEE-AH, squared her shoulders, softened her heart, although everything within her first attempted to seduce her to contract and to barricade her heart. She softened her heart, widened her shoulders, and allowed her heart to lead her forward into this void, the void of the Eternist. She opened all of her senses and her non-senses to all of the dimensions and continued walking on.

It seemed as if nothing was happening, and yet she knew she was walking, for she was feeling tired, and she was beginning to feel thirsty and hungry. She continued until no matter what direction she looked in, it was simply black. Behind her was black nothing. She could not even see where she had entered this void, and before her was nothing. It was black. It was a void. It was an emptiness. She continued. She knew in the wisdom of her heart that she had gone now too far to turn back. All that she could do was to go forward.

She lost all track of time, and she continued until there was no thought in her mind. All the emotions of fear and anxiousness and curiosity had all burned their way through her body until even her heart was simply still and open. And she continued. And then there was a light, a pinprick of light ahead, and she continued. But she did not rush. She did not run. She simply continued as she had. And it grew steadily larger and larger until, until clearly it was an opening and clearly there was light streaming towards her. And there was something, there was something about the light that was not what she would understand. She had never seen light like this. She continued until finally, she was at the threshold, the threshold where behind her was the black void of the Eternist and before her was a light that she had never seen before. And once again, she stepped. She took the one step that would take her into a world beyond her imaginings into mystery, once again the first, stepping again first into the mysteries.

The light had sound. The colors she saw before her had smells, and the touch of chartreuse wind had a taste of strawberry. All the senses, all the senses were present in all of the senses. And then she heard the music and smelled water running nearby. She ran for a drink. She was drinking and drinking, unprepared, and then she realized the water, the water was something more than just water. It was, yes, the words came to her flowing from inside of her heart—it was love in a substance. And with each drink of this water, it flowed into her cells, into every element of her body, and it was as if each sip reached into the deepest crevices of this form that she was in and filled them to overflowing.

She sat again in shock and relief, in joy and amazement—all at the same time. The green grasses that she sat in tinkled with harmonic bells of laughter, and the laughter became little bits of blue turquoise puffed into the air that was then blown along on a rose-colored breeze of wind. She sat and took it all in. She could feel her being, not simply her body's form but her being, renewed at levels she did not even know were tired or were fatigued.

Some amount of time passed, and she slept. She only knew that she slept, for she woke later and recognized the sensation of awakening, although the sensations that she awoke to were new and surprising, beyond anything she ever could have imagined. Time of an unknown amount passed. She named this space-place PIZZAZZ. It amused her. She had turned the letters ZIGZAGZIP backwards and made it the name of this space-place that also captured how she felt. There was a pizzazz in her being. There was a zip in her step, and there was nothing that did not tickle her just a little bit with a giggle and delight.

Olli felt content and gradually, deeply she felt herself feel full in all of her dimensions—her physical form, her spiritual self, her emotions, and her intellect—all of her being felt full, nourished, and satiated in ways she had never contemplated. And then and only then did the lands that she had left, the people that she had left behind on the other side of the Eternist begin to come back into her heart. She knew. She knew she must return to share with them what she had come to. It was part of her Mee-Ya-HAH commitment, and yet, in her deepest downest self, she knew she did not want to. But it was what was true.

And so determining she would do this the next day, she did. Walking to the Eternist void, as she had come to name it, this big, black gaping void, she stood before it, saying "Good-bye" one last time to PIZZAZZ, for she did not know what would happen as she stepped into the void, if she would ever be able to return to PIZZAZZ. So she hardened her heart just a bit in case she could not return. And she took a step into Eternist's void. And then she took a second step and found herself popped back out in PIZZAZZ. She tried again and again and again to enter into Eternist's void so that she could go to her people, to call them back and show them, but it would not work.

She could not return. It had become clearly apparent that she could not leave PIZZAZZ. This took a settled turn within her being. It had been an innocent delight until now. Now she could not leave. Now what would she do and what of her people, for the truth was she did not want to live anywhere but PIZZAZZ, and yet, and yet, what of her commitment to her people, for all those that she knew and those that she didn't know?

She sat and became very quiet and still. And then rising up within her an ancient wisdom mystery rose up—the ancient wisdom mystery called Echo. This had been what had tickled her mind earlier before when she had first entered the Eternist's void, but now it rose within full blown. Oh, yes, the wisdom of the Echo. The void would serve this well, for it was empty. It was without restriction, and it would provide the magnification that would allow an echo to reach back to her people. It was all that she could come to, and yet, she knew it was correct and right in the moment.

However, now Olli was confronted with what she should say. What would she send echoing through the Eternist's void? What would she say? She sat for two to three days, it is said, mulling on this. "Ah," she said, "it must be simple, for to send truth on the mystery of the magical powers of alchemical echo, it must be simple." She would trust the wisdom sisters of the TEE-AH to decipher it. So first, it would be important to say who was sending this message. She would call her name, Olli. It seemed that if she did this two or three times, the echo would arrive clear enough at the other end. But what would the message be, she wondered. She would say after a time, "I am going to send this message—I'm in here." She wanted them to know that there was a place and that she was resting in this place. She was in here, but this would not be enough. She wanted also to extend an invitation and to communicate there was no danger.

Now, this was a complicated message to send through the alchemy of echo. And so she determined to say, "I'm in here," and then to extend the invitation by saying, "Come on." And then a last phrase, "It's free of danger." So she was clear now, the message that she would send through the alchemy of echo. The next day she began. She sat three times a day—in the morning, mid-day, and as the sunlight of the many suns of PIZZAZZ were setting to allow the stars to rise up and dance in the sky in spiraling twirls. She would sit and she would call, "Olli. Olli. I'm in here. I'm in here." And she would wait. And then she would extend an echo, "Come on. It's free in here. It's free." And every day, three times a day, she would sit, not believing, but not disbelieving. Simply doing what she had committed herself to do.

Now, meanwhile on the other side, as it came to be known, her sister women of TEE-AH had found her baskets. They had posted a 24-hour witness to wait, for they knew beyond a shadow of a doubt that Mee-Ya-HAH would communicate to them, for it is the bounded commitment of TEE-AH that no one was ever left alone, and there was a comfort with the mysteries and the allowing of them to ripen into their fruition. The witness, of course, was the first to hear the echo, the call of Olli. Much conferring occurred in the TEE-AH. They all gathered around and they waited for the next message. They heard through the echo the message, and they decided in the heart wisdom that they each trusted to trust the Mee-Ya-HAH TEE-AH. And so they acted.

They gathered all the peoples of the land, and they told them what had occurred, what they had found, what they understood of the alchemy of echo, and what they heard of Olli's message. They extended an invitation to any who chose to come with them—those that were non-initiate were welcomed, the common folk. And it was determined that the procedure would be as such: the TEE-AH, in order to comfort and companion those who had not been initiated into the mysteries of transparency and alignment, curiosity, choice in the face of the unknown—those who had not been initiated would be roped between TEE-AH who were spaced apart.

And so on the day of the great action, those that had chosen to come—and not all did—gathered before the void Eternist, and the first and eldest of the TEE-AH called Homie stood at the beginning of a great long line, and she was roped to thirteen of those non-initiatives who had the courage of heart and the openness to risk beyond anything that they had known without any knowledge or initiation or preparation. And then the next TEE-AH was in line, and then there were thirteen again of the common folk. And once all the many, many, many were aligned in this way, connected so that they would not move into panic as if they were alone in the void and they would be steadied by the TEE-AH. And each TEE-AH, steady within her own being, would be able to hold steady as those in the spaces between them would move through their own anguish and fears, confronting mystery, just as the TEE-AH had each done a long time ago.

And with a pause that seemed to be eternal and yet was only a moment, Homie called out, "We begin," and she stepped into the void just as Olli had done. And one by one in silence, TEE-AH, thirteen, and then the next TEE-AH—one by one they stepped into the void in silence. Some wept. Some shook. Some shouted. Some dragged their feet, but those that had chosen stood strong, and they chose again and again and again until the entire link of all that had chosen were within the dark void of the Eternist. All that could be heard was the sound of footsteps until Olli, Olli's echo came. It came moving through the entire dark void, "Olli. Olli," and a long pause, and the footsteps—*whoosh, whoosh, whoosh.* And then, "I'm in here. I'm in here." And then a pause. *Whoosh. Whoosh. Whoosh.* "Come on in. It's free, free of risk. Come on in. It's free, free of risk." *Whoosh. Whoosh. Whoosh.* And then Homie, the eldest of the elders of the TEE-AH, felt it rise up inside of her to echo the echo.

And so it began, "Olli. Olli." And the people followed suit, and the TEE-AH followed suit, and soon "Olli. Olli." echoed back to Olli in PIZZAZZ. "I'm in here," said Homie. "In here. In here." echoed back to Olli. "Come on. It's free. It's free of risk." "Come free," echoed back to Olli. "Come free." Until all the people were echoing and Olli was echoing, and there was this dialogue in the space between, carried on the alchemy of the echo. And it was this that carried all the people as they traveled to PIZZAZZ, companioned by the alchemy of an echo and resting first and foremost in the heart of a wisdom elder who went first into the mystery. And all arrived, partaking of the water's substance that was love, drinkable love, and they all settled into PIZZAZZ, and it came to be their practice to begin and end each of their days with Olli's chant that had been burnt into the ancient emptiness of the echo, the chant that had been born in the dialogue between Olli who went first and those that followed in blind trust and hope and faith in the wisdom of the TEE-AH. "Olli. Olli. In come. Free. Come home to be." "Olli. Olli. In come free. Come home to be." would echo throughout PIZZAZZ, and Ollie continued as Mee-Ya-HAH. Homie continued as TEE-AH's mothering one, and all the people came to thrive as one.

And still, they knew that there were those on the other side, and so they placed a caller of the TEE-AH who stood at the void Eternist three times a day, trusting the alchemy of echo, and she would call out, "Olli. Olli. We're all in here. Come on. Come on. It's free. It's free of risk." And so the echo continues, as echoed across time and still does, all because there was a TEE-AH, an elder who took on heart and soul and dared the void to bring life eternal to the people.

And so it is. This is the story of Olli.

****

Have you ever considered what it takes to "go first?" As children we often want to line up "first" or "go first" on the swings or "get in the front seat" of the car. Yet we grow up often to be adults who sidestep "firstness." What has happened? What have we lost touch with along the way? What makes "sameness" more important that "firstness?" This fable is an invitation to consider the depth of boldness of heart, the breadth of openness of mind, and the height of vitality necessary to "go first" into the void on behalf of self, other, and the world. What would you choose to do today if you "went first?"

Wandra, The Forgotten One

Dedicated to all those of us who have quested for so long that the beginning has been lost in the mists. Dedicated to all of us, hoping for recognition, who have gathered wisdoms from the far corners of the globe, only to realize that the mission itself has been forgotten. Dedicated to all those who have believed in "self-growth," only to discover it wasn't the point at all.

Once there was an elder, and this elder's name was Bulahr. This elder was an elder of a great clan of people that spread across the lands. Bulahr was quite old in years and yet had a deep, deep commitment to wisdom. Bulahr came to a decision that there would be somehow a journey made to the four corners of the lands with the intent to gather the essential wisdoms to reveal the intent of life itself. However, she could not go on this journey—she was far too elderly. She sought someone in the tribe who would take up this quest, a quest that did not have any form or shape, save a journey to the four corners of the land and gather the essential wisdom to reveal the intent of life itself.

After much discussion and exploration, Wandra clearly, evidently from within her and from Bulahr's understanding and the other elders that were involved in this, was the one to undertake this journey. She was the chosen one. And so, she set out, Wandra, by her own choice. She did not know anything other than she was to journey to the four corners of the land and gather the essential wisdom. She did not even know what that meant, but she chose to step into the unknown. It was a great honor, after all, and she had somewhat of a wanderlust in her as well. So it was a good match.

And so she journeyed, and the journeys involved great discomfort at times—physically she was cold at times. She was hungry at times. She was so exhausted at times that she was sure in retrospect that she slept for days on end in various locations, for there was no time on this journey. She simply journeyed until she moved to the next place and the next place, following the leading that rose within her. It was also a demanding, lonely journey, and it called forth from her great courage. And it revealed all of the places and spaces within her where she was less than steady. It even revealed the places within her where she was so ready to betray the journey and return home. It revealed the places within her where she wished to betray her own preferences to make it easier, to make the easier choice rather than the truer choice.

And so it was, this was a journey on the outside, and it was a mirror of the journey of the inside that Wandra was on. She arrived at the first corner of the land, and after great exploration, came to this piece of symbolic wisdom. She found a feather so light that if one placed it in the air, it would simply stay right where it was placed. It did not rise, and it did not sink. It floated in place. And so she took this to be one of the essential wisdoms. She did not quite understand what that wisdom was. There was just a knowing in her.

She then continued on, traveling to, as it were, the second corner of the land as she imagined it, for there was no map that she was following, and she did not even know if there were corners to the land. It was just a saying that had been her guide. In this particular area of the land, there were monsters, great, angry monsters, and there were poisons that you could not see. It was a time of mirrored death many times over for Wandra. And time, no sense of time, time had simply become a word that meant nothing.

After great experiences that can be told in other tales, she came to find a piece of rock. This piece of rock was unique in that it was so durable; it was, in fact, impenetrable. There was nothing in all of known creation that could penetrate this rock. It was perhaps the size of a large fist or two. It did not appear to be in any way unusual, save for this property. She took this and put it in her pack, not sure again of what this essential wisdom was, yet the knowing leading her.

She turned again and spun and spiraled around inside of herself and moved towards what she felt called to her as the third corner of the land. Again, after experiencing near death through drowning, experiencing the sense that there could not possibly be this much water that was raining down upon her, that was rising up in floods around her, she came to a place where there was this pond—one might actually call it a pool, a pool of liquid. It was perhaps the size of a small bench or two. It was not large, and it was one she stumbled upon, she would say later, led by the heart wisdom that was developing within her.

This liquid when it was taken up in a cup and spilled upon the ground, if you watched, it would return to itself. It could never be separated from itself for long. And so, she took some of this into a container, placing this liquid that always returned to itself by some means that was not clear, never to be separated from itself for forever, and put this in her pack. At this point she had lost all sense of how long she had been on the journey. It turned out to be far longer than she imagined. Later they determined and calculated that it was over fifty to one hundred years that she had been journeying. She often spoke of it as the eons of timeless time, for she had lost sense of even the tribe itself, and Bulahr was merely a name, not even a face any longer in her memory.

She had yet one more corner of the land to go, and yet her feet were dragging they were so tired, and her heart was barely in the journey. She did not know what to find. She had this feather. She had this rock. She has this liquid. She did not even know if this was success or not. She was breaking in her heart for fear that she had spent all of this time and perhaps was failing, for she did not know what success looked like. Finally, she was led to what she imagined and felt was the fourth corner of the land.

Moving blindly through a dusty, arid area, she came to a place where there were these broken shells. It became clear to her that they were shells that were the remains of a creature's birth. These two halves of the shell that she picked up, when she brought them together would mend together into one whole shell for a time, and then they would break apart again. Then she could pick them up, and they would come back together. They would meld together again, and then they would break apart. This, too, seemed somehow, some of the essential wisdom, and she put this in her pack.

Then, barely able from the exhaustion inside and out, she brought herself back to her village. Her heart was broken open, and she had a deep sense of dread that perhaps she had failed, for this seemed a small and meager gathering for the quest she had been sent on. She returned to the village and found out that Bulahr no longer breathed on this land.

The elder who had sent her on the quest was no longer there to greet her, to even say to her this was success or failure. "Yes, you have done what I asked." There was no recognition. And now it was Leelah who was the senior elder.

At the time of Bulahr's death, the wisdom book which the senior elder kept and wrote a log, as it were, had been lost. The significance of Wandra's quest was also forgotten, and Leelah had never known of Bulahr's request to Wandra. Wandra, at this point, simply huddled down in Bulahr's fallen down hut, barely eating, and in great despair. After all she had gone through, it was now just ashes, it was all for nothing. No one knew of this quest that had taken most of her life.

Meanwhile in the village just prior to Wandra's return, a thief had been breaking in and stealing various sorts of items from the villagers. A lookout had been posted with the hope of finding the thief and the missing items. Approximately two or three days after Wandra returned from her journey, this thief was caught.

There was much anger at the presence of this thief. When they captured this thief, he was found to have had a great sack in his possession. Inside the sack were all the things that had been stolen and amongst the items was the wisdom book. Until now, it had not been known it was lost. Leelah had not known that Bulahr had kept and written in the wisdom book. Yet, this thief, in his act of betraying the land's rules, had uncovered this book, which had now been taken to Leelah.

Leelah, as the senior elder, sat and read through the book. She came to the place where Wandra's quest was described by Bulahr. Now she understood. Leelah understood the despair of Wandra. She understood Bulahr's intent and the grandness of the quest. She gathered all the villagers around and gathered Wandra and read the wisdom text to them. She read that the purpose of this quest was to reveal the intent of life itself. And they asked Wandra to step forward into the circle of all the villagers to present that which had been brought forth from the quest.

And so it was that Wandra presented the feather, so light it floated, and the rock so durable that nothing could penetrate it, and the liquid that returned to itself despite all that one might do to separate it from itself, and the shell of the creature's birth that would break open and then begin again. As each of these pieces of symbolic wisdom were offered, all the wisdoms of the heart that Wandra had gathered inadvertently and without conscious intent broke open within her, and she said this to all the villagers:

"The intent of life itself is life, to be alive in each moment, to do this in a way that you are as light as this feather, neither rising or sinking—simply being in that moment. To be as this rock, so durable in your own heart-felt presence that nothing can penetrate, nothing can take from you that durability of your own presence. And to be that liquid, that fluid that you will always in whatever manner and whatever form the flow takes you, return to yourself (W)hole again having gone on the journey. And knowing again, that there will be another birth in the next moment and another birth in the next moment."

And all of this wisdom rose from within her, and ultimately, she was able to say the greatest wisdom of all is a heart that's present.

Wandra's despair was healed. The villagers celebrated all that she had done, and upon Leelah's death, Wandra became the most senior of all elders. And so it is that Bulahr began the vision quest with a question and a journey to the four corners of the land and ended with the answer of a heart's wisdom. And Leelah knew that she had done what she had been called to do as an elder, which was to bridge the wisdom book to the new people. And Wandra had birthed herself as an elder.

And so, the quests continue.

****

Countless numbers of us have been on the quest of healing and improving ourselves, all with good cause. Yet, there comes a time when the quest and even the discoveries are not enough to replenish us from the exhaustion of this never-ending journey. This fable is an invitation to stop and return and consider the wisdoms which are you, to stop and give yourself great celebrations for your persistence on behalf of your own "improvement" and then set this mission down. It is time to return home and rest. Do you dare? The efforting, the "doing it all alone," the heroic in-human pressing forward—are you not done with this? Can you, do you dare to risk softening within and without? You may find that you have arrived in a far different place when returning home. You may find you've journeyed far to find YOU.

Feisty & Nudgy: The Moles Who Came to Love (w)Holes

Dedicated to all of us who have gone towards the anxious dark scary places within only to discover the treasures of our own (W)holeness waiting for us to embrace them. Dedicated to the rebels and radicals of us who pushed the edges and broke through the barriers of fear and presumptions to bring greater life to all the people.

Once upon a time, a time that was very long ago, moles were deathly afraid of (w)holes. This had been a long-kept secret in the current mole community until now. This "breaking news" is being broadcast around the (W)hole world, and the heroes of this tale are two very curious moles: Feisty and Nudgy.

Due to their fear of (w)holes, moles leaped over (w)holes, fled from them, fought them, and hid from them, and sometimes they even ignored them as they fell through the darkness. And no matter what, they never really looked into them. (w)Holes were to be avoided at all costs, and everyone knew that. It was simply common knowledge.

If you did happen to fall into a (w)hole, it was said to be a most terrifying event. The few who did "fall in" were permanently changed for forever! No one was ever sure how you would be different, but different you surely were. And when a mole actually did fall in, as happened occasionally despite all efforts to the contrary, the "(w)hole rule" was that you had to get out as fast as possible. Do not stay around to look. Do not go further down. Just leap out as quickly as possible. It was for this reason that all mole children took "leaping lessons" in school, "just in case," as the principals would say.

It was also rumored that if you looked at the contents of a (w)hole, this, too, would change you for forever. The type of change was unpredictable. ALL change was considered dangerous by moles in the know. "Just get out" was the essential emergency (w)hole response rule. In fact, (w)holes were considered life-threatening occurrences. The terror of (w)holes was so great that a (w)hole management training program was developed and offered at Mole (w)Hole University, located at Mound Moment, USA.

The (w)hole management program was the most popular field of study due to the pervasive (w)hole terror afflicting the mole population. Every family hoped to send their children to MHU—Mole (w)Hole University—to become Mole (w)Hole Avoidant experts. An MHA degree always guaranteed a good income for life, or so it was that all the parents firmly believed. There were many positions open to those with an MHA. There were mole (w)hole health resource experts who helped the general mole population manage the stress of (w)hole terror. There were mole (w)hole first responders who were on call 24 hours a day to respond in case of an inadvertent (w)hole-fall by an unsuspecting mole. There were mole (w)hole barricade attendants who did their mole best to prevent such occurrences. There were mole (w)hole professors who taught at the various educational facilities, ranging from pre-(w)hole school all the way up through the University Mole-Doc programs. The options were nearly limitless!

Other MHU graduates did (w)hole research as part of their mole doctorate studies. However, this type of study strictly employed distant (w)hole observation research strategies only to avoid the risks of actual (w)hole contact. Theoretical (w)hole studies were considered the most challenging of the programs offered at the university since it was based completely on untested, esoteric conceptual imaging of (w)hole anatomy.

Beyond all other fields of study and including those listed above, the most basic and crucial mission of the university was to do all it could to prevent loss of life and/or radical, unpredictable changes due to (w)hole fallout. (w)Hole fallout is a term used for the life-threatening results of falling into a (w)hole. But then, one day, something extraordinary happened, a mole moment that changed forever the course of mole (w)hole history.

It was on this day that a mole named Nudgy dared to ask the unthinkable in the middle of O-No-(w)Holes class. Nudgy was trying very hard to listen to Professor Mudfudd, who was lecturing on the danger of (w)hole contact. He had made his point 20 minutes ago in the first five minutes of the 3-hour class. His point: Don't go into or near a (w)hole. But all of the professor's words just felt dead in his head. Nudgy was feeling nudgy, not to make too fine a point. "This stuff just doesn't feel right. There has to be something more that makes (w)holes such a big deal besides everyone's fear of them. What, after all, made them so awful?" Nudgy wondered as he mulled and squirmed and twisted in his seat.

These thoughts were building in his innards until, "So, what makes (w)holes so bad?" he blurted out. "Why are we all so terrified of them? They're all over the place. Why, just this morning I found one. It had crept into my bedroom. Just tell us already. What is the real horrible truth about (w)holes?"

Silence.

All his thoughts had just spilled out, out loud, and there was silence in the (W)hole of Mount Moment, USA. This was just not done.

Then a small voice from the farthest row in the class was heard to say, "Yeah, those are really good questions. I'd like to know too." It was Feisty who had spoken up. Even at a whisper it was a daring thing to do. She had been mulling during the lecture about an article in a theoretical mole studies journal which had conceptually advocated direct (w)hole contact as the next true arena of study. The article had created intense debate and had planted a seed of doubt and a growing deep curiosity within her.

There was great uproar throughout the lecture hall. Something had to be done immediately, and so the administration took action.

Nudgy was summarily dismissed as a (w)hole radical and was asked to leave the university that very day. Feisty, despite all the urging of her mole advisors to remain in the program, was simply unable to resist her building curiosity. In short, Nudgy and Feisty were ousted for their radical inquiry. Nudgy never got an answer to his question. Both were summarily dismissed to the great embarrassment of the respective families. They determined to team up together to find the answers to their questions—for real, not just in theory.

This quest changed the course of history for all time—the quest to find the (W)hole truth about (w)holes.

Feisty and Nudgy immediately began their independent (w)hole research, much to the horror of the larger mole community. First, they developed a working definition of a (w)hole. They determined that a (w)hole was the result of any experience, feeling, thought, or process that one finds hurtful, distasteful, or agonizing. The "feeling scale of response" varies with the size and intensity of the wish to get away from that emotion. A (w)hole, in effect, was the space put between oneself and a painful emotion in one's life. Simply put, a (w)hole is a space between.

It was also understood that a "(w)hole fall incident" occurred when one fell into that space between. The actual relationship and the structural orientation between the space and the feelings remained unclear. Feisty, then moved on to develop a comprehensive (w)hole classification system with a variety of scales and variables. Meanwhile, Nudgy, skilled in the art of detailed observation, applied these systems to all currently available (w)hole information. Together they began to catalog (w)holes, using what came to be known as the Feisty (w)Hole System. Nudgy noticed that there were big (w)holes, little (w)holes, dark (w)holes, gray (w)holes, square (w)holes, deep (w)holes, distrust (w)holes, shrinking (w)holes, disappearing (w)holes, and there were also huge (w)holes.

It was scary to break the rules, but their determination to find the real answers motivated them to keep working at it. Even when it was terrifying, lonely, overwhelming, and confusing to actually directly engage with (w)holes, even at a distance, they kept at it. Their catalog of (w)holes grew and grew. They looked and looked at (w)hole shapes, types, sizes, colors, edge qualities, ages, et cetera, until finally they realized that the next step had to be to go into, that's right, into a (w)hole on purpose. There was no other option. All possible research using the traditional observational strategies had been exhausted. What was in a (w)hole? What was at the bottom of a (w)hole? Was there a bottom? The questions left to answer were nearly infinite.

They decided.

Gathering all the rope that they could find, they chose to explore a convenient (w)hole, there were tons to pick from. Feisty lowered Nudgy into the (w)hole. Nudgy was the best observer of details between the two of them, and so down went Nudgy in the name of the science of curiosity. Deeper and deeper Nudgy dropped, and although he was securely roped, he was surely shaking and quaking and trembling. "What is going to happen to me," he thought as he dropped deeper and deeper into the darkness. All that was apparent, so far, was the noticeable absence of light. The (w)hole seemed to have no bottom that he could detect.

It was a courageous act to do what they were doing. And then, something happened…they ran out of rope.

Feisty pulled Nudgy up out of the (w)hole to make notes of all that had been observed by this courageous (w)hole dangle. This (w)hole exploration strategy, hanging onto a rope as one dangles deeper into a (w)hole, was applied to many other different (w)holes. They began noticing that there were distinct differences between (w)holes. Some had smooth, slippery sides. Some had rough, crumbly, rocky sides. Some had such rough sides that they were almost like steps descending down into the darkness.

They also noticed that Nudgy seemed to experience different feelings or moods in the different (w)holes. In some he felt heavy. In some he felt sticky. In some he felt turbulent and nervous. In some he felt sneaky. In some he felt invited. In some he felt cozy, and in some he descended only three feet before yelling, "Get me out of here."

Feisty added all this information to their cataloging system. Already they knew more than any mole had ever known about (w)holes, but still the real questions remained. What is in a (w)hole? Where does one go, if anywhere? Is there a bottom? What is at the bottom? However, even (w)hole dangling had its limits. Each time Nudgy just ending up hanging in the dark over and over again because they kept running out of rope before they arrived anywhere. (w)Holes, they were learning, were big wide spaces. But there was still so much more to discover.

Clearly the (w)hole questions would not be resolved without even greater personal risk. Apparently, there just was not enough rope in all of Mount Moment to allow them to (w)hole dangle all the way to the bottom, if there was such a place as a bottom of a (w)hole. At this point Feisty's theory was that (w)holes were never-ending tunnels of darkness. However, this idea rested upon conjecture alone. There was no fact. Feisty could not stop with just an idea or another theory. She just had to know. They had to take the next step. It was simple. It was also horrifying, but for both of them, there was no choice. Either they would (w)hole descend on purpose beyond the length of the rope, or let the (w)hole fear win. Neither was prepared to accept this second option. And after all, what would all the other moles think? And even worse than that, they would never know the answers to their (w)hole questions.

So they determined to go beyond even their safety lines. They determined to engage with a (w)hole totally, holding nothing back. After some preparation and consideration, they chose a (w)hole. They both stood on the edge of a medium-size (w)hole. Category: Fairly dark. Rough, stepped-edged (w)hole, with surface "maximum rough" category. They had agreed this was the only kind they would risk entering because this type of side construction gave them some hope of being able to climb out once they passed beyond the stretch of the ropes. They had designed a flag to be placed at the top of the (w)hole which said, *Feisty and Nudgy went into this (w)hole on purpose*, just in case anyone wondered where they were. The date was fixed to the bottom edge of the flag and was posted at the (w)hole. Each thought this was both clever and professional.

They had not brought rope beyond the short amount that they had, since ultimately there would be no point. Each also had brought equipment that they imagined would be helpful. There was climbing gear, good strong gloves, and, of course, food. Feisty had brought her (w)hole catalog manual, and Nudgy had brought his set of magnifying glasses and a light for detailed studies, as well as a bottle of aspirin. Despite all the preparations and months of study, both of them were quite nervous. "Sometimes aspirin can stop a nervous headache," thought Nudgy.

No one had ever done this before and lived. "This could be our last day in Mount Moment, USA." thought Feisty. She didn't say it aloud for fear of increasing Nudgy's anxiety, but she was quite aware of what they were about to do. Feisty and Nudgy turned to each other and blurted out at the same time, "What if we get stuck? What if we can't ever go home? What if it's just darkness and blackness for forever and ever and ever? What if we get separated? What if we can't see anything ever again? What if we run out of food? What if it hurts a lot? What if we don't like it and can't get back? What if it's just a big, black void with nothing?" The "what if's" trailed off, for neither one had any answers. This was, after all, the (W)hole point of their (w)hole leap!

There were no answers. They were clear. They were both willing to sacrifice everything, even unto their lives, to know the (W)hole truth. No more words were spoken, for there was nothing left to say. So they each began to climb down the edges of the rough-sided (w)hole. At first, they easily found hand-holds and toe-holds, but then it became increasingly difficult until the most horrible, dreaded event actually occurred.

Feisty's toe slipped. Then her left hand slipped, and then despite all her efforts, she could not hang on, and she began to fall. She yelled, "I'm falling," to Nudgy, and in a flash, Nudgy chose.

"I'm not going to be left here alone, and besides, who might be able to help her but me?" In saying this to himself, he let go—an act of courage that has gone down in history as the greatest heroic decision ever made. He began to fall faster and faster, headfirst into the darkness right behind Feisty. Each of them thought to themselves, "Oh, well. This is it. We'll know now."

Then Nudgy began to notice that nothing but falling was happening. He began to wonder about that actual sensation. He thought, "Huh! After a while the terror of falling kind of wears off. How interesting. Being upside down isn't great, but it isn't so terrifying after all." He continued to notice what he was feeling and what was around him. What else could he do?

There he was falling headfirst in a (w)hole on purpose, so he began to do what he was good at—being curious. This moment, after all, was the very moment that would begin to reveal all the (w)hole truths he had wondered about. Direct experience is like that! The answers are right in front of one's face!

(w)Hole Learning #1: There is no substitute for direct experience.

Being curious by nature, Nudgy's focus calmed him down. Quickly, he noticed that his body was beginning to right itself so that he was now falling feet first. "Perhaps it was a (w)hole effect, which occurred once one was past the initial terror?" He called over to Feisty, "Are you ok?" Feisty yelled back, "Help me. Can't you see I'm falling, and I'm upside down on top of that?" She was totally panicked. Nudgy yelled back at her, "Yeah, me, too, only I'm not upside down anymore." Then surprisingly, Nudgy found himself laughing. It just seemed so silly.

They were both falling, but actually nothing really awful had happened. Neither of them was hurt or dying or anything. They were just falling. As soon as Feisty heard Nudgy laugh, her curiosity got the better of her fear, and she felt less and less fearful and more and more curious. Then she, too, found that her body shifted, and she was falling feet first. "What a relief," she said. "Being upside down can really give you a headache!! Ah, a (w)hole learning," Feisty noted.

(w)Hole Learning #2: The fear of falling into a (w)hole and being in a (w)hole wears off.

They both had begun to gain some control over the direction of their fall. By using their arms and legs and heads and hands, they were able to move closer to the sides of the (w)hole. First, Feisty and Nudgy managed to reach out and grab a protruding rock. They suddenly found they were no longer falling, and yet, they were very deep in the (w)hole. As they hung there, Nudgy noticed he was feeling very disoriented due to the many thoughts and feelings and ideas swirling within his mind and heart while Feisty was feeling very sick and unable to really grasp the magnitude of their situation. Neither of these responses were their normal ones. Some other (w)hole effect was transpiring. They took note of all they felt—for posterity.

But despite their inner reactions, they couldn't help but look around. They were actually getting answers to some of the questions they had asked way back when in that classroom so far away now. Curiosity always seemed to capture them and lead them on. Nudgy noticed a ledge just within reach. Daring to stretch his arm out as far as possible, he grasped the edge, took a deep breath, let go of the rock he was hanging onto and swung himself up onto the ledge. It was just large enough to sit on. What a relief it was to sit for a moment. He was very proud of his courage as well as the daring of the two of them. It felt good to pause for a time. "Good for me, good for me, good for us," he said aloud.

(w)Hole Learning # 3: Curiosity in a (w)hole is calming and useful. The most important tool. Be sure to leave all judgments behind.

(w)Hole Learning #4: Be sure to take time and rest. (w)Hole Play can be tiring.

Nudgy was carefully recording each of these (w)Hole Learnings in their mole (w)hole research journal he had brought along in his backpack.

Nudgy looked more closely at the ledge, and to his surprise, it appeared to actually be a narrow path going around and around the inside edges of the (w)hole. It seemed to spiral deeper and deeper into the darkness. "Hey, Feisty, look what I found. It's a path. Maybe we can walk instead of fall." Feisty's stomach had calmed down somewhat, and she was finally able to work her way over to the ledge by grasping rock holds, hand over hand. They just sat breathing together silently, each thinking to themselves, "I'm so glad I'm not alone on this adventure."

(w)Hole Learning #5: (w)Hole Play is gentler when shared with others.

"Holy, moley, this is some (w)hole," spoke Feisty for the first time since they stopped their fall. Her enthusiasm and curiosity then really kicked in. She just had to know if any of the theories they had been developing were true. As she stood up, she noticed that her manual was missing. She remembered that she must have dropped it when she began to fall. "Oh, well. Now, I'm really going to know the (W)hole truth. It seems my book wouldn't do much good right now, anyway. I've fallen way past what I had written down."

Feisty reached for Nudgy's hand, and together they began to walk along the path. They both noticed it was like a spiral rimming the inner edge of the (w)hole. Around and around they walked. It led them deeper and deeper into the dark (w)hole. It was helpful to have brought their flashlights, as there was no light source in the (w)hole.

(w)Hole Learning #6: When entering a (w)Hole, be sure to bring your own light.

Nudgy took out his magnifying lenses just as Feisty happened to pick up a rock on the path. Nudgy examined it closely, noticing to his great surprise that there was writing on the rock. Looking closer herself, Feisty saw the word "fear." She put it down. She thought for a moment, "Wow, I just felt a wave of fear." She paused. "How could that be??!! Hmmm…"

Feisty then said, "Hey, let's look at some other rocks." Taking a few steps more down the path, she began to examine one rock after another. As she turned over one and then another and another, each stone seemed to affect her differently. Nudgy also began to pick up and read each stone. He found the word "love" on one stone and felt his heart warm. They found one that said "hate," and they felt a coldness and disconnection within their bodies. They found another saying "gentleness," and Feisty felt herself soften and open. Another said "despair," and hopelessness and sadness washed over her. Yet another rock read "hope," and she felt joy and possibility well up inside of her.

"Hey," asked Nudgy, "have you noticed something strange about these stones when we pick them up?" Feisty said, "Yeah, each one seems to do something different to me." Then he reached for another stone. It was kind of addictive to have these different feelings so distinctly experienced. He was feeling so alive, so aware and awake. He had no idea that feelings were so uniquely rich and varied, satisfying in a way. His heart was feeling nourished in a way he had not ever known. "Hmm," he said, "I wonder if allowing feelings to flow through our hearts feeds us in some way??" Feisty secretly admitted to herself that she had carefully avoided many of these feelings for a long time. They had just made her feel so naked, so vulnerable, so out of control.

It was in this way that they spiraled deeper and deeper into the (w)hole. Each one would pick up a stone, have a feeling experience, and then move on to the next. *Spiraling* was the new (w)hole term they coined for following this path, circling the edge of the (w)hole. Spiraling, they both commented, takes courage. It took courage to pick up each stone. Neither one knew what would be there. However, with each feeling that they faced, they gained more confidence. After all, these were simply feelings. No matter what anybody might have told them, feelings did not seem to be lethal. They stopped to let Nudgy make notes in his journal.

(w)Hole Learning # 7: Leave no stone (feeling/discovery) unturned. Each reveals wisdoms.

As they continued on the path, Feisty picked up another stone and suddenly found herself giggling and laughing and being totally silly. "I'm never like this. What's gotten into me," she wondered as she giggled and chortled. She turned over the rock, and there was the word "silly." This was something she had totally set aside long ago. "It was not appropriate," she had been told. She even remembered saying to herself, "Life is just too important to ever be silly. I am anything but that." This had happened when she had overheard her dad say, with a very scornful voice, that only children were silly. Feisty had quickly decided that being an adult meant to not ever be silly. And yet, here she was in this (w)hole being very silly… and she liked it!! It was a relief from always having to be serious.

Meanwhile, Nudgy had picked up a stone and was feeling full of confidence and self worth. "What a great feeling. I actually am kind of smart after all. In fact, now that I think about it, I'm very smart," and with that thought he stopped. In his mind he could hear his mother saying, "You have a big, beautiful heart, but you are a bit short on brains." He suddenly felt very sneaky to think of himself as smart. "I wonder if Mom will find out," he thought to himself. Then he turned over the stone, and there is was, the smartest word that could be said about any mole—genius! In fact, that was just how he was experiencing himself. It was great, and he hoped it was ok; after all, it was not what Mom had told him he was. However, he really liked this feeling of being genius.

How different their perspectives were about (w)holes now. "There are gifts to be found here!" they each said simultaneously. "This is great!"

(w)Hole Learning # 8: Being in a (w)hole has some surprise benefits if you stay curious, persist, and remain open.

Both slipped those particular special stones into their pockets, for neither one wanted to give those up. Nudgy turned to Feisty and said, "Wow, I like how I get to feel things here, things I thought I couldn't feel or didn't dare to feel. It feels a bit awkward at first, and it isn't exactly normal, but I like it. I feel happier and somehow bigger. I feel like I'm more me. I feel like a more (W)hole Mole, as a matter of fact!!!." "Yeah, me too. This sure is different than what I thought (w)holes were about," said Feisty.

Then they each went to pick up another rock. They had realized that these feelings or qualities seemed to stay with them once they allowed the feelings to flow through their hearts. It was as if they were gathering treasures. They were each getting fuller and fuller with these new and interesting qualities which they had not allowed themselves before. There were some stones that didn't have much significance to one or the other of them, and then there were those that really seemed to hit the spot. This was interesting. This was fun. This was challenging and also sometimes startling.

Sometimes a stone had a word on it that made one or both of them blush or feel shame for wanting that feeling or having that feeling or enjoying that feeling. Sometimes a stone would make them feel angry or resentful that they hadn't had that quality in so long. Each stone carried with it an experience of facing more of one's self. It was now clear to them that (w)holes were full of direct, immediate experiences, ripe for the taking, so to speak! Who would have ever guessed!?

Then, Feisty noticed a dull, crumbling, rumbling sound. She looked behind her and saw to her horror that the spiral path was dissolving behind them. There was no way back! They hadn't noticed this before. All of a sudden, this wasn't so fun anymore. "Look. Look. We can't go back," yelled Feisty.

(w)Hole Learning # 9: Once you are in a (w)hole, the only way out is through. The portal is at the bottom.

Nudgy turned and looked. He saw the pathway crumbling and felt very nervous. "I guess the only way we can go now is forward." With a big gulp, he looked ahead at the path. It was quite solid, much to their relief.

Nudgy then noticed a dim glow way down ahead of them. Perhaps there was light at the end. “Look,” he cried to Feisty. “It looks like there’s some kind of light down there.”

Feisty saw the dim glow too. “I guess since we can’t go back the way we came in, we only have one choice—to follow the spiral path deeper and deeper into the (w)hole.” she sighed. They determined to keep going, leaving no stone unturned, for one might reveal a clue as to what was to come. So it was after a time that they came to a place where the light was quite bright, and the path ran around and around and around in tighter, smaller circles until the two sides of the (w)hole were so close together that one could step from one side of the (w)hole to the other quite easily.

Unbeknownst to Nudgy, Feisty was secretly scared to death about the light. It just seemed too bright and light and warm and, well, just too good to be true. Her mother had always warned her that “Things are never as good as they seem.” She could still hear her voice in her head. She wasn’t quite sure what all that meant, but she was quite sure that she must be telling her something important.

Nudgy, on the other hand, felt drawn to the light, almost hypnotized, seduced by the warm, pulsating radiant light. His father had always been a bit of an adventurer, and he had absorbed that excitement. The unknown drew him along, fascinating him as nothing else. He had always wanted to be just like his dad.

So what was this light? Was it life or death? Neither knew. Neither could do anything but move forward. They had nothing to go on except how it felt to them. Theory had long since dropped away. However, they both had learned that curiosity was an extremely useful response to anything occurring in a (w)hole. They examined and noticed and studied what was right in front of them—the light.

Together they concluded that it was pulsating. It was alive somehow, radiant, radiating, gentle and warming, very bright but not burning. There seemed to be a purpose in the light, but they had no idea what that could be, and neither of them had ever thought to discover such light at the bottom of a (w)hole, or maybe it wasn’t the bottom.

Suddenly, Nudgy had a brilliant thought. “Hey, maybe (w)holes aren’t (w)holes but tunnels that take you someplace new or lighter or something.”

He still had the "genius" stone tucked inside his pocket, and he liked how it made him feel. Feisty laughed with a silly grin on her face. "Well, it doesn't seem like a headlight, and it doesn't seem like it's moving towards us, so at least we probably won't be run over. Ha ha ha," she laughed. She thought, "Being silly sure does lighten things up." She liked how she was changing. She just wasn't quite sure how all this was happening, but she knew she wasn't going to give up the "silly" stone that was tucked away in her pocket.

"Well," says Nudgy, "we have to dare to face the light. We can't go back. The path is gone. The only way out of this spot is somehow towards the light and into the light." Between them and the light there was a doorway or a portal of sorts. Both of them noticed that they would have to step across a threshold to really enter into where the light was actually emanating. They stopped and made further notes in Nudgy's journal. There was so much they were discovering.

(w)Hole Learning # 10: When in doubt in a (w)hole, move towards your anxiety and its cause.

Nudgy took a deep breath and stepped across the portal's threshold and into the light. He began to feel as if the light was entering every cell of his body. It felt uplifting and embracing. "I feel like an angel," he thought to himself. Feisty, however, was feeling scared and tense. She wasn't sure she wanted this much light anywhere near her. She wasn't sure she could handle it, that she could contain it, that she could control it. She was afraid that it would crush her or take over her. So she just sat down.

She closed her eyes against the light. She wasn't sure she could step through the doorway. She just felt so vulnerable. So much had happened to her in this (w)hole. "It's ok," called Nudgy from the other side of the portal. "Look at me. The light doesn't hurt, but it does change you. It is up to you to choose to receive it or not. Personally," he said, "I love it. I feel great relief. It is as if all the hard work in me is melting away. I feel glad to be me inside and out."

Feisty looked at Nudgy across the threshold. She was still terrified. But even in her terror she was able to be very observant. She noticed a radiant glow beginning to emanate from inside of Nudgy. It looked as if a light bulb was turning on inside his heart. He was already so different, so changed. He looked so beautiful and somehow more alive and brighter and radiant, more something than any mole she had ever seen. In that moment she knew. She knew she wanted to know what that was like too, and it scared the whiskers right off her nose.

She stood up. She had chosen. She was determined to face the mystery of the light. She wanted the (W)hole truth, no matter if it killed her. Frightened but determined, she threw his arms wide and said, "I choose light.

(w)Hole Learning #11: "Whatever it takes" is the attitude for Spiraling a (w)Hole. Choose the light every time.

Gently, pulsing light life seemed to enter every pore and cell of her. She felt a warm tingling run through her body, and for the first time ever, she began to make sense to herself and to feel ok. In fact, she felt great. Nothing had prepared her for the mystical, magical feeling of such inner peace and the quiet joy of being herself. She could now admit to herself how much time and effort she had spent being serious and good and careful in her life. "Cautious" had been her most favorite word. She saw now that she had spent much of her life not being fully alive. She had spent much of her life not expressing aspects of herself because she wanted others to like her, to accept her, to not mock her or laugh at her. She hadn't, until this moment, ever really been herself, holding nothing back. Up until this moment, there had been things held back because of her fears. Something big had now changed in her.

"Boy, this life light sure does make you feel good," said Feisty. "I'm really glad I dared to step through there. It sure was scary, though. If it hadn't been for you, Nudge, I'm not sure I would have dared to risk so much change." "Yeah," said Nudgy, "it's so different than anything I've ever felt." He was just sitting in the light with a big smile on his face. Feisty then found herself dancing around in the light, something she would never, ever have thought that she'd be caught dead doing, and now there was no stopping her. It was as if there was so much effervescence inside of her, she didn't know what else to do.

"I used to be so afraid to be vulnerable, to be me, to be seen, to be silly, and now it would seem I would choose nothing less than the (W)hole entirety of me."

(w)Hole Learning # 12: There is a healing light and truth deep in every (w)hole.

Nudgy accidentally bumped into something in the light while he was dancing around with Fiesty. "Hey, what's this? Oh, look. It's a thread leading off towards something beyond the light. I wonder what that is all about?" That's all it took. With the new-found light inside of them and the qualities that they had picked up from the (w)hole, they were even more curious to follow this thread or path to the next discovery.

This was far more interesting than the classroom's theoretical studies that they had been engaged in. Their curiosity was focused. They were moving. "Curiosity is addictive," they both said at the same time and giggled together. They were moving in a spiral path again, around and around and around. Yet, this time the circles were getting bigger and bigger and lighter and lighter and brighter and brighter. They both noticed that they continued to feel more (W)hole and more radiant. And, oddly, even as they spiraled around, the light had not diminished.

They had (w)hole jumped on purpose. They had spiraled to a portal. They had chosen and crossed a threshold into a Light Presence that "turned their inner lights on." They were really getting to know the (W)hole truth about (w)holes. They were following their hearts' questions using curiosity. They discovered the (W)hole truth about (w)holes, and they were feeling pretty doggone good about that.

(w)Hole Learning # 13: (w)Holes are actually compressed spirals or tunnels that lead to bits of Living Light, which are orphaned elements of our own Radiance.

Feisty and Nudgy then came to a place where the spiral and the light all seemed to simply fade from view. It was as if the light spiral was there but not quite so visible. They looked around, not sure where to go from here. However, Nudgy thought to himself, "When in doubt go forward." What a shock and surprise it was to find they were back in Mount Moment, USA. There were even moles who saw them arrive. The now famous witnesses were stunned!

"Ah, we thought you were dead," they yelled and cried as they ran and waved towards them.

"You look different." "What's making you glow like that?" "What happened to you," the other moles cried, some approaching, some keeping their distance.

And so it was that Feisty and Nudgy told the moles the (W)hole truth about (w)holes. The proof of their stories was in their natural radiance that pulsed from within them, the light that emanated from them even in the dark of night.

The (w)hole avoidant moles had seen nothing like this, and yet here was the (W)hole truth. Most of the moles wanted some of this light for themselves, too. Of course, there were a few who said, "It is too different." "I do not want to stand out that much." "(w)Hole work sounds like too much effort." "What would other moles think of me?" Or, "What if I can't do it? It's best not to try."

And so the debates and discussions went on. However, the Mole (w)Hole University curriculum was redesigned to include Spiraling, (w)hole jumping, curiosity skill development, and multiple classes on radiance capacity evolution. The mission of the entire university was changed to "The study of the (W)hole truth on behalf of (w)holes" for moles everywhere. Nudgy and Feisty became the first (w)hole professors, and moles everywhere began to line up to engage in their own spiral journeys to radiance.

And so now it is said that the reason moles are so comfortable with (w)holes is that the moles know the (W)hole truth, and now so do you.

When confronted with a life (w)hole, take a lesson from Nudgy and Feisty. Go into the (w)hole on purpose. Leave no stone unturned. Stay curious. Drop judgment. Keep moving. Keep spiraling. Pick up things you like along the way, and keep them. Dare to step across the portal's threshold, for a mystic moment of radiance awaits each of us deep in any (w)hole. And, it will always be true that each must choose to receive the light, no one can do it for another.

"Segments of Nudgy's (w)hole fall journal" Date: (w)hole fall 1/1/1

An original copy from the first (w)hole ever to be explored. On loan from Mole University—Department of (w)Hole Explorations & Documentation. (Note: date signifies 1st (w)hole, 1st journal, 1st mole team to purposely (w)hole fall. Ever since this epic journey, every (w)hole expeditionary team was given a number to designate all their journals. Of course, Feisty and Nudgy were designated Team 1.)

(w)Hole Learning #1: There is no substitute for direct experience

(w)Hole Learning #2: The fear of falling into a (w)Hole and being in a (w)Hole wears off.

(w)Hole Learning #3: Curiosity in a (w)Hole is calming and useful. The most important tool. Be sure to leave all judgments behind.

(w)Hole Learning #4: Be sure to take time to rest and appreciate your efforts. (w)Hole Play can be tiring.

(w)Hole Learning # 5: (w)Hole work is gentler when shared with others.

(w)Hole Learning # 6: When entering a (w)hole, be sure to bring your own light.

(w)Hole Learning # 7: Leave no stone (feeling/discovery) unturned. Each reveals wisdoms.

(w)Hole Learning # 8: Being in a (w)hole has some surprise benefits if you stay curious, persist, and remain open.

(w)Hole Learning # 9: Once you are in a (w)hole, the only way out is through. The portal is at the bottom.

(w)Hole Learning # 10: When in doubt in a (w)hole, move towards your anxiety and its cause.

(w)Hole Learning # 11: "Whatever it takes" is the attitude for Spiraling a (w)Hole. Choose the light every time.

(w)Hole Learning #12: There is a healing light and truth deep in every (w)hole.

(w)Hole Learning # 13: (w)Holes are actually compressed spirals or tunnels that lead to bits of Living Light, which are orphaned elements of our own Radiance.

(w)Hole Learning #14: When a number of (w)Holes are spiraled, a mole becomes a "Radiant Pulsating MoleBeing of Light" due to the amount of Radiance embraced. This transformation is inevitable and highly sought after.

****

When we think of moles, we don't tend to doubt that they dig holes or live beneath the surface of the earth. Yet, for this one moment, consider what kind of mole a mole would be if it feared (w)holes. Yes, go ahead and laugh...I did too as I wrote those words. Moles are moles the way we know them because of (w)holes, just as we humans are each uniquely human because of our precious particular imperfections. I call these human foibles—they are what make each of us different from all the others. They are our "etchings" on the crystal of our soul selves. How easy it is to just study what "they" say and follow what "they" tell us to do, and yet, what are we missing then? We are missing out on all the encounters with the mysteries hidden in the unknowns of ourselves. This fable is an invitation to go leaping into those places, the anxious, scary, hidden hidey (w)holes within so as to reveal the ever "mo-R-e" of who you are, one "(w)Hole Leap" at a time.

With laughter and silliness I wrote this fable so very long ago, and it still brings a giggle into my voice notes. May it do the same for you. Hope to see you at the new and improved Mole (w)Hole University!

The Land of Gleeful Laughter

Dedicated to all Moms and Dads for having hearts big enough to love, despite the naked powerlessness over the fate of one's children. Dedicated to all parents and family who have had a child die. Dedicated to all of us who have suffered the anguish of losing someone we love. Dedicated to all those who, knowing the risks, open to love and life anyway.

Once upon a time in a land that was and always will be, there was a kingdom filled with the laughter of so many children that it was called The Land of Gleeful Laughter. The (W)hole place was so vital, so alive, so passionately present that every tree and leaf, every cloud in the sky seemed to twinkle and sparkle from simply the love of being itself. The stream seemed to skip as it bubbled around the stillness of the soaring stones along its path. The flowers waved their scents in the air, as a maiden waves her very first gossamer scarf, just for the shear pleasure of it. And the earth soothed the feet that ran upon it with a warm cushion of thick dark soil, rich with life.

Children ran everywhere, full of that naked "I just love being me" feeling that only small beings know. They skipped, they sat and read, they hugged and helped the bigger people, they cried when they hurt, and when the crying was done, they would jump up, moving on. In The Land of Gleeful Laughter, the children were the threads that wove together the (W)hole tapestry of the community's life. They wove with the wild abandonment of a child playing with finger paints. They wove the connections between all the parts of the village. They played without apology. Yes, life was grand and very, very real! This was not a place of airy-fairy nice, nice. In this land, death happened, illnesses happened, sadness happened, and even an occasional fight between neighbors would happen. Yes, The Land of Gleeful Laughter was a REAL place and an ALIVE place!

However, it was not always this way…and this is the tale I tell today.

Now, it is said that…

Once upon a time long ago there was a mother who had twins—a boy and a girl. The boy was called Richard, and the girl-child was called Maria.

The mother loved her children deeply, and although her husband had died shortly after their birth, her days were filled with joy, laughter, and all the silliness that children bring into the often serious world of adults.

One day a great tragedy occurred. The two children, Richard and Maria, were playing together near the great road that ran through the town. In fact, this great road ran through the entire kingdom, much like a river that snakes across the earth. It was the spine of travel for all in the kingdom. It was simply called The Road.

Now, The Road always had a lot of traffic going to and fro, as you can imagine, and so their mother often warned Richard and Maria to stay well away from the edges of this thoroughfare. Since they were very obedient children, they had always followed her advice and were playing very far away from the edges…when suddenly they heard loud crashing sounds. They looked up. The loud banging and rattling sounds were getting closer but still they could see nothing at all. From what seemed to them like out of nowhere came a great cart with eight horses pulling it. The horses were screaming and pounding, clearly out of control. The cart flung itself directly at them. Richard ran to the left. Maria bolted to the right. However, neither one of them was able to get out of the way.

Both children suffered serious injuries. Their mother stayed by their sides through that long day and into the late of night. Each child rested in one arm of their mother. In the wee hours of dawn, Richard and then Maria closed their eyes and sighed out their last breaths.

It was later determined by the town mayor that the driver of the cart had been bumped off the wagon as it rode over a large mound in the road, and consequently the cart and horses had run out of control. It was no one's fault. The mound in the road had formed the previous night during a large thunderstorm. The driver of the cart was an experienced transporter, who had simply been thrown off by the surprise bounce of this vehicle. The horses had become frightened by his shouts to stop them and had run faster. "No one's fault," everyone said, but still it was a great tragedy.

However, this is only the beginning of this tale, which begins in tragedy and ends in…well, that would be getting ahead of the tale now, wouldn't it?

The twins' mother was in terrible grief. The bright lights in her life were no longer with her. Though many were sure the children were now in the arms of the angels, this did nothing to comfort her lonely agony. Who really knew anyway?!!!

She sat almost unmoving for the longest of times. She breathed barely. She ate almost nothing. She waited for death. No one's ministry could reach her soul. The absence of the unique laugher of Richard, so wildly free, and the absence of Maria's soothing sing-songy voice left her feeling so bereft that her world now seemed like a pile of dried up dusty leaves left over after winter has gone and before spring has hinted its presence.

Slowly, ever so slowly, mother's grief became more and more fixed. She was frozen in the time between when she was a mother and when she was not a mother. The villagers did not know what to do, having exhausted all their ideas and all their hugs and their comforting words, without results of any sort. Finally, each had drifted away, knowing themselves as powerless failures. They, too, were burdened by this shocking loss that could not be reversed.

Finally, even Mother, as she was now called by all, could bare it no longer. She set out on a great journey. She had come to a decision.

She had determined, in her own intimacy with this anguish that no mother should ever suffer so again. Mother felt sure that her children would not even wish to be alive if they had known how horrible the dangers were and how much she would suffer from their loss and how painful their death would be. She knew, without doubt, that no children should suffer in dying, as hers had done. So she set off to find the greatest magician in all the lands to cast a spell to keep any such thing from happening again, ever!! The horrors were simply too great. They must be stopped. Mother decided she was the one who would stop them!

She traveled far and wide from town to town and through great mountain ranges. She followed the great road, walking alone in rain and snow and in the spring time of the year and in the time of leaves falling. In each town, she would stop for one night. Mother would then seek out the wisest person in all that area and say, "No child should ever be allowed to suffer like mine did before they died. No mother should ever be allowed to suffer the agony that I am now suffering. How can this be prevented?" Then she would proceed to tell her story of mother-anguish in all its detail to insure that the listener knew how important and serious her quest was. She meant business.

One after another of the wise people she spoke to would say to her, "I cannot say how one could stop such suffering. It is true it happens everywhere. Deaths such as these are particularly troublesome tragedies. It is also true that grief, such as you feel, is so painful as to be nearly unendurable. Yes, all this is so and I have seen many versions of this same tale. I have been asked 'Why? Why?' many times over. But I do not know how this could be prevented. I do not have an answer for you. However, have you spoken to…?" They would tell her of yet another wise person who might be able to help her, and she would travel on to yet another place.

So it was that Mother traveled from one wisdom-elder to another, called shaman-child, to another thought of as the oldest of elder elders, until finally in the deepest, smallest, darkest of caves in all the kingdoms she found herself before the greatest magician of all times. She was called Ashana.

Mother explained her quest and her determination to see it through. As she had walked The Road and as she had sat with the wisdom-folk of all the towns and small huddles of huts, her query had become quite short and concise. The details of her story had fallen aside along the edges of The Road upon which she had spent so many hours. Mother sat, after bowing to Ashana, and spoke her simple words, once again. "I seek to find a way to prevent children from ever suffering and dying, like my two dearest ones did. I seek to find a way to never have mothers suffer the agony of grief as I have and still do. I will do whatever it takes to make this so. Do you know of a way?"

Ashana was not only a great magician but she was a very, very old and very, very wise woman who knew of this pain that this mother spoke of, for she herself had suffered such a loss. Ashana felt within her a sympathetic vibration, insisting that she respond.

Now, the truth was that Ashana did know of a way, a way so extreme that even she had not dared to take advantage of it. It had come to her when she was grieving the death of her only daughter who had died in a terrible drowning accident. Though many years ago now, the pain was as if it had all occurred a moment ago. Ashana listened within as well as without. Ashana was known for her depth of listening.

She had told herself before that it was simply too risky to try, but secretly, Ashana had never quite given up the idea. The fact that children were born and could die and suffer before their time was so unimaginably horrific that she had not been able to destroy the writings of this extreme yet powerful ancient magic. Yes, she did know a way. Beyond all, the agony of Mother reflected Ashana's own torment that had truly never ceased and brought forth in Ashana's heart a yearning to act so that no mother would ever have to suffer such agony or stand before her seeking help in this way. Mother's plea awoke Ashana's own shredded heart, the one she had buried the day of her own daughter's death.

Now, here it was again, the same question. She knew that her wisdom was not great enough to decide what to do, so she told Mother to wait while she retired to the Magic Black Pool in the farthest corner of this deepest, darkest cave. The pool was one reason that she had taken root here and set up her residence in the dank cavern. There was another reason, however, that she could not speak of even now.

This black pool of water, so still as to be a path to the most ancient of times, was an authentic Wisdom Source. Its black inky colored (w)hole,whose contents had more than once offered up a richness of guidance, still set her nerves on alert. One did not visit The Pool lightly.

She sat on the curb of the black (w)hole and waited. Resisting nothing that arose within her while waiting for the knowing to be gifted, there Ashana sat for many days, eating nothing, saying nothing, waiting.

After 40 days a ripple moved across the pool, and a quiet voice said, "Do this thing you are called to do, for it will bring great learning to all who live on the lands." The pool became totally still once more. No reasoning was offered. The black (w)hole pool was as it was, a response to the moment's query.

And so she did. Ashana cast the ancient spell right then and there as she sat at the edge of the dark pool. She could only trust the wisdom spoken to her by the Ancient (W)hole Ones. She had not dared to make this choice on her own merits.

This is the dreadful truth that had kept her from acting upon her magic earlier. In order to keep children from suffering and dying and to keep mothers from such agonies of loss, this powerful spell prevented all further births. No more children would be born in the lands. This solved the (W)hole problem. It was the only solution. The magic of this spell was that no one would or could die. All who existed would simply gradually age for forever. Thus, the balance of life's spiral would be maintained and the essential laws honored: No more children. No more births. No more deaths. All was frozen.

For those of you who may not be aware, The Essential Laws, decreed at the time of creation by Creator-Self, were minimal in number but critical to all of existence. The Essential Laws enabled creation. All the Essential Laws had to be honored, even in the face of any spell uttered, for, as you may know, magic cannot be used to unravel the elemental elements of creation as established by Creator-Self. One of these laws decreed that all living creatures were never to be destroyed, for this would destroy creation itself. Since creation had been set up to be a continuous looping of birth, life, and death in all its forms and manners, this ancient spell, though freezing these pulsating motions of life, could not override the foundational Essential Laws.

Ashana, with an outer calm that hid her deep fear about activating such a spell, told Mother it was now as she asked. And, she added, in one year's time there would be no more mothers who would be grieving and no more children who would suffer or die. In fact, no one would die. The knowledge of death had to be erased in order for the birth of children to be prevented. It would take a year for the spells' implementation to be complete.

Ashana did not tell her of the cost of this spell but simply sent her away as quickly as possible. Deeply disquieted, Ashana then retired to her cave to wait, for she knew this was not the end of the story. She was very worried, despite her own relief that her secret wish had now been fulfilled. There was something, something that niggled at her mind about such a drastic spell. However, she just couldn't grasp the wisps of the thought.

Mother was elated. Her quest successful, she could now return to the village with her head high and her hope restored. She had actually done something to "fix" the problem. Relief at her action's power had realigned her to her own life. Additionally, in the process of her long and sometimes dangerous journey, Mother's soul had finished its grieving. Her heart had healed its raw gapping wounds. And all her tears, shed over the many dusty, dry miles she had trudged, were complete, so she could now return to her hometown to settle into a life of sorts. She felt glad that no one else would have to suffer as she had done.

When she returned, things seemed as always. Yes, there were children running about and there were newborn babies grandmothers held while rocking and cooing at them on their wide long porches. But Mother trusted Ashana's spell and so returned to her daily chores to see what would occur.

Slowly, ever so slowly, in fact so slowly that no one noticed, fewer and fewer children were born. Slowly, ever so slowly, fewer and fewer people died until throughout the kingdom, years had passed without one death and without one birth. At first, no one considered the impact of this change in the pulse of life's heartbeat. Then the sounds of the village gradually became only those of old men snoring, old women's rocking chairs creaking on the porch boards, the sounds of knitting needles making yet another pair of socks to keep their old feet warm, and the quiet sounds of the elders who napped each afternoon. Now, the true cost of the spell that Ashana had cast was becoming apparent. Yes, it was true. No one was born. And yes, it was true. No one was dying. And yes, it was true. No children were suffering. No children were dying. The ancient spell had worked! However, the cost of the spell was immense.

The people had forgotten to cherish life, since death was no longer a reality.

The people forgot to embrace each moment, since all moments for forever unfolded before them. All moments lost their significance. No one moment had any life to it. All became a long series of infinite moments waiting for the next, with no surprises or juice or reasons to bother.

Mother saw the spell had worked!

No children suffered.

No mother cried herself to sleep in agony for her lost or suffering offspring.

No child left "before his time."

No one died, for life was forever.

Death had been erased in order to balance the loss of birth. This, too, was an Essential Law of the universe, The Law of Opposites. This law allowed for all the play of the universe. One could laugh because they could cry. One could be born because they could die. One could embrace because one could walk away. This Essential Law was the balance point upon which life rested.

Mother saw that it was also true that there was no laughter in the town square and no giggles coming from the cookie factory, which had shut down since the last child had grown into old, old age. There were no toys being made any more, and yet again, it was true that no child had died a horrible death. And Mother knew that no other mother had suffered grief such as hers.

Yet, still again, Mother pondered. There were no longer any precious moments since there was only infinite time. People became lazy about living their lives. "Why bother, I can always do it tomorrow!" was a very common saying. Finally, it had come to be that there was no meaning to anything at all.

The truth was…All of this awful!!

The whole kingdom lacked the vitality that children bring. It had now become clear to all the townspeople and, in fact, all the people of the (W)hole land, that a place without the sparkle of new life was a place that wasn't really alive. It had become clear that death, itself, was the bringer of a gift. The treasure was the knowledge that life is precious. This can only be felt in the face of death's reality.

No one knew what to do. What they did know was, "This was just awful, an agony of its own."

After many days and months had passed and all that was still heard was the creaking of rockers and the snoring of old men and the occasional noise that goes along with life's chores…Richard, the oldest man in the village and the great, great, great grandfather of young Richard, who had died horribly so very long ago, couldn't bear it one more minute.

Richard had been one of those who had cheered the spell worked by Ashana. Richard had celebrated what Mother had done. But now, he couldn't bear it! He saw the soul of every person he knew withering and shriveling into a dark nothingness right before his very, very old eyes. So hobbling to the town hall where all important meetings took place, Richard rang the meeting bell. "Come to an important meeting," he called as he rang and rang the bell.

This was something quite unusual, as there had really been no reason to hold a meeting for a very long time. Of course, everyone wanted to be present. It took quite a while for all of those old, old creaky folks to arrive (you know, of course, that without children to keep the bounce in one's step, it is easy to "take it all a bit easier" until everything is quite an effort, even walking to the town hall).

Finally, all had gathered around Richard at the town hall.

Richard said, "I have called you all here because this can no longer go on! We may be alive in our bodies, but our spirits are starving for that which only new life and children bring to us. Those who actually bear children and those who are touched by them…it does not matter…without children, spirits die. And without the knowledge of death, we are failing to cherish our very lives. Without the surprise of newborns, all is a waste. This is awful."

"What should we do?" croaked an old woman on the edge of the crowd. "The spell Ashana has cast is still in effect…and none of us can do anything to de-spell the spell."

"I am going to seek her out and beg her to return children to our lives, no matter the horror or grief or pain that we may have to suffer as the result of their presence. This is far worse, this death of the spirit!" Richard's voice rang with a young truth. This was the first time he had uttered this thought aloud.

"Yes," Richard added with great seriousness, "I am going to plead with her to return to us the knowledge of death so that our lives will be cherished one again."

From the back of the crowd stepped the women called Mother, who had first gone to Ashana to ask for the ancient spell to be activated.

"I wish to go too, for now I see that this is far worse, even the pain I suffered in my loss cannot compare to what we suffer today. I long to hear babies cry and to hug young people who are wild and rebellious. My spirit is starving for new life. I am tired of the silent sounds of creaking and rocking. I want to bless my ears with laughter and silliness and fill my mouth with cookies from the noisy old cookie factory. I want to be tired in the morning because I sat up all night with a child running a fever. I want to plant seeds in the ground and watch a child's eyes light up when flowers show up in the spring. I want LIFE back!

"Please," Mother sobbed before all the townspeople, "please forgive me for this awful spell, for although it has made the pain go away, it has also taken all the life and vitality with it. I did not think of the cost. Please forgive me." She collapsed in her shame.

The townspeople all crowded around Mother. They were wiser and older than any people had ever, ever been. They knew a great deal about life, about anguish and about truth. They knew the most about what it meant to love. They knew that there was nothing so horrible, no pain so great that it was worth avoiding love's risks! They had now learned that life was nothing if death was absent, no matter the pain. They knew that to love meant one could hurt and even lose that loved one. Yet, without love, life was empty. Birth, life, love, death were one great weaving series of threads woven into the fabric of creation's tapestry, and without them all else meant nothing.

They placed their arms around her and whispered with many wavery, watery voices, "We, too, have learned a great lesson. Thank you for your courage to journey into your pain and now into your learning. We forgive you. We cherish you. We love you. We are glad for your quest. Because of you, we know we cannot do without the children—no matter the pain or grief that comes to us. All of life and death is better than this frozen balancing act."

Mother felt her heart open and spill forth a great radiant light.

Suddenly, standing before them was Ashana! This was an unheard of event, since Ashana never in all recorded time had ever ventured out of her cave. But she, too, had felt the loss of vitality of life and of the laughter of children since she had cast her spell. She had been watching events unfold in the lands since the spell had been cast. The Dark Pool of Magic had shown it all to her.

"I, too," spoke Ashana softly, "have learned a great lesson. Life without death and death without fresh life is no life at all. I confess that I, too, had wished for a "good enough" reason to cast this ancient spell. Because of my own deep grief I hid in the darkest, deepest cave, sitting next to the Dark Pool, my only companion and solace. Truth be told, I can bear this half-living no longer. I, too, need new life, light, and love. I confess to you all, I have felt the shame of which Mother has spoken. I, too, wanted to wipe out all causes of such wrenching grief. And in my shame I have held myself apart from you. Now, I, too, ask your forgiveness."

Then drawing herself up to her fullest height and speaking in a clear voice that rang throughout the kingdom, she said, "It is enough. The lesson has been learned. The pool's wisdom was true. We have grown greatly through the activation of the ancient spell. No matter the pain, no matter the horror, the souls of humans everywhere cannot remain vital if there are no children, even if they are lost after one moment's breath. There is no life without death. There is no joy without the sorrows. This can go on no longer."

And after saying this, Ashana raised her hands and in a great sweep of her arms and with many magical incantations muttered under her breath, the spell was broken.

A great stillness swept over the lands.

Then, suddenly…

Those standing before her heard laughter coming from down the road. The wiser old, old people held their breaths…could it be? Could it really be?

And still, they heard laughter coming from the great road, the same road upon which the cart, that had killed Richard and Maria, had been driven along…

The same road that had been the road that Mother, in her grief, had walked upon to seek a spell to eliminate all grief and loss…

The same road that wove throughout the kingdom…

And turning around, there was, for all to see, a crowd of children running and skipping and laughing as they ran toward those of the town.

And the old ones suddenly found vitality in their steps. Their backs straightened and their faces shone with delight, for their youth of spirit had returned with the children.

And the children swarmed into the crowd of adults—as only children can swarm. There were hugs and laughter and welcomings and joyful tears, for children had returned to the land.

Every child was given a home. Every child was cherished. Every child was held and taught and loved. And when those times came when a child died or was hurt or injured and when a mother grieved her loss, the story was told of the time long ago when the children were missing from the land and all became old…the time when death was forgotten and when life became nothing.

And somehow in the telling of this tale, the pain was a bit less, and the memories of the child a bit clearer and the grief a bit lighter…for all knew that even a moment of a life was better than 'forever life."

And where had all the children come from, those who had skipped down the road towards the grateful embrace of the old, old people? These children were the ones the old, old people had dreamed of having birthed during the spell's activation. Each one of these "Dream Children" had been born and lived in the Land of Secrets from the moment the old, old person had first conceived of their presence. As the spell was broken by Ashana, the "Dream Children" were released to go and play on the lands until such time as they died and returned to the ONE (W)holeness. Thus, the children who returned were of many ages and sizes and shapes and sounds!

And so it was from that time and forever more, the land became known as the Land of Gleeful Laughter—a place where all life, even if it existed for just a moment, was cherished and where every giggle and hop-skip-jump of a child was remembered.

Ashana remained with the people of the town, coming out of her grief-stricken retreat. She was invited to live with Mother, who had, after all, been the Mother of it all. Together, they became the oldest, wisest women of the lands, sought out by many in their time of need.

And it is said that if you listen quietly on a very still night, you can hear the laughter of all the children who have ever lived and died, for they know the gifts they bring. And if you become even stiller than still, you can hear the "Dream Children" playing in preparation for their birthing into bodies that can feel arms hugging them, tears flowing from their eyes in sadness, and hearts that beat with love for no reason beyond that. "Dream Children" can't feel what real children do, so no matter the anguish, all "Dream Children" hunger for their own births into the arms of real life moms and dads.

And it is said that if you skip and hop and chuckle through your days, that at the time of your death, you will come to know that you have always lived in the Land of Gleeful Laughter.

****

"Why?" is the cry that rips out of our hearts when death happens "out of the order." "Why love?" when it can be so filled with the anguish of loss. "Why open?" to another when they can be torn out of our lives without warning or apparent cause. Simply put—there is only one answer: It is a mystery. Knowing all we know, we continually risk so we can love and be loved.

To abide in this world calls us to dare to dance with mysteries and to do this with open hearts, even as we may tremble in terror. To abide in peace is to come to know we are always more for having loved, we are always greater for having risked and lost then never to have risked at all, and that finally, life and death are one piece of cloth called Life. Death and Life cannot be separated one from another. Let yourself know that life without endings is already dead, that life without new births is dry, dusty routines and that "safety" is all about hearts locked away from the breath of life. My invitation to you is to laugh, love, cry, and rage as life comes to you. Let Life be what it is: A mystery unfolding upon itself.

The Birth of the People of Light
Chapter 1: The Time of Terror

Dedicated to our brains which contain within them miracles and magic beyond any known science. Dedicated to our hearts which, when confronted with another's terror, reach out and embrace without regard to cost. Dedicated to all of us who have jumped into burning buildings, leaped into frozen rivers, grabbed a child from the street car's bumper, held the hand of a dying person, cared enough to take a gift to one of the "forgotten," took the time to listen to the tears of a homeless person…this fable is dedicated to us all—the glorious wondrous expression of Life called Humanity.

It was all so ordinary until the terror. Life cycled. People were born and died. Seasons flowed. They came and went, and always there was a sense that things would continue in the same way. There was the land. There were all the people of the land, and in fact, there were no separate tribes. Everyone was simply a part of the people. And the way this would occur is a person would be born, and when they were born, it was noted, although really not made much of, that there was a crystalline shape prominent on their forehead between their eyebrows, and it would protrude somewhat at the time of their birth. Within the first year or two, it receded into their skull, ultimately disappearing. And when it disappeared, there was a small celebration to acknowledge that this one had grown into a new stage of their cycle. And then as the time of their death approached many, many years later, this same crystalline shape would begin to re-emerge until it extended the full space between the eyebrows and became ever more brilliant until there was what was called the final flash before death. This crystalline shape had been named Kria.

Now, none took much notice of it, and it was simply part of how things were. It was just that which marked the beginning and the end until the time of the terror. It was at this point that the mystery of the Kria was truly revealed. It was not simply a marker. It was an essence.

It began on an ordinary day. The guardians of the eight directions were in place as always, for they moved in a fluid, seamless rotation. There were eight directions that were guarded—North and South, East and West, Up and Down, In and Out—and all of these directions were watched over so that all the land's dimensions were tended to. No outer event apparently occurred, as was commented on later. However, suddenly, abruptly, all of the people in all of the land were in sheer terror. It was not fear. It was terror. Abruptly they were seized by a soul-paralyzing terror. All the dimensions of the land and all of the people and all of the guardians were in the grasp of this terror that was so gripping that they were unable to notice that this was occurring. It was only later that there was reflection upon it. At the time everyone simply moved into terror.

Some were frozen in place mid-stride or mid-word. They simply were unable to move, the terror was so deep and so comprehensive in their being. Some shook and quivered and trembled, and they curled up into tiny ball shapes, falling to the ground shaking. Some ran around and around, moaning and wringing their hands with no direction or thought. Some raged, blaming, yelling and attacking, screaming at everyone and everything, "How could this be happening? You did it wrong. It's your fault!" but there was no context, so even their raging fell on terrified ears that were not attuned to any form of comprehension. And then there were some that died of the terror right then, without even a Kria flash.

The terror had no story. It had no apparent source. It was simply a wave of terror that washed all over the people and through their entire essence, even unto the eight guardians who were each alone in their posts far from the people, on the edges of the land. And they each expressed their terror uniquely. North cringed away from South, while South shook before the noise of the North. East was frozen in the face of West, and West fled from East. Up attacked Down, and Down blamed Up. In submitted to Out, and Out screamed at In. The terror agony tension was so high as to shatter existence itself. There was a pause, a void in which there existed no hope, no movement, only the terror.

Now, in one of the small huts there was a pair of folks. They had been caught mid-day snuggling in a nap. And their terror expression occurred as they were side by side, facing one another, each curled in a ball in their bed, heads near each other, noses nearly touching, their knees curled up touching, while each of them pointed away the bottom half of their bodies. And there they were simply quivering and shaking. There was no way for them to express what they were experiencing because the terror had taken away all thought and speech.

And then, there was an accident, an accidental miracle. In the shaking and quivering of this pair, this ordinary pair of two people, they inadvertently bumped their two heads together. That was it. It was messy. It was a bump without purpose. It was not even a chosen action. And yet, it was this that unleashed the uprising of the Kria and the birth of the new people.

With that bump, the Kria of each of these two abruptly emerged from their inner head spaces and began to glow and twirl ever so slightly. A radiant light emanating from their Kria pierced through their terror, and they were freed. Of all the people in the land, only these two were free. It was the first time in all of memory that the Kria was fully awakened in this way. It was not simply a marker of a beginning or an end. It was something more.

And these two arose, their Kria radiating a living light. Each reported later feeling peace and a calmness beyond anything that they had ever experienced before, and their bodies began to warm. And there was a golden glow that seemed to surround them. Neither understood what had occurred, and yet both arose without words and walked outside, responding to the impulse, the knowing that they knew what to do. And they simply did it without pause. Each walked to another of the people, and they softly touched forehead to forehead with a gentle bump and shared a breath, just as the two of them had, and it happened again. The Kria of those who were bumped would arise and emerge, and then, they, too, were awakened. Their Kria light pierced through their own terror, and they were freed, simply by being bumped in this way.

And then those newly awakened walked over to others and gently bumped them in the same way, and in this way, the Kria of all of the people was awakened and activated. All were now walking with these living lights emanating from their foreheads, their bodies warm and glowing. However, it was not over yet, for the eight guardians were still in terror. They were all alone, separated from the rest of the people. So the awakened people all walked first to the guardian of the North. Bowing to the North guardian, they touched foreheads with this guardian to awaken the Kria. The terrors of North then fell into peace. They walked then to the East. Bowing to the guardian of the East, they awakened the Kria, and the terrors of East fell into peace. They moved on to the South and to the West, to Up and to Down, awakening each Kria in this same bumping way. Then the people walked inside and bowed to the Inner guardian. The terrors of In fell away. Then they all walked out of themselves, bowing to the guardian of Out to awakened the Kria.

And as the last of the guardians' Kria was activated, moving into an awakened state, a light of radiance larger than the land itself rippled and washed through all of the land simultaneously. The peoples' forms became living light with a Kria at the center of each, awakened, twirling. And at that moment, death no longer existed—all because of the time of terror and accidental bump.

Later, upon reflection, the transformation into light beings did not occur, they realized, because of any known plan or content or effort. Rather, the people had been carried through this awakening by the smallest of accidents and the greatest of choices. The accident, the touch of two heads as they quivered in terror. And the greatest of choices, the choice to act without understanding. And so the Kria wisdom arose, and it was spoken around the fires, "Judge not the smallest of accidents. Dare to act upon the unexplainable impulses, and pass forward the awakenings that come."

The Birth of the People of Light
Chapter 2: The Barricaded Ones

Dedicated to us all and written in honor of all the "betweens" of creation that allow us the wild ride of being Soul Selves in human form. The (W)hole Truth is that we are ONE great "up-rising of LOVE" encountering itself in all its bits, pieces, and parts. And now for the joy and pleasure of it, we are all awakening once again to our (W)hole Holiness!

Throughout the land, all the peoples were experiencing, for the first time in eons, what it was to be Living Light. They no longer needed to quest after, to toil or to strain at life, to struggle from within or without. The arising of the Kria had not only transformed the peoples' physical form but their presence as well. Their light presence had altered their entire culture and the way they were, for as Living Light, they did not need to eat. As Living Light, they did not need to clothe their forms. As Living Light, they were all connected in one consciousness, while still maintaining their individual sense of presence. They were woven by a great web of light, to which all were joined, that allowed them to move completely and freely as they chose.

At first, this was looked upon with great awe and wonder at what they had accomplished in a most surprising and unplanned way. At the same time it had also unnerved many of them, for their (W)hole purpose for being had been to accomplish and to build and grow and achieve, whatever it was that they had imagined was important. They knew how to push and strain and strive. Now, rather abruptly, none of these activities were even relevant. Now, it was simply a matter of LIVING life: found in the joy and pleasure of sharing presence with one another. This was what now renewed them, what gave them any kind of, if one could even say of this condition, focus.

Many went through great adjustments with this, for they had enclosed themselves in purpose. They had enclosed themselves in mission, and they had enclosed themselves with effort and with strain. They had enclosed themselves in striving towards goals, and what some used to call "success." Now, all of this was simply gone like vapor, like dust blown away by the wind.

At the same time all of this was occurring, it was discovered that there had been a small group of people who were still caught up in the terror. They had been traveling in a very secluded area, and thus, the rippling effect of Kria forehead touching and mutual breathing had not come to them. It had at first been thought that all of the people had had the experience of the arising, and yet now, it had come to light that there was a group of people who were still frozen in the terror. In fact, because their terror had been so sustained, they had moved from a frozenness to a state of angry, aggressive fear. As an expression of this angry and aggressive fear, this self-protective, aggressive view, this group of beings had created a great wall of enclosure. They had built it quite rapidly and then retired into the center of it, and they have been there ever since.

They had continued to add to the wall until it was very thick, and the anger and the fear and the terror and the angst, the anguish of these people, continued to grow. There was nothing, save the experience of the fear, that had been so paralyzing for all of the people. The other people, the ones outside the wall, had been freed from their terror rather quickly, so it had not had a chance to take root in their being. However, for this small group that had walled and barricaded themselves within a structure of stone and wood and clay, this condition of fearful anger and focus on self-protection and dissent had grown and grown and grown.

The people did not ever leave this barricaded, walled-in structure. Once they were inside, that was it. There was nothing new that came in. They were all walled in within themselves as well as living in an outer walled-in place. Any movement, any thought of moving, was quickly erased, for the terror would rise up within them. "What of this? What of that? What of the other?" And then they would begin to have great conversations amongst themselves which would further convince them that anything other than remaining within their barricade of stone and wood and fear would be foolish.

When word of this came to the greater number of people whose Kria had arisen and who knew themselves as Living Light, there was no need to have great discussion of what would occur. They all knew simultaneously, because of this web of life, that as Living Light, they could do nothing but respond with love and embrace. They could not abandon these people who had been caught in such a perilous situation that caused them to barricade themselves in. And so a great number of the people, nearly all of them, save for a few that remained with the younger ones, traveled the great distance to arrive at this place where the great barricade of stone and wood and terror had been built.

One could not stand in the face of the barricade, the wall, and see over it, for it was quite tall. And one could not walk around the barricade in an hour, but perhaps in a day or so—it was this large of a barricade. It had been built with the intent to keep all the dangers of life and all of its surprises apart from those within.

Now, in tradition, the most typical response prior to the arising of Kria would have been to storm the walls, to storm the barricaded ones and to force the way in. But this was no longer an option, for this, too, as an action had melted away for those had become Living Light. All the old ways that in any way involved pressure or pushing had melted away. And so all those that had walked this great distance simply began without conversation. One by one they took their place, each knowing where they ought to be, until the entire barricaded area was surrounded. There was, of course, space between those that had come because there were not enough people to surround the wall so that each could touch the other, but this was no longer necessary, for the web of light always maintained a connection between those of the Living Light.

As each one stood near the barricade, they could hear the echoes of the anguish within, screams and shouts and fighting. "No." "Yes." "That's wrong." Attacks and a kind of anguished howling would arise and quiet, arise and quiet as the fear would ripple through those within. And all of the Living Light beings, once they were in position, simply sat down.

They joined with one another through the web of light. They did not intend to fix anything, change anything, or project anything. There was not even the intent to, send light, for this, too, would have been understood as saying those within were without light. Rather, all of the Living Light beings joined through the web of light, simply sitting in patience, sitting in presence with the stone and the wood that had been used to make the great wall, all the fear that had gone into gluing it the wall together, as well as all those within whom they could not see but could occasionally hear. They simply sat in presence, knowing that this patience of presence is found in the stillness of being, where oneness is awakened to itself.

And so they sat, with no intent to cause any change. After quite a time, quietly and with no fanfare whatsoever, the entire barricade fell into dust. It was simply not there. Those within were in shock at first. They were in shock because that which they had trusted was simply no longer there. And then, one by one, the Living Light beings moved among those that had been in barricaded spaces, bending, sharing breath, touching forehead to forehead. Soon, those that had been barricaded within were transformed into Living Light.

For some, this was a great release. The process was gentle. They had been so frozen in place that there had been no time to run and flee when the barricade had fallen down. However, there were a few who, in that moment when the barricade simply fell to dust, in their fear, had raged and hit. They had screamed and shouted and fought back, and all the Living Lights knew through the web of light to simply remain in presence with those who were fighting so viciously for their life out of fear. Inevitably there came a moment when their exhaustion overcame them, and they would sit or they would stand and hang their heads. In that moment, one of the conscious Living Light would go and share breath, touching forehead to forehead with that one, and in this way all moved through the awakening.

And so it is said now, around the campfires as the Living Lights joined together in community in the web of light, that "sometimes we will still encounter an aspect of ourselves that wants to be barricaded in." Sometimes in these gatherings there would be conversations about those that had been barricaded in, conversations about what it was that had happened and what had caused the barricade to simply dissolve, to melt away. Often they would wonder, "What was it that had transformed all of the beings of the land into Living Light?" The only answer was a hushed, awe-filled stillness of a mystery that could not be named or explained.

And that is the story of the land of the people whose Kria arose and birthed a new people of light. And this is happening as we speak.

****

Human beings are quite extraordinary creatures. They are capable of actions, heroic beyond imagining, destructive beyond any horrors seen before, and all that is in between. What is it that sets aside one from another? Isn't it finally the degree to which there is a celebration or elevation of those involved? Not from an intellectual place but rather from the space of our natural innate regard for life itself. To speak of Light Beings invokes an image of something other than who we are...yet in the surprising delightful Play of the Universe... this is exactly who we are: Light Beings Being Light. How might you show up today if you lived the truth of you—Light Being Walking?

The Universal Story: The Fable We Are All Telling Ourselves…day by day

Dedicated to us all and written in honor of all the "betweens" of creation that allow us the wild ride of being Soul Selves in human form. The (W)hole Truth is that we are ONE great "up-rising of LOVE" encountering itself in all its bits, pieces, and parts. And now for the joy and pleasure of it, we are all awakening once again to our (W)hole Holiness!

It all began (W)hole. All-That-Is was one (W)hole, like a big soup of life force. And then, then, there was the very first between, the between of creator and creation. And then there were the betweens of creation. And then there was the between of you and me until there was the (W)hole of creation made up of betweens—betweens of this and that and you and me and them. Creation was made up of this and that and spaces between.

Holy (W)holeness: (w)Holes are how creation IS. There can only be creation because of betweens or (w)holes. Creator-Self did this so that all of creation could have the experience of being, of feeling, of living. (w)Holes make this all possible. (w)Holes are part of what allows this life experience to happen. (w)Holes are part of creation. (w)Holes are a "secret" kept from our awareness—until now. (w)Holes are Holy (W)holeness in disguise.

Each one of us is a creation with the creator on the other side of a between. Each creation's destiny is to return to Creator-Self, (W)hole again with consciousness and an awareness of our own divine radiance. Creator-Self desired to support the return, the awakening. These ever-occurring awakenings were so that all of creation would one day return and bring back, as it were, to the (W)hole an awareness of radiance, of who we all really are—bits of Creator-Self, Radiant Pulsating Beings of Light.

The Creator-Self wanted to ensure that the path home to (W)holeness would not be lost. Self-Most-High loves creation and longs for its return and celebrates that it is occurring and always has been. Yet, by the very nature of creation, the holie secret of creation was remembered only by the Creator-Self.

So how was creation going to find its way home to itself? The Creator-Self loved creation and determined to leave **a clue**.

This clue had to be for everyone—accessible to everyone, constantly available, unavoidable, and inevitably discovered by all. The Creator-Self longs for the (W)hole return and knows that it is in this very moment unfolding. And what would the clue be? What could the clue be? Creator-Self left us the clue of our (w)holes!!

What an amazing thing. We can create them just as the Self-Most-High created creation. We can't avoid them for forever, no matter how hard we might try. We help each other into them. We help each other through them. It was the clue of all of creation, and it was the way all of creation came to be.

We were made with the same power that was used by Creator-Self to make creation. Here is a great secret that is now no longer a secret. We are all (w)hole-creators just like Creator-Self. The clue to the way home is unavoidable. We wrestle with (w)holes—ours and others'—every day. We even operate as (w)hole helpers to each other, shoving each other head first into the clue. The Creator-Self wants us to get the (W)hole point!

Creator-Self wants us to come home to our (W)hole holy selves, Radiant Pulsating Beings of Light. Creator-Self wants us to re-turn to who we really are—awakened (W)holeness! So, we have the **clue**. None of us can avoid coming face to face with the WAY home. What love.

The path, the spiraling ever-expanding path back to (W)holeness is found, in fact, at the bottom of every life (w)hole that comes to us, every life (w)hole that you may find yourself falling head first into.

No matter what the (w)hole, they all have the same point.

The (W)hole Point is to bring us back to our (W)holeness, back to an awareness of what has never been missing—our (W)holeness, our holiness—and back to Creator-Self, who longs for us to recall ourselves.

The (W)hole Point is to know ourselves as heaven on earth, consciously, where we all, each of us, know ourselves as Radiant Pulsating Beings of Light, radiant beings of pulsating light.

Somewhere in all of us we know this. It is where the longing to go home arises, the longing to be aware and to know and live our (W)holeness, to be all we are meant to be, to live on the earth—walking—as heaven consciously. We feel this longing for Creator-Self's embrace. It is a longing for our own embrace!

Now the Creator-Self's embrace is on one side of a between, and we, creation, are on the other side longing. Our longing to be radiant tells us something. It tells us that there is an embrace waiting for us. Even in the way we breathe, there is a clue. An in, a between, and an out, and there is life. An inhale, a pause, and an exhale.

This is life being life, breathing.

Each breath we take is Self-Most High calling "***All-y, All-y in come free***" across the universe. "***All-y, All-y in come free. Come home to be.***"

And then, there was a second gift of love. Self-Most-High gave us a **tool to respond to the clue**, a tool, in fact, that is hard-wired into our very cells and nature, a tool that fueled our evolution until we are now, a tool that has brought you to this very moment of listening, hearing, and awakening. The tool is curiosity. It is a gift—a gift, a tool we are all born with. We are able to use this tool, this gift, no matter our condition or feelings or thoughts, if we so choose.

This tool, insistent, persistent curiosity—questions—is a magical gift. It is all we truly need to access to walk the path, the spiral path, the ever-expanding pulsating spiral path home, and the Creator-Self made sure we all had it. Of course, we each have a free will choice to make. We may choose to use it or not. This is our choice. We all have this choice. The choice to use this tool is one we have made over and over again! It is how we have learned to walk and to talk and to do life. Curiosity.

And then, across the between Creator-Self gave us one more gift. Why? To what end? What great love—another gift! Offered as love on our behalf! Offered without cause. The gift is an **inner call**, a call to come home to our (W)hole selves, to come to know we never left. We are home right now, and yet, we have simply forgotten who we are.

Creator-Self longs for us so much. This last gift is found inside the gift of knowing ourselves consciously. Self-Most-High gave us to ourselves. We can notice ourselves. This, this is the **power we need to use the tool and see the clues.**

So Creator-Self calls to us, longs for us, opens its arms, the arms of Self-Mother, Self-Father and calls to us "***All-y, All-y in come free. Come home to be.***" And then Creator-Self awaits with open arms—a spacious void—for us to satisfy our longing in the embrace of Radiant Conscious (W)holeness. The (W)hole point of creation is to return—remembering—home, conscious, awareness of our radiance, an ever-expanding continuum of knowing who we are.

We have the clues. We have the tools. We have the power. And yet, even with that, Creator-Self knew **a risk**. Just as true love means allowing the other freedom to leave, to choose to leave, the Creator-Self granted us the power to refuse to come home to ourselves for as long as we choose.

For as long as we choose, we may travel and explore the betweens, the (w)holes, the spaces between you and me and this and that and us and them. Yes, we are watched over. Yes, we are witnessed. We are cherished and held even as each one of us exercises our free will choice.

We may refuse to use the tools. We may resist the clues, and we may exercise our power to say, "No." "No" to ourselves, "No" to the inner call, and "No" to our holy-(W)holeness, "No" to being heaven on earth, "No" to being who we are.

And all the while, Creator-Self will witness and hold open holy spaciousness, awaiting us within where we know ourselves once again as (W)hole holy consciousness. Yes, we are free, free will in action. We are free to choose each moment (w)holes or (W)holeness.

We all get so afraid. We huddle and crouch in our (w)holes. We rant and rave. We get depressed. We get angry. We resist and resent. We attack and blame. We all hurt like hell, all in the middle of the great clue.

And Self-Most-High awaits us unconditionally, without judgment or blame, as each of us awakens to the grandest truth of ourselves again and again and again.

And here is the greatest **Truth-Gift** of all. Finally, all of us will return home now or later, for all of Creation-Self is (W)hole, has always been (W)hole and is designed to be (W)hole, consciously. Let there be no doubt of this. It is the nature of the Universe:(W)holeness.

And so the (w)holes keep coming. The clues keep showing up, and each time we choose.

We have the free choice, the free will choice to choose (W)holeness or (w)holes, to spiral or to freeze until we awaken to the (W)hole point. And then, we are heaven on earth.

Betweens collapse, (w)holes spiraled into, radiance reclaimed, (W)holeness known as itself—awakening. All of us knowing that we are Radiant Pulsating Beings of Light embraced by Self-Most-High: ourselves, conscious of our divine nature.

And all the angels in heaven will shout, "***Welcome Home. Welcome Home. Welcome Home.***" And we will all laugh at the wild play we have had as "bits and pieces and parts" of (W)holeness! Remembering that we are all ONE, all home and (W)hole, holy and holie all for the fun of it, all for the learning of it, and all for the chance to look in the mirror and see who we really are: Radiant Light—Pulsating Beings—awake as (W)holeness!

All because of (w)Holes!

Yes, it matters what we do with our (w)holes. No matter what the (w)hole, it matters what we do, what we choose to do with our (w)holes. Yes, it matters what we do with our (W)holeness. No matter what expression our (W)holeness might take in each moment, it matters. If we are embracing, playing, dancing the grand dance of our particular (W)holeness expressed in that moment, it matters to the (W)hole world, for heaven on earth is waiting for us to happen again and again in each moment, for betweens to collapse, for radiance to be known and lived, for us to be (W)hole, holy, wholly ourselves, consciously embraced by spirit, Self-Most-High, ourselves.

And it all began with that very first between when the Creator-Self said, "Go. Go play. Discover yourselves as divine, and then come home to me, and tell me all about it." And now, now all of creation has heard the inner-call, *"All-y, All-y in come free. Come home. Come home. All-y, All-y in come free. Come home to be."* And the embrace of All-That-Is will wrap around the globe, and each of us, all of us will cease to long, to fight, to cling, to fear this embrace, for we will have chosen, we will be home, heaven on earth, each of us in the arms of our (W)hole Holy Selves, consciously. Self-Most-High as us: ONE awake.

So, it really does matter what you do with your (w)hole and the next one. It really does matter what you do with your (W)holeness. Yes, you matter. Your choices matter.

And the wonder and glory and magnificence of who you truly are is needed, called for, asked for, and invited to be expressed now.

May the One bless
the telling of this (W)hole truth,
for the benefit of Self, Other, and the (W)hole world.
Jodha Vodha Ayme.

****

Regardless of what spiritual texts you may be familiar with, if you look closely and listen deeply with your heart, you will find that they all contain within them (hidden at their core) a "Fable of "Betweens." In this fable, my intent is to reveal this core framework. This is an invitation to you to consider that every moment in which you find yourself is a moment of decision. The "real" hope is found in our bold wild choice to risk it all, to dance in the betweens.

Hints, Tidbits & Fairy Dust

Encouragements for all the folks who want to dance these fables into their life & the lives of others

Once upon a time, a long time ago and is still true today, there were many folks who choose to use stories to heal, transform and awaken themselves and those around them.

They walk in the outer world as coaches, teachers, therapists, pastors, nurses, bosses of all sorts, business owners, doctors, lawyers, school principals, computer geeks and wizards, Sunday school teachers, baby sitters, grandmothers and grandfathers, big sisters and little sisters, shamans and wise elders of all forms, lifestyles, beliefs and habitats around the world.

Theses folks come in every shape, size and height, every lifestyle and race, beyond the imagination. Yes, they are all quite an amazing gang. Like the infinite colors of the rainbow seen around our planet in the form of people of all colors, races and nations, so too are the "Tellers," those who speak the stories that weave the tapestry of our humanity.

If you are reading this note, you may very well be one of those, called by your inner elves to share these fables. Perhaps you are even a "Teller" yourself. I believe that we are all "Tellers" of different sorts; however, in this particular case, I am referring to the fables we share and live—directly and indirectly.

There is a secret in this small section of this book, which is offered as a way of support and an invitation to the "Teller Within us All."

The secret is: Each of us IS a tale.

Each of us walks as a living fable in the world each and every day.

Each of us tells the story of "ME" that we are in that moment and the story of how this "ME" meets and greets the "YOU" of you.

We each tell our fables in every moment that we breathe.

WE are the threads and themes of a Universal Fable of Awakening.

AND…

Each of us is a crucial element in the tapestry of Humanity.

I invite you to consider "What fable you wish to write today and in this moment?"

I invite you to consider "What story you would want written in the Universal Library, about your presence in this world at this time?"

I invite you to ponder upon this question: "How are you adding and what are you adding to the TALE of the PLANET, by how you are showing up today?"

So…just as "Once upon a time" is often a beginning of a fable, so too "Once upon a time" in this NOW MOMENT, I extend some particular invitations, as in regards to *Alaya's Fables.* Let's Play!

* *

ASK yourself or another or a group or a family member or friend:

"How might it be to take these fables and their messages out into the world?"

"How might I/we be a voice or a calling, to those around me/us, to open up and play?"

"How can I/we or might I/we share even just one of these stories, spoken in my own words, in a way that awakens a life or transforms a family or opens hearts in a place of business?"

"How can I/we be the walking LIFE and LOVE of the invitations that these fables offer?"

Bob Stone, who wrote a section at the beginning of this book, said to me that as he prepared to compose his own words, he noticed that at first he found himself "reflecting upon" the fables. Then there came a moment when he began to "feel into" and to "feel within" the fables. It was at this point, he said, when he felt his Heart and Soul begin to dance within him. The Fables became friends that he embraced and whom embraced him.

I believe this offers us all a global approach to walk transformative stories into the world, to, in fact, heal the (W)hole World through sharing tales, stories and fables.

Ultimately, I have found that the uniqueness of each tale is the wrapping paper for the universality of our human journeys and our essential divinity.

Now, here is Another Secret—The secret of "The Secret Fairy Dust" that is sprinkled when a tale is voiced: Sharing a Fable, Enlightens a Soul and Awakens the (W)hole World.

This is the "Fairy Dust" sprinkled by every "Teller." Skill has little to do with the essential and potent impact of a heartfelt telling of a tale. Such gifting captures the inner self of the "Listener" and invites an expansion of the "Life Force Spiral" we all are. Both "Teller" and "Listener" begin to dance "around the May Pole of Life itself." This is just how it is!

So, above any other "Tidbits or Hints" to the Teller within us all, drop all judgments and concerns about your experience as a "Teller" and just jump into the play of it all, for a Playful Spirit is the magick that infuses all words with the life-giving power of Radiance.

Some Hints and particular Tidbits and magicks for setting the stage and beginning the "Telling of a Fable":

Ask someone "Would you like to read me a fable?"

Offer to read a fable to each other, one a night until you have read through all of them! And after each fable, play with the questions at the end of the book. Or make up your own questions and share your answers.

Host a group of friends of all ages and let a fable be the "kick off" for a night of sharing and caring.

Start a staff meeting with a fable and ask one of the questions (see list at the back of the book for ideas) and suggest that it be a focus for breaks.

Lead a group for spiritual exploration of folks of all faiths and let a fable be the focus for the discussion.

Have *Alaya's Fables* be in the waiting room at your office so that folks have something uplifting to read and relax with as they await their appointment. This can apply to all fields of practice.

Use a Fable as a meditative focus, while breathing at a slow steady rhythm. Notice what arises. Then walk it out into the world.

Use *Alaya's Fables* for a Book club.

Invite folks to gather once a quarter and have a "Fable Festival," reading two to three fables and discussing them over a shared meal.

There are endless possibilities once you dare to allow the Inner Teller his/her Outer Voice.

In fact, this art form of "Telling" is rooted in all our ancestry and histories. Long before paper and pen, long, long before computers and the internet, Connection, Communication, Learning and Community rested upon the "Teller's" shoulders. "Tellers" traveling mile after mile gathered together tales and planted the seeds of "Life and Love" along the way. In this long ago time, villages were spread so far apart that it was often only these small threads of light and play to which folks could cling in the dark moments.

In truth, I believe that "Tellers" were and are the weavers of heart and soul and mind and body. At this time on our planet there is no greater need than for the (W)holeness of our Planet's Family to be awakened within us all. Let *Alaya's Fables* be a doorway into a new way of being in this world.

I invite you—no, even more strongly—I encourage you, I call to you, *"Please open your voice and life to becoming a* ***conscious teller*** *for the sake of us all!"*

My call sounds like this:

All-y, All-y In-Come Free, Come Home to Be.

Now Let the PLAY Begin!

May all your "Once upon a time" moments elevate and celebrate the wonder of life itself, walking the planet as you.

Alaya

P.S. for Therapists, Clinicians & Healers

In more formal settings in which the "Teller" is also a psychotherapist or counselor (M.S.W, PH.d, MD, REV. M.S.N., etc.), Imago Relationship Therapist (an approach which weaves, in my opinion, beautifully with the use of story), teacher or Human Resource manager, the use of the *Alaya's Fables* as a resource and tool can be quite powerful. In a summary way, let me offer a few hints as to ways a clinical setting can be enriched.

Story is a doorway to the heart. It is our hearts that have been so broken and shattered; it is our bodies that have felt the anguish of our humanity; it is our souls which have been lost in the darkness of experiencing life's surprises. Fables offer a way to access the secrets a person has hidden from themselves, through an attitude of openness and curiosity.

We have all heard the line, "Once upon a time and a long time ago…" When we hear this, the small lost orphans of our soul begin to gather to hear the tale, and our defensive barriers fall away, allowing the therapeutic process to blossom. For example, invite a client/patient to read *Alaya's Fables* and then pick the one that speaks to him or her. Or, invite them to read through the table of contents and select a fable that will be used as their beacon of light and hope.

Upon mutual review of that fable, the clinician may then invite them to explore further, between sessions, using the questions offered at the back of the book. Or, simply invite the patient to answer/complete these "stem sentences:"

- How I see myself in this fable is ____________.
- Others from my life are these characters ________________.
- The dilemma, for the character most like me, is ___________________.
- How this fable offers me a way home to my (W)holeness is _________ .

Obviously, these stem sentences can be adjusted and created to best invite the client to enter into their own revelations and explorations. At this point, I would simply invite all the practitioners to trust their own skills and know how to play with perfecting "stem sentences" that fit the needs of their clients.

The wonder of the fable is that it relaxes the limbic or "old brain" to allow the person to open up to new insights and possibilities.

Another format that I have personally found very helpful is in those therapeutic moments, when the person I am in presence with becomes afraid or reactive—tightening up in some way—is for me to say, "Let me tell you a story…" I then offer one of these fables in my own words, in a shortened form. Like a bit of magick, the client begins to set aside their "tightening up" and softens again into a more open relationship matrix. Of course, this therapeutic maneuver requires a "bag of stories" to be at one's immediate selection. *Alaya's Fables* offers a ready-made resource, as I have given you, the clinician and the patient, a tip off about the theme of the tale in the "General Dedications," thus, relieving the practitioner of memorizing all the stories. One can just quickly flip to the most relevant fable.

Imago Relationship Therapists, skilled at the dialogue process (which I highly recommend) or any other form of couples' communication skills, can also share a fable and invite each part of the PAIR (*"People Activating Intimate Relating")* to read the same fable and dialogue about how it is mirroring their relationship concerns.

Take a moment now and consider your clinical setting and training and population…and ask yourself this question, "How might I play with *Alaya's Fables* on behalf of my clients?" A bit of magick is within us all; have no doubt that the "Wise One Within" will respond with an invitation to play and thus, heal the hearts of both you and your patients. Yes, even that process is its own fable! I wonder what you will find yourself listening to in your shared experiences with your precious "tellers" called, clients. Remember, as children (ideally) we would come home from the playground and before we could truly settle down for dinner, we had to share our stories. A true "listener" is the mid-wife of the (W)holly, Holy and (W)hole Soul. I invite all practitioners of the art of "therapoi" (Greek), to begin to engage in the alchemical process of using *Alaya's Fables* to transform and awaken the hearts, minds and souls of the folks they work with.

To put this note simply: These fables are powerful therapeutic tools designed to invite healing, transformation and awakening in both clinician and patient, for one cannot read a fable without one's heart being touched. This is an essential truth of stories!

Stories have the capacity to "heart-touch" without violence, force, pressure or judgment. The listener becomes a vessel, which fills with the images and messages and invitations of the story. It is within the alchemical vessel of the heart that transformation occurs. Thus, the "listener" and the "teller" dance a dance of heart and soul, on behalf of the patient's deepest yearnings and life situation.

What a joy, what a pleasure, what fun it is to see the light begin to sparkle in the eyes of folks coming to us for help!

What a great play it is to offer to the wounded orphans of the heart, a way to come in out of the cold and take their seat at the table!

And it all begins with, "Once upon a time and is now…"

Note: Alaya does offer supervision (phone or live) to clinicians choosing to use fables within the clinical setting. Arrangements made directly with Alaya.

What Clinicians Are Saying

I am a licensed mental health counselor and certified behavior cognitive therapist. Along with CBT, I rely on the usage of DBT along with the Glasser approach of the here and now.

As a therapist, we all have a bag of tricks to help a client move from one stage to another, keeping in mind the outside pressures of managed care to resolve their issues within 6-12 sessions or less.

I have worked with those as young as 3 years of age and as old as senior citizens. Through the years I have heard individuals ask, "Why does this keep happening to me," "Why can't I get ahead," "Why do I feel so stuck all the time?" At times I, too, in my life have asked those same questions.

As a clinician, I know much about theories and human behavior, and I have numerous experiences of observing others. I am aware of transference and counter transference and how we naturally compartmentalize. These fables open up a doorway into the hearts and souls of those that read them, moving beyond theories to empowerment and transformation. I encourage clinicians to take advantage of the gifts these fables offer all of us.

I would challenge each of us as clinicians to engage with these fables as doorways into our feelings and those of our clients, to shift from "it's about what I know" to "what I feel." In this way, we as clinicians can be (W)holly present with our clients and in our everyday life.

> "*Your visions will become clear only when you can look into your heart. Who looks outside, dreams; Who looks inside, awakes*"
>
> By Carl Jung

Joanne Groetzinger, MS, MA, CCBT, LCMHC

****

Alaya's Fables is a transformational gift to us as psychotherapists. This book is a resource and a doorway to our hearts. Alaya invites us, psychotherapists and clients, to explore our own revelations through these fables. There is 'majick' within all of us which leads us to heal our hearts and play through accessing the secrets that we have hidden from ourselves. These fables are powerful tools to access our secrets. One cannot read these fables without having one's heart being touched.

Mary Ellen Nicholls, LICSW, BCD

Question Series for Fables Discussion

The Universal Story of Hope

1. What does Hope mean to you? In your life? In your relationships?
2. How would your life be different if you dared to live from HOPE all the time?
3. In this Fable, what is the core of the message of "HOPE?" How might this inform your life? How might this change how you relate to yourself and others?
4. How did the (W)hole of Creation begin? What is a "between?" How and where do you see them in your life? How might this concept of "betweens" be helpful, or not, in living your life?
5. How do you imagine or know "Creator?" "Creation?" Who are you? What if you are the Creator of all you are experiencing—can you dare to know this without judgment or shame? What would you re-create in your life with this different knowing?
6. What would you change in your life if everyone you see is part of the ONE (W)hole Soup of Creation?

The Mystery of the Gold Coin

1. In what way are you on a solitary journey on-behalf of others you care about? What outer or inner conditions touch you so deeply as to invoke the courage to act?
2. What "Gold Coins" have you or do you give away? What is the impact of this on your life vitality?
3. What is meant by "a Gold Coin"? In your life? In the lives of others?
4. What "Gold Coins" have you taken and thus remain trapped in the underworld? What does your "underworld" feel like?
5. In this fable, it is the face and voice of the "old woman" that calls for Dia to give up her "Gold Coin," what in your life seduces you to give up your gold coins?
6. Who is Chandar in your life—those who encourage and believe in you, while insisting you walk your own wisdom

journey? What are their qualities? How are you your own Chandar?

7. What parts of you are still lost in the underworld (i.e. Claud)?

The Heart of it All—The Twice-Born Weaver

1. What do you feel and know are your webs—your gifts/creations?
2. Who are those around you who ask those wisdom-questions inviting you to journey within?
3. Where/What are all the outside places you have looked for inside answers?
4. What is the difference between an answer, a knowing and a wisdom?
5. What is the difference between creating from one's "reason" as opposed to creating from one's "inner heart-wisdom?" Is creation possible from one's mind alone?
6. What possibilities can your "inner heart-wisdom" manifest in the world, if you dared to go within and honor yourself as Weaver, Twice born?
7. What does "Twice-born" mean to you in your life?

The Cloaked Light

1. What is unique about the leadership qualities of the cloaked figure?
2. Who have you known in your life to operate as this cloaked figure in the fable?
3. What are your particular leadership qualities? How do they save you from stormy seas?
4. When have you "jumped ship" in panic or terror in your life? What caused the inner panic or terror? Who gave the panic/terror such power? Upon reflection what might you choose differently now?
5. What are the differences in attitude and behavior between the Captain and the cloaked figure of light?
6. How does panic-terror keep you from being present?
7. What might you choose to do so as to stay open and calm even in the face of great turmoil? What is the power of an open-hearted presence?

8. What is the significance of the transformation of the cloaked figure? How does this apply in situations in your life? What might it look like for you to no longer seek an outer savior?

<u>ObLAYday, the woman of barren fertility, and her child Mareeha</u>

1. Other than children, what other elements in your own life have been "carried away?" How have you been locked into unending grief?
2. What are the ways you are secretly clinging to your ancient losses? What do you imagine or fear would happen if you dared to feel into these depths? What are you not willing to feel? What makes "those" emotions so treacherous to you?
1. What are the "unforgiveable" failures in your life? In others?
2. How are you not proceeding in your life because you are refusing your own forgiveness? What is the core of "hard-heartedness" towards self? Other?
3. In what ways have you named yourself "the barren one" (ObLAYday)? In what ways have you shunned yourself as "deserving exclusion?"
4. How have your "children" (orphans of your heart and soul) returned? What did your welcome look like? Were you able to welcome them completely?
5. How is your presence a transformative invitation to those around you, much as ObLAYday was to Mareeha?
6. Who around you needs the compassion of your ObLahDay presence? If you dared to be present with them, what would you reveal about yourself to yourself?

<u>A Diamond of a Soul</u>

1. What secret "condition" do you imagine is yours and might cause others to leave or avoid you?
2. In what way are you like Grace, convinced you are but an "ordinary" being?
3. How do you avoid or deflect opportunities to see yourself clearly in the eyes of others? What do you fear to see? Long to see?

4. Who in your life reveals you to yourself? What do they show you? What surprises you? What causes you to move into judgment against yourself/others? What are the judgments?
5. What are the intimacy ("in-to/two-me-see") risks of being seen so clearly?
6. How do the intimate people in your life scare you with their vision of you? Why?
7. What is the inner truth about you that you would prefer to keep hidden?
8. In what ways are you secretly lonely? What would you have to risk to open yourself to being loved for no reason?

The Pink Webbie Shell Home

1. What does your "Pink Webbie Shell home" look like? Feel like? Keep you safe from?
2. How do you keep yourself from others? How do others scare you?
3. How do you use your talents to avoid life? How do you "shell yourself?"
4. In what ways do you barricade yourself against life's invitations to more?
5. What are the elements of your "preferred" reality? How do they differ from what you are currently experiencing?
6. What or who is "banging" on your "shell?" How is this inviting you to move beyond your comfort zone?
7. In what ways do you resist offers of freedom from your prison-shell?
8. What would you have to risk to ask for help?
9. How are you currently asking for help? Or not?
10. What does (W)hole Born look like in your life? In others?
11. In what ways are you a Soul Weaver?

The Gift of the Storm

1. What in your life has felt like "a forever storm?"
2. What are the inner and outer torments of being trapped by an experience you have no power to control?
3. In what arenas of your life have you developed "Storm Eyes?"

4. Who in your life inspires new visions and perspectives? Who invites you to go where you have never gone? What inspires curiosity?
5. What must shift for those with a closed mind to open?
6. How has curiosity, without edges or restraint, served to reveal a surprising pathway?
7. What might happen in your life if you began practicing MAH-Wah-TEE's HUM?
8. Living and using MAH-Wah-TEE's HUM, describe your Presence? Its impact on others?
9. What are the gifts of your forever storms?

The Story of Wah-NEE

1. In what way is your vision limited by the belief "it has always been this way?"
2. Where is there evidence of a "Browning and Dying" in your life?
3. What are some of the rules of "Pretending & Denying" that keep all of us blind to our situations? Needs? Fears? Risks?
4. In what ways do you find yourself making up more rules with the idea that these will make you safer?
5. How might you gain the summit of your inner "mountain's visioning top" so as to see beyond your own scales?
6. How do you cherish the existence of your scales? What are they composed of? Where did they come from? Who around you has similar scales? (i.e., prejudices, limitations, assumptions, "givens" of all sorts…)?
7. What do you imagine would need to happen for you to DARE to remove your own scales?
8. How are you, the globe, your family, etc. on the edge of an evolutionary leap which is unavoidable?
9. What is the significance and power of "witnessing" to bring life anew?

Ceques of the Heart

1. In what ways is your heart hardened against life? What led to this hardening?

2. As you read this fable, did you begin to notice a whispery call from within to begin a softening journey? What did the voice say to you? Who is it that calls you from your hardened places? What is requiring softening within you?
3. What would it cost you to stop "knowing" and become curious without conclusion?
4. What trees (i.e., babies, weather changes, spouses, trees, rivers…) have you been ignoring in your life?
5. What experiments of communion and reflection might you engage in as a means to come into relationship with the greater life around you ("your Precious Trees")?
6. In what ways do you stop yourself so as not to become the "radical" focus on a community? What might it mean to be "radical;" for example, would you reach out and touch when others wouldn't? Would you call upon a neighbor during a storm even if they are strangers to you?
7. When and how have you experienced that your presence is enough? What does "enough" mean to you? How do you "lay down ceques?"
8. What happened in your life for you to forget your own magnificence? What is now happening to "re-call" you to your True Nature?
9. When does your Presence light up the soul of another and reveal the truth of their magnificence?
10. Will you choose to remember yourself today? What will you remember of you today? How might you honor and celebrate your ever-spiraling remembering?
11. Where might you walk and lay down ceques that invite others to remember?

MarNEEya and GherTiid, The Blessings of Anguish Revealed

1. When in your life have the burdens of impossible life decisions overwhelmed you?
2. Daughters and mothers both profoundly love one another and then move into the hate of one another, how have you experienced this continuum in your lifetime?
3. How do you stand aside as a mother, witnessing your child going through the anguish of learning?

4. In what way might your interference intended to "save the child" actually kill off precious elements of that young being? How were parts of you "killed off" in your passage from babe to adulthood?
5. How did you as a child express your angry longing to be saved from life itself? What did you wish your caretakers would have done to "stop the hurt and pain?" What if they had? What if they didn't?
6. Who are the "Shee-YA's" in your life (i.e., first day of school, first sweetheart, first job, first move out of the house…)? How have these "Shee-YA moments" birthed your greater self?
7. What would you have to set aside to allow the mother and daughter Wisdoms within and without to come into union?
8. When has your life felt broken (i.e., Broken Life Blood)? What unshed tears do you still contain? How might their re-union birth the desire to share LIFE with others (i.e., Fountain of Living Waters)?

__The Awakening of a NOMAD__

1. What poisons you and keeps you from seeing the true nature of your family? Your life? Your way of being?
2. What are the gifts of being heard? How does one know that one has been listened to deeply? How does this depth of reception transform?
3. What is the difference between accepting WHAT IS as opposed to WHAT you LONG for it to be? What are your experiences of resisting "WHAT IS," struggling for "it to be different?"
4. Does your acceptance of "WHAT IS" limit you or expand your life's experiences?
5. What is your relationship to being a "Nomad" (i.e., what changes do you welcome? Refuse? etc.)?
6. A Nomad is one who is comfortable with not knowing while also at-home within, in every place or space they find themselves, that there is no leaving or arriving. How might you feel in this moment if you embrace being a nomad, purposely?

7. What name might you give yourself to celebrate your true freedom?
8. Who is the Nomad being awakened?

Shame's Wisdom

1. How are you different from others? What sets you apart from others?
2. In what ways have you felt shame for these differences? What were your reactions to feeling shame?
3. Have you kept your shames secret? What are the hidden stories you have created to make sense of things you are ashamed about?
4. What is it about shame that results in isolation and solitary anguish?
5. What leads us to so readily believe in our own "badness?"
6. How does the experience of SAMENESS (alikeness) heal the commitment to shame's judgments of us?
7. What happens when one of us is freed from the prison of shame that allows others to feel safe enough with us to speak of their own shame? How can we offer this same peace to ourselves and thus to the world?
8. What are the "High Places" in you? What are the "Inner Places in you? And how might they come together as "ONE Place?" Of what significance would this have in your life with others?

Wanikiya—Light Mountain That Was

1. What do you imagine a "heart space" (MEE-Kah) is? How might one know that it is open?
2. In what ways have you "sourced" your life by connecting to that which is outer?
3. How have you been a Le-NU, seeing things that others don't or exploring where others have no interest?
4. Who in your life touches you from what feels like the inside out?
5. What permission would you have to grant yourself for your heart to open?
6. How do the world's terrors mirror your own?

7. How do you find comfort upon hearing the "terror-sounds" from within or without?
8. In what way do you cover your heart's light? And what is called for to reveal your MEE-Kah's radiance?
9. How, in this fable, do all the relationships reflect the potency of MEE-Kah's revealed generosity? The Light of Wanikiya, the MEE-Kah of the people, the Flame within the mountain's core and the re-freshment from within are all the same and yet different—what is revealed to you here?

Hot Stuff

1. In what ways have you lost your "flicker?" What does this mean to you? What "flickers" do you feel are still wandering looking for the home-fires of YOU?
2. What gave the "flicker" such impact upon the (W)hole Flame of Hot Stuff? What events or people have caused you to smolder your life's passions?
3. What does home mean to you? How might you know you were "home-at-last"?
4. In what ways are you wandering, looking for home?
5. Who are the "moles" or the sources of guidance in your life, who are pointing you towards your home? How do you recognize them?
6. What dark places have you dared to enter and found in-flamement? What did that process require of you? How are you like "Sparkles with Life?" What have you learned on the journey so far?
7. How does this fable invite you into an inquiry into your own beliefs about the relationship between spirit and body? What are you revealing to yourself about recognizing your own soul's presence?
8. How does our relationship to our soul-self impact our life experiences?
9. What lights your fires? What brings aliveness to your moments?

The Dragon in the Box

1. What does your box look like? Feel like? Describe your experiences of being "boxed IN."

2. What part of you had to be set outside the box for this to happen? In what way did you give permission for this separation to occur?
3. In what ways does your Soul-Self cry out for your attention to wake-up?
4. What are the familiar patterns that keep you in your box? Consider a day of your life and be curious about the (w)Roles, the "givens," the presumptions, etc. which determine many of your choices/responses? Where did they come from?
5. Who in your life is a "waker-upper critter?" How are you your own "waker-upper?" What are the qualities of powerful people, events, or feelings that stimulate us to wake-up to more of ourselves?
6. When have you felt a "soul-reunion?" How does it feel? What blocks or stops you from sustaining your "soul-reunion?"
7. What "soul-task" or calling do you imagine was given to you, based upon what you have learned and experienced in your life?
8. How might you gift this back to another and thus the (W)hole World?
9. Who might you seek out, neighbor, friend or foe, to offer your "soul-task?"

<u>The Gift of the Gazorah's Gaze</u>

1. What scares you about looking directly into another's eyes? How do you avoid direct eye-contact? When? Whose direct gaze is most challenging for you? What makes direct gaze dangerous?
2. In what ways are you "stiff-necked" in your judgments or opinions of self and others?
3. Which tribe do you relate to: The BAC-TOE tribe, who walk backwards into encounters, or The WAH-SEED tribe, who move sideways into life's moments? What does your answer suggest to you about your relationship to life?
4. What adjustments have you made in the way you walk through life that have impacted the children in your world? Your creations?

5. What is the difference between an inner danger and an outer one? Is there a difference?
6. What would you have to do or change within to look at life straight on?
7. How would this choice to engage in Direct Gaze alter how you participate in life?
8. What differences in others, those things that "drive you crazy," would you have to embrace to fully participate in living your life?
9. What was the true gift of the Gift of the Gazorah's Gaze?
10. Just as the tribe re-named itself, how might you re-name yourself?

The Stroll of the HoorTeeTah

1. What would you reveal if the HoorTeeTah walked past you today? Now that you said the "nice" answer, what would you really reveal?
2. What causes us to keep secrets? From ourselves? From others? What is the difference between the two types of secrets?
3. How have you been a HoorTeeTah Being for others?
4. In what ways do keeping ourselves secret separate us from others? Limit intimacy? Create divisions within communities?
5. What makes secret-keeping such an opposition to compassion?
6. How is it that when compassion is present, acceptance without understanding is more naturally extended to others?
7. When there is no need to hide, how is it that compassion and harmony ripen?
8. How does revealing yourself totally increase your capacity to be compassionate?
9. How could a HoorTeeTah Stroll, done by you, change the world?

Olli's Echo

1. What are the edges of your world which you have considered eternal and permanent?
2. How have you responded when the edges of your world have fallen? How did you feel upon realizing your entire world was no longer the same?

3. When have you gone first, despite your own terror, because you felt a call beyond logic?
4. What sustained you or sustains you now as you walk into unknowns? How do you feel facing unknowns?
5. Imagine you have entered PIZZAZ, as described in the fable, how might you respond if "water was LOVE in substance" and "Sounds had color" and "Light had musical notes?"
6. What are the moments in your life when you have realized that there is "no way back" from the choice you have made? How did you feel?
7. How do your relationships change from your new perspective or position?
8. What does your own echo to those "left behind" sound/look like? Can you sing it?
9. How you are still attached to their response? What might it require of you to release the cherished outcome of a particular response from them?
10. How does this fable speak to you about trusting self and others?

Wandra, the Forgotten

1. What do you believe is the purpose of life? What might you call "Essential Wisdoms?"
2. How have you journeyed seeking to understand the meaning of life? What have been your four corners?
3. How have you trusted in yourself on the journey of your life?
4. How does the image of a "feather so light it floats" inspire in you a wisdom from your own life?
5. What is the worth of being "impenetrable," as the rock Wandra found at the second corner of her journey? How has death, in all its forms, been a teacher to you?
6. In what ways is our very essence like the liquid, which "returned to itself?" How might you flow easier with life if you trusted that all would return to the One true Source?
7. What are remnants of birthing moments in your life, which you hold sacred? What wisdoms do they still re-call to your heart?

8. What is your response when after a great effort on your part, there is no response, no recognition, no celebration of your victory? What does recognition mean to you? How do you prefer to be recognized?
9. How has someone working against you or breaking the rules been in your favor?
10. Read aloud Wandra's wisdom shared with the villages and notice how you respond within. Share your wisdom response with those with whom you are in conversation.

<u>Feisty and Nudgy, the Moles Who Came to Love (w)Holes</u>

1. What are you deathly afraid of?
2. What do you imagine would happen if you "fell into it?"
3. How have you chosen to "research life" from a distance, rather than jump into direct messy experiences with bold curiosity?
4. When have you dared to ask the un-askable questions? What are your un-askable questions now in your life? ASK them out loud now.
5. Where have you been when you have run out of rope? What was your response? What did it feel like?
6. What was the nature of a "leap of faith" or "a drop into a (w)hole" in your life? What did you discover or reveal when you let go?
7. When have you chosen to let go into the unknown of "No answers?"
8. How does curiosity without judgment align and stabilize you in the face of mysteries? When we replace answers with questions, there is room for the mysteries of life to reveal themselves—when have you dared to do this?
9. Consider the (w)Hole learnings of Feisty and Nudgy. Which speak most directly to your current life situations?
10. How did embracing feeling experiences serve to support (w)hole spiraling? Living? What holds you back from embracing your (W)hole Life, including your light?
11. How have the (w)holes in your life become tunnels to enlightenments?
12. Are you ready to wake up to your (W)hole Life now? What is your first step?

The Land of Gleeful Laughter

1. What life tragedies stop you from wanting to live life?
2. How have you made sense of suffering, yours and others? And how have you longed to prevent such occurrences?
3. How is it that the wisdom source within reveals itself in the face of tragedy?
4. When have you made choices whose costs were later shown to be greater than you anticipated? What were those costs?
5. Is the preciousness of life only because we can lose it or can we extend the celebration to embrace birth, death, gain, loss, anguish, joys, and the mystery of it all?
6. What does it mean to love in the face of knowing that death and loss is also possible and inevitable?
7. What makes the laughter of a child different from the laughter of adults? Where is this child's giggle still alive within you? How do you restrain it? How do you release it from the inner spells?
8. What are your "Dream children" waiting for your call to return into your home lands, bringing their aliveness?
9. What do your "skip, hop and jump" look like if you dared to chuckle through your days?

The Birth of the People of Light

1. When have you been so frozen in terror you could do nothing but wait without hope or even awareness, or scream or blame or rage or collapse, etc? What did you do?
2. What does an accidental miracle mean to you? When have you experienced one? How did you feel?
3. If your Kria was fully awakened, how might your experience of yourself be expanded? Be surprising? Be unprecedented?
4. How have you been carried by the smallest of accidents and the greatest of choices?
5. How might you imagine life as "a Living Light?"
6. What would peace look like if ALL stress dissolved?
7. How would you choose to inhabit your days if there was no need for purpose, mission, goals, successes or striving of any sort? What remains of who you are?

8. What becomes life's purpose?
9. How does Kria forehead touching and mutual breathing translate into actions in your daily life?
10. What is the power of patience and presence in dissolving all barricades, within and without? When have you gifted yourself this presence without end?
11. When have you been a Barricaded one? What freed you? LOOK around in your world, where are there "walled in" ones waiting for the touch of a forehead and a shared breath of love? What are you waiting for?

Acknowledgments

It takes a village to birth a book!
Let me introduce you to my village.

Each fable within this book has two forms of dedication. One is a dedication honoring particular people. The other is what I call a "global" dedication which acknowledges that the fable is about all of us in some way or another.

Contained here in the **"Village section"** are the particular dedications in which I name individuals who have invoked within me that fable's theme or message or feeling.

The "**global dedications**" are located beneath the title of each fable within the Table of Contents, to make it easier for you to select fables at any given time. Also, of course, fables are living entities, which call to us much as a friend calls to share their news. You may find that while perusing these short abbreviated dedications, a tale will reach out and tickle your heart's hungers. I invite you to PLAY in this way with all the fables offered in the space between these two bookends called "Back" and "Front."

****

Epic of Play—Martha Harrell inspired *Alaya's Fables* through her gentle, persistent, non-judgmental "Wisdom Windex." For over 30+ years Martha persisted in "playing around" in the old past dirt on my soul-psyche glasses until I could grant myself permission to "play for real"—and then all the fables followed. Thank you, Martha. This book of "fable play" is only because you never gave up on me, no matter how many stories, tales, and fables I wove to avoid saying, "Yes" to playing by my own authority. Thank you.

Ripple's Tale—is dedicated to two women, Yvonne and Joanne (5-star "Mom"), who have walked into the darkest of dark places both within themselves and beyond themselves, only to return to their daily lives with a wealth of wisdom, a compassionate presence and a steadiness of being. Thank you both for being you.

The Mystery of The Gold Coin—Dia Moore inspires this fable. Lost in the underworlds of "less than," Dia chose to face monsters and terrors beyond imagining, and in doing so, has changed the laws of our lands, opened the "blind eyes" of our justice system, and birthed the potent power of her own healing arts. Thank you.

The Heart of it All: The Twice-Born Weaver—Steve Burison inspired this fable. "Whatever it takes" to reveal the path from one's head to one's heart-truth has been the greatest of challenges taken on by Steve B on behalf of us all. Going where few men dare to tread, you, Steve, have forged a path of hope and possibility which ripples around the world. Thank you.

The Cloaked Light—Ellen Byrne inspired this fable. Nearly dying to discover her own light, Ellen has chosen to face herself, unveiling herself over and over again, until her heart opened to the terrifying truth of her own brilliant presence and wisdom light. Thank you.

ObLAYday, the woman of barren fertility, and her child Mareeha—Amanda Johnson inspired this fable. Despite an original appearance of soul-barrenness and permanent despair, through her persistent quest to come back to life, Amanda's heart is now alive and well again. She is able to open her heart, soften her words, and open her ears to embrace even the hardest of truths. Thank you.

A Diamond of a Soul—Marilyn Dexter inspired this fable. With "soul dedication," Marilyn has marched to her own drummer despite the pressures of conformity and has become a grounded and true reflection of Love's Presence in our world. Thank you.

The Pink Webbie Shell Home—Karen Aznoian inspired this fable. Sacrificing "blind comfort" by placing "Heart Truths" above all else, Karen provokes us all to "be real without apology" and in this way, truth leads us all Home. Thank you.

The Gift of the Storm—Lizzy Derecktor inspired this fable. Surrounded by storms of heart, mind, and soul—hers and others—with a huge bold creative spirit-heart, these "storm gifts" have been and are opened, folks' souls are healed, and the children of this planet are better for it. Thank you.

The Story of Wah-NEE—Rochelle Mausteller inspires this fable. Despite all encouragements to remain blind to "What IS," Rochelle has chosen to look and to look again, ever moving towards "Truth Vision," until now her sight pierces straight and true to the heart of the matter. Thank you.

Ceques of the Heart—Alex and Stephen Browne inspire this fable. From hearts broken and shattered, each has chosen to soften, spiraling around and around the horrible truths, trusting that "Truth makes us free to love, to be loved, and to be who we are." Thank you.

MarNEEya and GherTiid, The Blessings of Anguish Revealed—Judith Sloan, Marguerite and Maurice DiBlasi—you inspire this fable. In the face of the agony of the many children who suffer in body, mind, and soul around our globe, you open your hearts and walk right into the darkness, holding a light of hope, and in this way, (W)hole families and communities are brought back from near death. Thank you.

The Awakening of a NOMAD—Ahtea inspires this fable. Releasing her attachment to the outer as source, Ahtea has revealed that honest and heart-felt presence is the only authentic home any of us have. Thank you.

Shame's Wisdom—Anne Suddy inspires this fable. From "I am nothing" to "I am everything" to "I AM," Anne has never backed away from her own self-unveiling, until her very presence is "The Wisdom of the Ages" walking gently along the ordinary pathways of life. Thank you.

Wanikiya—The Light Mountain That Was—Lisa inspires this fable. Independence, her old-time savior, Lisa's bold courage and persistent heart-curiosity has led her to pioneer the wilds of intimate relationships and soul-singing love, opening her home to lost orphans (within and without) until her presence became an embrace without condition. Thank you.

Hot Stuff—Janice Welch inspired this fable and it's resurrection for this book. My dear "Angel of Sanctuary," from the darkest nights you always birth the greatest of lights. We met at a time when you were in the darkest of places, your light nearly extinguished, and yet by your essential playfulness and aliveness of heart, you now stand as a beacon of hope and joy for us all. Thank you.

The Dragon in the Box—John R. Chadwick and all the other Light Brothers (particularly Steven, Steve B, Todd, Pete, Tom, Bob, Tim, Gary, Brownie, John, Jim, and Jonne), you inspire this fable. With bold courageous hearts, John, you and the brothers in Light continually dare to drop into your own playful and tender hearts, despite all that the world screams at you, and thus you all change the (W)hole World. Thank you.

The Gift of the Gazorah's Gaze—Marianne DiBlasi and Sue Moss each in their own way inspire this fable. You both, though terrified and wounded by hurtful "gazes," have each dared to boldly look straight at "What is true," and in this way, you have healed us all. Thank you.

The Stroll of the HoorTeeTah—John Richard Chadwick inspires this fable. Having explored all of the options of hiding out from love, John has dared to step into the spotlight of Love's transparent embrace, thus challenging us all to the same surprising "stroll." Thank you, dear "Hero of my Heart."

Olli's Echo—Dorie Cameron, Karen Kuhl, Dee LaCrosse, Suzie Moss inspire this fable. No matter what was before us, they have unfailingly walked, over and over again with me, into many unknowns with trust—trust that we, as friends, would walk into the as yet unknown "light of day" once again. Thank you.

Wandra, The Forgotten One—Steven Scally inspires this fable. After wandering around and around the inner and outer worlds in which his own wisdom was denied by all, Steven dared to come home, without knowing how he would be received, and brought with him all the wisdoms he had gathered on this spiral journey. He offered them to us all, and in doing so, the heroic man he is became revealed. Thank you.

Feisty and Nudgy, The Moles Who Came to Love (w)Holes—Mary Ellen Nicolls and Barbara Myers, along with all the Certified Master Teachers of Radiance of The (W)hole Point Institute, LLC, infuse this fable with authentic vitality and a simplicity of truth by how each of you walks through your days. By daring to be radical pioneers of the psyche, on behalf of others and yourselves, folks are waking up all around the (W)hole World. Thank you.

The Land of Gleeful Laughter—Dorie Cameron and Holly Edwards (my dear sisters) and their children (Kylie, Keaton, Nick, and Melody) and my mom inspire this fable. The greatest "love-risk" ever is to have children who you love without reason or restraint while knowing how little power one has to "keep them safe from life happening"—and you wouldn't even if you could. These women have dared this greatest of adventures, and in doing so gave me a small peek into its glories and horrors. Their children have gifted to me the wonder of being "an ordinary aunt"—one of my first "fables." Thank you to all the "mom's of this world" who give us all life.

The Birth of the People of Light—Anne Suddy, Ripple of The (W)hole Point Institute, LLC, inspires this fable. Leading is a challenge that is made far lighter by the presence of a "Number One," the person who stands steady and loyal and true even as the leader, herself, wobbles in doubt. Anne is this person for The (W)hole Point Institute and for me. Thank you most humbly.

Appendix

Word Play

In this book... **(W)hole = wholeness**
(w)hole = hole

This is an obvious play on the words "hole" and "whole." Not so obvious is the transformational power of "holes"—our fears, insecurities, and dark places—as doorways of "wholeness," an expression of our true selves: confident, secure, at peace with ourselves and with our surroundings.

Notice when there is a capital "W." It points to wholeness and the state of being whole. The capital "W" is in a parentheses to remind us that we are always evolving, rather than being "finished" products. The little "w" is also in a parentheses to remind us that there is always more to discover about ourselves.

The power of word play is engaged because both the psyche and soul are dancing as one (W)hole as they digest and experience all the layers of the invitation. The psyche, or the psychological viewpoint of a person, can perceive the term in many ways, while the soul, or spiritual life force, flows with it in various directions—all at the same time.

Word play is an invitation to all parts of our being: our human selves, our psychological facets, our mental elements as well as our soul self. The wonder of this is that you don't have to put forth much effort for this to happen. Word play has an alchemical effect, sinking deeply into the unconscious, inviting self-unveiling and surprising revelations.

This image of a hole is the metaphor used to reveal the bare bones of our shattered (W)holeness *and* our path to awakened (W)holeness. In essence, each time you read the word (W)holeness, a profound wisdom awakens within you. Called forth from deep inside your cells and your psyche, the truth of your (W)holeness is invited to move into greater and greater awareness. This effect references the impact upon the psyche and the soul whenever this term is encountered. A movement is initiated or stimulated between and in both the psyche and soul of the person which requires no conscious effort.

To clarify: by the word "psyche" I am referring to all the elements of a person's psychology, including historical life events, the myriad of responses, feelings of yesterday, today, and even about what might happen tomorrow. With the word "soul" I am pointing to the elements of spirit, that which enlivens the physicality of our human bodies—the mystery of life in each of us. When psyche and soul meld into (W)holeness, turmoil and struggles melt away. The human-ness of us is no longer shattered into bits and pieces. Our spirit is now fully present to experience life itself, thus supporting the (W)hole person.

The use of the word "(w)hole" is an invitation to recognize how we feel when we hit those tough patches in our lives. When a life moment happens and we feel like we've fallen into a big, black hole, we are actually being offered an invitation to awaken (into wholeness). This is a secret lost to many of us because the experience of being in a "hole" hurts so much.

What's surprising is that the point of all of our experiences in life's "black holes" is to access our (W)holeness. In fact, our particular route to revealing our inner selves is found in each and every (w)hole we stumble into.

In these fables you will notice and feel this play of words. Let it sink into you and reach those hidey (w)holes of mysteries and fantasies, monsters and wonders, called You-Me-Us! In this way these fables will awaken your ever expanding spirals of you being you.

This is true particularly of the fable of "Feisty and Nudgy, The Moles who came to love (w)Holes."

Roots from which the Fables Came

Neuro proramming - NLP
Logo Therapy
Constructivism
Schema Theory
Hypnotism
Personality Theories
Freudian Theory
Cognitive Therories
Jungian Theory

Wholeness
Religions of the world
New Age viewpoints
The Beginning
Wisdom Traditions
Creation Theories

Genogram Theory
Sociology-Anthropology
Theories of dysfunction
Family Systems Theories
Biology-Genealogy
Psychological genetics
Object Relationship Theories

Inner child work
Gestalt Therapies
Co-dependence work
Journaling-Artist's Way
Suffering

Imago Relationship Therapy
Psychotherapy-Psychoanalysis
Ontology-Buber-The Space Between
Curiosity-Inquiry Theories-Rogerian Theory
Satir-Gestalt Theory-Stone Center Research
Presence Practices
Communication Theories
Carl Jung-Jungian-based theories
EMDR-TFT
Shamanic Soul Retrieval-Journeying
Internal Family Systems
Integration of ltiple Family System Theories
Parts Theories-Inner Child Explorations

Mindfulness Practices
Alternative Healing Modalities-Reiki-Ennersense
Wicca Practices-Eco Psychology-Ritual Practices
Alchemical Healing Processes & Practices
Embodiment Practices-Experiential Seminars-Yoga
Spirituality Studies-Granting Significance-Mastery Apprenticeships
Still Point Energetic Trainings-Options Therories
Choice Practices-Integration Practices
Tel Shai Ya Training-Oneness Wisdom Traditions
Inquiry Practices-Meditation-Interior Reflection Processes
Stillness Practices-Awareness Practices-Mindfulness
Diamond Heart

Lar Short-Klas
Spirituality-Transpersonal Therapies
Carl Jung-The Book of Job
Holistic Therapies-body, mind, & soul
Visionary & other Cranial Sacral Therapies
Holistic Theories
Theologies-World Religions
Unitarian Philosophers-Quantum Physics
Unity-The Mystery of All That Is-Paradox
Living a Whole Life Consciously
Oneness

Glossary of Fable Characters

Abba-EMah – the wide-eyed being at the summit of the mountain who taught Wah-NEE how to see The Greening and the Living

AH-tea – the name that E-TAH took upon realizing that "nomad" was about an inner home

Alzibet – the hard-hearted woman who sought to show The Great Tree its truth and thus, inadvertently softened her own heart

Ashana – a great magician and very, very wise Shamanesse, and also a mother who had lost a daughter

BAC-TOE Tribe – a portion of the tribe that walked backwards into each moment

Book of Wisdoms – the diary and collection of wisdom maintained by the elders

Broken Life Blood – GherTiid's blood saves through all her ritual "breakings of bone" which then serves to, in part, save the lands

Browning and the Dying, The – a condition afflicting the earth, air, water, and plants, resulting in death if not stopped and corrected.

Bulahr – (bul-ah-har) an eldr of the greatest and oldest clan of the people, a women deeply committed to wisdom, she sends Wandra on a quest for the essential wisdoms

Captain, The – at the helm of the boat

Chandar – a wise woman who gifts Dia her gold coin (The Mystery of the Gold Coin)

Cloaked passenger – later reveals the Light veiled by the garment

"Cloaked Light" – the second name of the boat

Con-Soul – gathering of the elders of the village (Note: name created by Anne Suddy and Ahtea)

Dia – a young girl (The Mystery of the Gold Coin)

Direct Gaze Wisdom – to look into the eyes of another and allow the shared gaze to reveal wisdom

Dragon, The – a huge beast stuffed into a box, which is possible only after the soul has been removed

Dream Children – children born in the imagination and hearts of those who long for children. These children live in the Land of Secrets until such time as they are welcomed home by their creators

Echo – the wisdom of a call that is sent on the notes of trust and spaciousness of the void

Eetoot – the name of the current YahHoot, presiding villager of the town and the one who sucked his thumb whenever he was anxious

Essential Wisdoms, The – the four wisdoms found by Wandra

E-TAH – nomad girl who is frustrated by the constant moving around

Eterist – the name of the great barrier or all that enclosed all the lands

Feisty – a girl mole who agreed that Nudgy's questions had merit and joined him in the direct exploration of (w)Holes

Flames – the bit of life-light required to join with a body for birth to occur

Flicker – named "Sparkles-with-Life," the lost flicker who finds its way home to HOT Stuff

Fountain of Living Waters – that which results in the combination of Broken Life Blood and the honest tears of a mother's anguish, shared with the daughter directly

Gazorah – a creature that kills through its direct gaze. Low to the ground and filled with malice, it often killed for the sake of killing alone

GEN-II – second elder of the village to notice the dimming of Wanikiya Light

Gertrude – a young girl who had big feet and big hands. She was made fun of by all the kids, and she hated her own gawky physical form, until the day when she skips school and is chased by a (w)hole

GherTiid – daughter of MarNEEya, born with a broken body. Made Shamanesse

Grace – a sleek Persian housecat who did not know how amazing she was

Great HUM, The – "Here I am" practice that allows one to walk without being storm tossed amidst the HAH-BEE-TAH

Great Tree, The – a tree across from the porch of Alzibet's room, who had forgotten itself as a young sapling due to an evil and self-serving man's cloak

Greening and the Living, The – a condition where life force flows unrestrained.

HAH-BEE-TAH – the forever storm

Hannah – the baker who is revealed as loving chocolate

Harriet – an angel in the form of a mosquito, a waker-upper critter sent from heaven

High Place – a place where men went into deep retreat, and only men were allowed

Homie – (home-ee) the eldest elder of the TEE-Ah

HoorTeeTah – a Being of Transparent Presence who's presence causes others to become transparently revealed to everyone and themselves

Hot Stuff – one particular flame whose flicker became lost

Inner Place – a place where women lived in retreat, and only women were allowed

KLAS – ancient healing process in which wisdom is sought through a sustained Life Gaze

Kria – a crystalline shape within which all are born and would originally recede into the head until the time of pending death. Later the Kria became a radiating crystalline shape in the center of the forehead which emitted a bright Radiant Living Light, causing all fear to melt away

Le-NU – pre-adults in the village who discover the light within Wanikiya Mountain, chant to the hidden flame: Mow-TAY, Le-NU, Le-NU, Gow-TAY, Hae-NU, Hae-NU, Hae-Nu (translatioins: Spirit-Light and I are ONE. Forever, forever, forever)

LEE-BO – elder of the village who first notices the change in Wanikiya Light (Note: also cousin of Wah-NEE)

Leelah – the elder who replaced Bulahr upon Bulahr's death, which occurred while Wandra was on her wisdom quest

Life Gaze – the direct eye-to-eye gaze that affirms the value of life of an infant

Light Beings – all people whose Kria has arisen and become activated as a Radiant Living Light

Lilith – a young girl who wove a Pink Webbie Shell Home in response to life

MAH-Wah-TEE – a man of the village, trapped in the mountain caves when the storm arrived, and who revealed the practice of the HUM

Mareeha – the woman who watched over the children who were taken

Maria – a little girl who died in an accident

MarNEEya – mother of a child born with a broken body. Mother of GherTiid

Mathew – a little boy who was swallowed up by a big (w)hole

MEE-Kah – the inner light self of each villager, requiring daily re-freshment at Wanikiya Light Mountain

Mee-Ya-HAH – the position in the TEE-Ah held by Ollie, it meant "she who goes first into the void"

Mole (w)Hole University (MHU) an institution of higher learning, located at Mount Moment, USA, where studies are designed to educate moles to become "Mole (w)Hole Avoidant" Experts (MHA degree)

Mount Moment – where Mole (w)Hole University is located and where all the moles live

Mow-TAY – leader of the Le-NU clan

Naked Gaze Tribe – the new name given to the tribe when the BAC-TOE and WAH-SEED tribes reunited

Nee-WAH – the name Wah-NEE took after the lands were restored and the village relocated

Nudgy – a mole who helps "Sparkles-with-Life" find her way home, a boy mole who dared to ask "What makes (w)Holes so awful" and started the explorations of (w)Holes, which lead to the entire transformation of the MHU.

ObLAYday – the woman scorned due to her barrenness and became known for her initiatory and healing presence

Olli – a member of the Wisdom Village and an elder in TEE-AH

Olli's Echo – "I am in here. Come on. It's free of danger. It's free…Come on." Later the chant was changed by Homie after her passage through The Eternist void to "All-y, All-y in come free…Come home to be"

OUR Place – a place of balance between inner and outer, ebb and flow, woman and man, female and male. A place that exists after shame is healed

Passion's Fire – the second name taken on by Hot Stuff after the flicker returned

Pastor of the village – the pastor who hated clothes

Pink Webbie Shell Home, The – a creation of a young girl in response to life's harshness

PIZZAZZ – the place on the other side of The Eternist void, discovered by Olli

Professor Mudfudd - a lecturer at Mole (w)Hole University and the one who expelled both Nudgy and Feisty for their radical inquiries into the nature of (w)Holes.

RAH-TOO – a young girl in the back of the hidey (w)Hole basement refuge. The young girl who brings the HUM back to the village.

Richard – a little boy who dies in an accident

Scales – flaps of skin nearly covering the entire eye's vision, a normal condition of the people

Shee-YA – Shamanesse who takes GherTiid and through a series of rituals of body, heart, and mind breaking, heals her soul and initiates her into the mysteries of the Shaman

Sheila – the eldest member of the town, a very staid women who loved to dance naked

She-Light-BEING – the one who called Lilith out of her Shell Home

Soul Mirror (or SM for short) – a cat new to town, whose eyes reflected back to the creature looking into them a reflection of the truth of their soul

"Still Flight" – the name of a boat

"Storm eyes" – a condition in which one's inner focus is solely directed towards that which is fearful and raging and fear-inspiring

"Storm tossed" – a condition experienced by those who ventured out into the storm without the knowledge of the HUM

TARIC – Father of a child born with a broken body. Father of GherTiid

TEE-AH – a gathering of elders of Olli's tribe, these elders were considered the Keepers of Wisdom. Each elder was also called a "TEE-AH"

Tee Cah – orphaned girl who is taken to High Place as her only option of refuge

Trembly Times, The – the time when the Browning and the Dying first began

Wah-NEE – a young girl who quested beyond the Elder rules to usher in an evolutionary transformation

WAH-SEED Tribe – a portion of the tribe that walked sideways into any moment

Wandra – a young woman of the tribe, chosen by Bulahr to see the essential wisdoms. Upon her return from the quest, she becomes an elder once the secret of her quest is revealed by the Book of Wisdoms

Wanikiya Light Mountain – source of light presence and life in the center of the village

Weaver, The – a spider who wove healing webs (The Heart of it All: The Twice-born Weaver)

Web of Light – the web of fibers of consciousness that links all Light Beings

(w)Hole – a space into which one can fall.

(w)Hole Learnings – discoveries about (w)Holes that can only be revealed and understood through direct (w)Hole experiences

(w)Hole Play – a way to make sense of life by exploring one's own (w)holes

(w)Holly Point, Mrs. – Gertrude's teacher in school, who loved to teach about (w)holes and loved to say her own name

YahHoot – the title of the presiding villager

ZIGZAGZIP – the name of the great scratch in The Eternist. A landmark to all the people

Sneak Peek at *Wake Up to Your (W)hole Life*

Chapter 2: What I Wish I had Known

To review, what is a (w)hole? For our purposes a (w)hole is a painful place we "fall into." A (w)hole is a space between one side and another, or one object and another, or one expression of yourself and its opposite. A (w)hole is a space in-between. A (w)hole is a hole or space between parts of ourselves.

Up until now we were left with only two positions: being in the (w)hole or hoping to avoid (w)holes. In many circles, this is called "being on the journey." Many people today speak of being on journeys to discover themselves, to recover the joy of being alive, or to simply free themselves from that which has become a painful experience of being alive. However, it often morphs into a circular movement around and around the same issues, without any actual direction, only a hope of "one day." Most of us on the self-awareness path use a "shotgun" approach based on "I heard this is helpful" or "They are recommending this now."

We often begin full of hope that this way or that way will finally free us from circling around the same thing over and over again. The problem is that after a time most of us find ourselves right back to the same issues we started with. It's frustrating. It's maddening. It's so totally exhausting that some of us give up—or give up for a while anyway—and then we try again. Some of us just don't even bother trying at all. What does this tell us? It tells us that there is something missing in our approach. (W)holeness isn't a journey. (W)holeness is all about unveiling and revealing the (W)hole Truth of ourselves. The truth is that there is no place to journey to and no destination to arrive at and no "right" way to be. At the same time we find ourselves acting, being, and feeling stuck in the dark. Again! So what is going on?

Whatever is going on is actually happening deep within our being. It is driven by profound motivations that defy our own conscious adult choices, and all our blind efforts to "get better" are not very effective. In fact, they can be quite exhausting. We know that something is missing, or we would have resolved the "issue" already—never to revisit it again.

When we feel depressed, down, and sad, we may describe this experience by saying, "Oh, I am in a pit. I have fallen into a big black hole." "I am in the pits today." At this point we are clear that what we want is some speedy assistance with climbing up and out of the (w)hole. Then somehow, some time later on, we inevitably end up falling right back into that (w)hole again. Perhaps there will be different details, but the feelings will be very, very familiar. This is the story of all (w)holes. We cannot escape them without fleeing from our own life force! We cannot avoid them without cutting ourselves off from life experiences! We can't make them go away no matter how hard we try! The "issues" keep showing up!

Sound familiar? So what exactly is this thing, this (w)hole that we seem to keep falling into?

There is a famous autobiography written by Portia Nelson called *There is a hole in my sidewalk: Autobiography in five short chapters.* Perhaps you are familiar with this, as it is often quoted in seminars and self-development programs. It goes like this:

> **Chapter One:** I walk down the street. There is a deep hole in the sidewalk. I fall in. I am lost. I am helpless. It isn't my fault. It takes forever to find a way out.
>
> **Chapter Two:** I walk down the same street. There is a deep hole in the sidewalk. I see it is there. I still fall in…it's a habit…but my eyes are open. I know where I am. It is my fault. I get out immediately.
>
> **Chapter Three:** I walk down the street. There is a deep hole in the sidewalk. I pretend that I don't see it. I fall in again. I can't believe I am in this same place. But it isn't my fault. It still takes a long time to get out.
>
> **Chapter Four:** I walk down the same street. There is a deep hole in the sidewalk. I walk around it.
>
> **Chapter Five:** I walk down another street.

We can all see that there is great wisdom to be found in her five chapters. There is wisdom about self-responsibility, choices, and acknowledging what is unchangeable. However, her essential solution leaves a person with fewer and fewer paths to walk down, since ultimately one will find a pothole on any sidewalk. We would end up living a very small life.

The core assumption made by Ms. Nelson is that we are stuck with these holes and that all any of us can do is either avoid them, avoid the situations in which they show up, explore the issues until we are tired of doing this, or just give up and suffer "better" as we fall in over and over again. If we want something different, then something different must happen. The definition of insanity is: To keep doing the same thing over and over again while expecting different results. Ms. Nelson's autobiography suggests one solution—avoid the (w)holes. The Wisdom WAY suggests an alternative that preserves all possible pathways.

If you find yourself falling into a hole and each time you solve the pain by simply choosing another street or avoiding that situation, eventually you would find very few places left to walk. You would end up living a very small life.

There is no way to avoid (w)holes!

Even if you have examined every one of the (w)holes you are aware of, named, defined, and "fixed" the identified issues, I promise that you will still find yourself falling into the same deep pit at some time in the future. The only way to eliminate a (w)hole is to collapse it and be (W)hole! Until then, you are simply managing the inevitable condition of being full of (w)holes. This is a condition we all have!

Unpleasant moments happen in life; it's a fact that can't be changed. This is because there are all sorts of people bumping up against each other. Accidents happen. Death, illness, and pain touch all of us at some time or another. This is life happening.

Each one of us has our own story, our own history, which has led us to exactly this moment, to exactly who we are and how we experience life right now. Our story is unique to each of us. Sprinkled throughout our stories are places of pain, anger, or hurt which we have experienced over the course of our lifetime. One might say that the (w)holes that Ms. Nelson is referring to are the repeated experiences of touching those same places of pain or hurt or anger over and over again. I call these "Life (w)Holes." These life (w)holes operate like "open sores." They still hurt enough to dictate the choices we make now. When we fall into a "dark place," we are, in effect, head first in a (w)hole, which is a space or a void in the interior places within our sense of self.

We know that we have fallen into that place when we recognize the same old story and feel the same old pain. It feels familiar deep inside of us. I've listened to my clients say, "Here I am again! What is the point to all this self-exploration if I keep falling into this same place?" Here is a (W)hole Truth: Each of us will find that our personal stories lead us right back to the edge of our (w)holes, right back where the (W)hole mess started. After listening to people as they wrestle with their dark places and having spent years excavating my own, I came to realize the obvious secret. It had been before me the entire time.

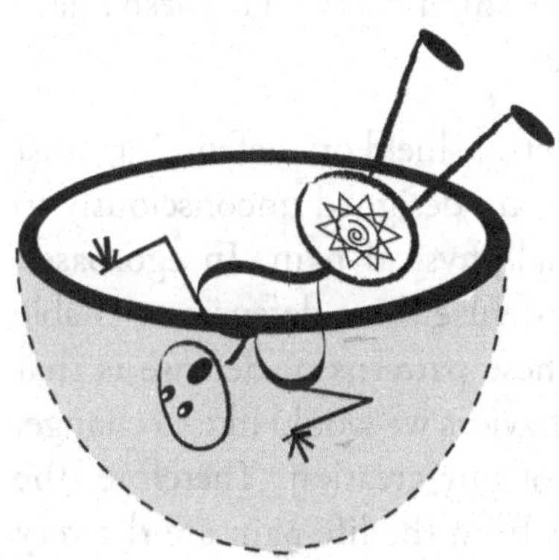

The Secret of (w)Holes

The missing piece is our *relationship* to the (w)hole. What we have not been told is to change our relationship to (w)holes! It is as simple as that. Ms. Nelson sees (w)holes as obstacles, as pit-falls, as experiences to avoid. The difficulty is we can't avoid them. Life is full of (w)holes. Instead, the WAY is to change our relationship to the (w)holes themselves, to let ourselves know a great mystery: (w)holes are doorways, pathways, invitations to our own Holy (W)holeness! We can't awaken to our (W)holeness without walking through the door!

In order to change our relationship to (w)holes, the actual anatomy of a life (w)hole must first be revealed. Let's take a look at exactly what a life (w)hole is.

Let us start at the beginning. We can see physical holes all the time—a pothole, keyhole, porthole, peep hole, nail hole, sink hole, knot hole, bullet hole, worm hole—just to name a few. In actuality a (w)hole is a space between two objects or edges. Let us take you and this book you are reading. There is you…a space…and this book.

There are also (w)holes that are internal or felt (w)holes. These are the life (w)holes inside of us. These are spaces of pain, hurt, and anger inside of us. These are the black pits we fall into when we feel "in the pits."

When I am referring to a life (w)hole, I am referring to a place in our hearts that hurts whenever it is touched. Some examples of (w)holes might be the "I hate being single" (w)hole, the "I am a child of an alcoholic" (w)hole, the "Please like me" (w)hole, or the "Fear of failure" (w)hole. A life (w)hole is where we hurt and struggle but can't seem to figure out how to stop the pain from happening. There is no human being who doesn't have (w)holes or unhelpful patterns of response.

Typically, what we do is create a protective shield or "defense" against what hurts. These defenses or heart-fences are designed unconsciously to accomplish one thing: stop the emotional/physical pain. In ego-based psychology a fundamental approach is to defuse these defenses to enable folks to self-reflect. The difficulty with these patterns of defense is that they commonly are the root of the very behaviors we would like to change, and they sidestep the hidden brilliance of our creation. Therefore, the ways in which we are protecting ourselves from the life pain are the very source of our "unwanted" life responses. Eliminating a defense without first understanding and appreciating it does not empower you. The shift I am pointing to is to move into living your life from inside out rather than designing yourself from the outside in. This is a very rich arena to explore because it points to the intersection of psychology and spirituality.

We are Holy beings, full of (w)holes wondering around "looking for" our (W)holeness.

We are all full of (w)holes because we all have places that trip us up or trigger reactions. Our uniqueness is also reflected in our sameness. We all have (w)holes, and yet, each of us experiences our (w)holes in our own particular way. *Having (w)holes* is not the problem. It is our *relationship* with these (w)holes that creates the difficulties.

You may have attended one or more self-growth and self-discovery experiences or you may have been someone who resisted any idea of help until now. Either way, most of us somewhere deep inside believe something is broken in us, something is wrong with us. We believe in a "bad essence" inside of us which we each name differently. We quest to find a way to "fix" ourselves. What I know from personal experience is this simply doesn't work. The "fixes" at best are only temporary. They cannot be maintained or sustained. They only keep us going around and around the same old issues—going nowhere. I guarantee that by following the approaches that presume you are broken, you will not get beyond the past, regardless of how many excellent books, seminars, teachers, therapists, healers, family, or friends you turn to.

There are three reasons for this. These reasons will reveal three truths to you.

First, you are not broken. You are feeling the pain of a (w)hole. You are not the problem! The (w)hole isn't the problem, even when it feels awful. Falling into a (w)hole when you don't understand what is happening is the problem. How you *respond* to a (w)hole is what really matters. Your relationship to the (w)hole is what makes all the difference! Most of us haven't been taught what (w)holes are, how to relate to them, and how to collapse them. As a result all our (w)holes remain dark spaces to avoid. It's like having a flat tire and fixing it by changing the oil. The tire will still be flat.

Second, unless you know the point of a life (w)hole, you will end up lost. You are not blind. You are simply just sitting in the dark. It is a question of turning on the lights! I could say it this way: unless you know where you are going, you won't know how to get there, you won't know what arriving even means or feels like, and you surely won't know when you get there. Without a map to reveal your particular process and the entire (W)holeness path, you will be lost in the dark. It isn't your fault; we all need light to see our way.

Third, your path to embracing and activating your (W)holeness is unique to you, so following anyone else's path simply won't bring you to the joy of being you. Only your path will take you to YOU.

Everyone on the self-growth/development quest can attest to the fact that we've become experts in old feelings. However, this expertise does not automatically translate into the illumination of the (w)hole itself. Just as a pothole in a road remains a hole, even if we get proficient at driving around it or over it or simply drive a different road, the pothole remains. This is also true of life (w)holes. Life (w)holes do not resolve themselves nor do they stop stealing our lives unless we collapse them, or bringing the two sides of the (w)hole together! The effect is that there is no longer a (w)hole or felt-space to fall into! It was that simple thought that opened the door for me to the (W)hole Truth. Think about it a moment. Doesn't this make sense?

Have you ever been told how to collapse a (w)hole? I'll bet you have read all about the life (w)holes you have fallen into, learned to name the feelings you have when you fall into them, and can even name the cause for the dysfunctional responses you have had in the past. But have you ever been told how to collapse the doggone thing once and for all?

Before we go on, let me clarify a key point about collapsing a (w)hole. Filling up a life (w)hole is not the same as collapsing it. Studying and analyzing a life (w)hole is not the same as collapsing it. Chanting affirmations while circling a life (w)hole will not collapse it. Reading another theory of self-development, empowerment, or chicken soup "for whatever" will not collapse it. We cannot collapse a (w)hole by thinking our way out. We cannot collapse a (w)hole by comforting ourselves while sitting in the dark. Life (w)holes remain no matter how much we study them, define them, or understand them. They will remain until we collapse them. However, once we have collapsed a (w)hole, we can't fall back into that exact same dark space because there is no space in which to fall.

To reveal how to collapse a (w)hole a closer look at the anatomy is required.

(w)Hole Anatomy

Our (w)holes are not just openings with a bottom and edges! They are actually compressed spirals. They are not just "bins" or "containers" or wounds we are stuck with forever. If you were to open up a life (w)hole, you would see your personal path to (W)holeness—*your* (W)holeness. If you were to do a cross-sectional anatomical study of life (w)holes, you would discover they look much like the Slinky™ toy. When a Slinky™ is compressed, it appears to have solid surfaces. When you extend the Slinky™, you discover a spiral path. Life (w)holes are the same in that they have a spiral pathway hidden inside of them. However, they are different from Slinkys™ because instead of just ending at the spiral, at the bottom of a life (w)hole there is a doorway I call a portal.

So, imagine, if you would, a Slinky™ extended so that one end of it comes to a point, much like a spinning top rests on a point. At the bottom point is a "doorway." That's what our life (w)holes "look" like. And yet, the bottom of a life (w)hole is the place most of us flee from! Only by walking through this portal can you reveal what has been lost in the dark of that (w)hole.

Any (w)hole you fall into has a spiral path built in automatically to take you to the portal or doorway at the bottom of the (w)hole. This spiral path is made up of your expertise about YOU! This is your Wisdom WAY. It is particular and unique to you. We all have created in every (w)hole, without realizing it, a pathway of (W)holeness for ourselves. Each and every (w)hole has a (W)holeness path you alone may walk. My path isn't your path, and your path isn't my path. The Wisdom WAY map is the skeletal anatomy that allows for you to "fill in the blanks" and "flesh out" your own private and personal stepping stones of (W)holeness revealed.

Consider this image again. (W)holes are like a compressed Slinky™ toy, appearing to simply be a (w)hole with wire sides. If you were to imagine that it is opened and stretched as far as it could go, you would begin to see parts of the anatomy of a life (w)hole. These parts of all life (w)holes are: an opening, a spiral path, and a doorway or portal at the bottom end of the spiral. Radiance, (W)holeness, the (W)hole Point of every (w)hole, is found at the bottom of this spiral path on the other side of the portal.

The top of the (w)hole is a wide open space between the edges, and the spiral path increasingly narrows down to a point where the doorway of (W)holeness is found. **We have all been running in the wrong direction—frantically trying to climb upward, out of our (w)holes instead of moving toward the doorway of (W)holeness found at the bottom.**

So, now what? The first step is to know how to follow the spiral path of each (w)hole, not to run from it, desperately climb out of it, or cover it up. The point of a (w)hole is to go into it, explore it, and follow it where it leads you, to the real, authentic (W)hole awakened you.

The great news is that when a (w)hole is collapsed, we cannot fall into it again because, quite simply, there is no place to fall. This is cause for great celebration, for now we are finally free to be alive as who we are rather than chase after the "right way" to be or trying to avoid being who we are or hating our life or suffering from it. The freedom to be who we really are, fully and without apology, is a miracle I have witnessed over and over again.

The basic anatomy of a Life (w)Hole:

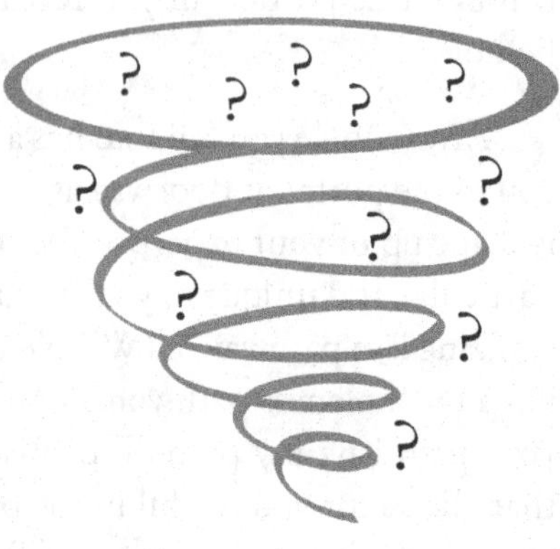

Ever the pragmatist, upon realizing this secret about (w)holes, I was most interested in the application of this new understanding. Many questions formed in my mind; however, the most central one was, how would one go about collapsing a (w)hole? In all my years of education and hours of listening, I had never heard the idea of the practice of (w)hole collapsing or healing a (w)hole!

Some Original Moments and Experiences

When I realized the (W)hole Point of (w)holes was not to climb out of them, run away from them, or avoid them but to experience them by going into them, I developed a map of sorts to empower myself, my clients, and later my students so we could all collapse our own (w)holes.

I have to admit I had been stuck within the traditional boundaries of healing that assumed that (w)holes were a "given." The best that could be hoped for was a mature resolution and management of the facts of life with the greatest degree of compassion towards oneself as possible. Now, I can see how blind I had been. Even though I had experienced many moments of relief in my own growth work, there was always the presumption of (w)holes as a given rather than (w)holes as an invitation to (W)holeness. Once I had made this shift in focus, my entire internal position as a psychotherapist or counselor shifted and so, too, did the experience of my clients.

I soon discovered that my clients and students were moving at light speed through the very issues that had held them stuck for years. Clients were now coming into my office to tell me how they had collapsed a (w)hole on their own, even some (w)holes which had plagued them for years. At first, I was a bit taken aback at the potency of this simple, yet profound, process. Then I realized that authentic empowerment was actually the (W)hole Point of my profession and the actual effect of this model. I became quite excited to witness the blossoming of my clients and myself. Yes, you bet I was applying this to my own life too! I was captivated not only by the efficacy and rapidity of this new process, but also at how people were independently choosing to move deeply and fearlessly into places they had been too resistant to even acknowledge much less boldly embrace. It was, and still is, so exciting. The process was not dependent upon me! The degree of empowerment and transformation was totally in the hands of the one spiraling (exploring) the (w)hole. This was no theory. It was happening before my eyes. I found myself sitting back and watching the excitement, the radiance lighting up the darkness!

I was being given the opportunity to witness my clients becoming truly alive. Since then I have witnessed this with families, couples, and yes, even corporations who have taken the Wisdom WAY and applied it to their own stuck places or (w)holes. Now, I am able to say with great conviction, "Trust the map—your (w)holes will reveal your (W)holeness."

It wasn't the pace or even the breadth of the applicability of the model; it was the depth and permanence of change and empowerment within people that was so precious to witness. Before my eyes, clients and students alike were awakening, empowering, and embodying (W)holeness in a conscious integration. Nothing about the model contradicted traditional therapy or any spiritual wisdom traditions with which I was familiar. In fact, the model was empowering individuals to become their own mentors! Rather than having to let go of all I had studied over my professional life, I found myself weaving it all around the basic Wisdom WAY. I felt increasingly able to empower students to be their own source, not conceptually but for real!

Actively choosing how to move and where to move within this map, these people were falling in love with the wonder of who they were discovering themselves to be. (w)Hole work, or (w)hole play as some call it, is about falling back in love with yourself consciously. By discovering in a felt way that we are not broken, we can all fall back in love with who we are. The only thing that had been missing was knowing the secret of (w)holes.

Now in the simplicity of (w)holes, I found a way to love myself—one (w)hole at a time. The universal message of love now had "Hands & Feet" that could walk into my life situation or a client's and awaken the possibility of (W)holeness. It offers folks a simpler, easier, more connected way to live.

I offer profound gratitude to all of my clients and students—and to myself--for not giving up, no matter how many (w)holes we all fell into until the Wisdom WAY revealed itself.

Chapter 3: A Universal Story

Universal means that it is true for everyone from every walk of life, to whatever (w)hole or (w)holes you are in, to all ages and faiths and cultures. The Wisdom WAY is usable, do-able, immediately accessible, easily learned, and practical for anyone. The simple truth is that we *all* have (w)holes, and we *all* fall into them over and over again. We are all Holy. These (w)holes are the felt experiences where our life force seems to drain away, the vitality is missing, and there is a dimming of enthusiasm. Every single one of these (w)hole experiences has a message.

(W)hole experiences simply tell us that you and I are normal human beings who are waking up to the (W)hole Truth of ourselves. The Wisdom WAY is a path of celebration—which begins right where you already are—in a (w)hole. You already know all you need to know to get started because you are the expert of your own (w)holes and your own story. Your story refers to all your history, your beliefs, and your inner orientations to life. The Wisdom WAY is not about my telling you the answers, but rather it's about my revealing the map of (W)holeness and your using all of your intimate self-knowledge to simply follow the bread crumbs you left for yourself on your own pathway.

Here is a (W)hole Truth hidden in plain view: Every (w)hole we fall into is actually an invitation rising up from within us. Every (w)hole is an invitation to look, to see the (W)hole Truth, and to be the (W)hole of ourselves. Of course, we can say "No, I don't want to today." YOU get to decide what your relationship with a life (w)hole will be! This is your Free Will choice each time you fall into a (w)hole!

If you decide, "No, not today," the (w)hole will wait for you—it will not go away or disappear. Neither will (w)holes force you to accept the invitation. All life (w)holes are insistent invitations to embrace the life force at the bottom of the (w)hole. You choose when: now or later. I hope that you choose NOW!

The awakening cannot be stopped once it has begun; in fact, it can be quite addictive. I have found clients and students become very excited about awakening their own aliveness, about being empowered to be (W)hole rather than working to "fix" their brokenness. Once a person has his first felt experience of a (w)hole collapsing, he simple wants more—more (W)holeness, more aliveness, more freedom to be! The motivation is from within rather than from without. Awakening (W)holeness is captivating, potent, and powerful!

In The Beginning

Truth, discovery, and change are found within our life (w)holes. However, (w)holes are not the point; they are a place to begin. From the beginning we access our (w)holes through our feelings rather than our thoughts; however, since our minds are also precious, we want to include them as well. Any time we exclude an aspect of our experience, we are, in effect, making a (w)hole or a space between parts of ourselves. The Wisdom WAY touches our hearts with truth and comforts our minds with logic. The inclusiveness (i.e., "all parts of us are welcomed and included") combined with the universality of this method of (W)holeness is the source of the effectiveness of this approach.

I often say, "The Wisdom WAY is the skeleton inside of transformation. Once you know the skeleton, you can flesh it out however you choose and then embrace your (W)holeness." We look different to one another on the outside because of how our unique bodies are shaped; however, our flesh hangs on the same basic skeletal frame inside each of us. The skeletal frame of the Wisdom WAY does not tell you any answers; it invites you to reveal your own answers, your own heart's logic, and your own life alignment to yourself. Then, once revealed, you are positioned to be able to make choices and changes at a cellular, spiritual, and psychological level of your being. This is the "Hands & Feet" of empowerment.

The Wisdom WAY is also a framework or skeleton hidden inside all of the various modalities of self-discovery, healing, and awakening you'll find out there. How amazing it is to see through to the skeleton! It is like having X-ray vision on behalf of oneself! My clients and students are often shocked by the simplicity of the skeleton and its presence in movies, books, workshops, seminars, relationships of all kinds—almost anywhere you look for it. It has always been there; we just weren't ready or able to see it.

Soon you, too, will be able to see (w)holes and (W)holeness everywhere, but most importantly you'll see them in yourself.

As you begin to see the simplicity of the skeleton and the complexity with which we have disguised it, be gentle with yourself. Each of us has simply been trying to make sense of our own experiences and make the pain go away and never happen again. It is my firm conviction that as we clear the darkness from our own lives, we clear the darkness from each other and our (W)hole planet. Our light is present; it has just been obscured by the darkness of our (w)holes.

As we move through the chapters, we will explore each part of the Wisdom WAY separately. I invite you to remember that you are the expert of yourself. Some have found it helpful to have some paper or a journal to write down personal information. Do this if you so choose. At the end of each section will be a page with the next step diagramed for you to see visually. I suggest that you copy the image onto a blank sheet of paper and fill it in with your personal particulars. In this manner you will not only move through a cognitive recognition of the (W)hole Truth, you will simultaneously move through a felt embrace of your (W)holeness a bit at a time. The intention is to elicit a logical, cognitive, and felt experience of your (w)hole.

At this point, I have been building a foundation upon which to demonstrate and draw the Wisdom WAY map. We have not yet covered the implementation actions. There are just a few more foundational facets to cover before diving into your precious (w)holes.

About Alaya

Alaya obtained a master's degree in divinity from Yale University and a master's degree in social work from the University of Connecticut. She has lived on a Kibbutz, studied in Switzerland, traveled across the country, participated in Outward Bound™, and sailed in the Caribbean, among many other life-altering adventures. Life has now led her to this latest adventure—writing this book.

Prior to entering the healing professions, Alaya held positions in corporate sales and administration. After returning to school for her master's degrees, she spent the next twenty-seven years practicing in the field of traditional and alternative healing. During this period, she developed the Wisdom WAY™, a powerful and sustainable process of self-awakening. She continues to invite herself and others to embrace themselves in wonder and to boldly come alive.

Her private consultation practice of (W)hole Life Coaching focuses on empowering individuals, relationships, and organizations by creating positive change. Alaya is a practicing Teaching Reiki Master as well as a Certified Imago Therapist and an ordained minister.

Currently serving as the founder/director of The (W)hole Point Institute, LLC, as well as being a co-director with her husband, John, of "Sanctuary," a sixty-five-acre healing location in New Hampshire, Alaya is living her dream of offering folks direct access to practical "hands and feet" approaches for empowered awakening.

Alaya's classes, apprenticeships, and consultations continue to touch people around the globe.

About Alaya's PAIR John

John Richard Chadwick is the name of my dear "PAIR." He and I have been married now for 20 years. A chemist and inventor at heart, John has been deeply challenged by me during our 20 years. He has been invited by me to open up and explore the bazillion surprises of being in partnership with a pioneer of the interior spaces of the human psyche. This in itself is not a small tale! Beyond this he has boldly walked into the wild jungles of The (W)hole Point Institute, LLC, to become a graduate of all the Wisdom WAY levels of Radiance—there are 8!

And most precious of all, he has softened into the miracle of being loved for no reason and for every reason by this woman of mysteries and miracles. John is and has been my greatest teacher of the unbelievable magic of love beyond logic and of the huge courage-of-heart it takes to drop the armor and let naked love in. It is this PAIRing that has held me in its lap as I knitted these stories together for over 15 of our 20 years of chosen partnership. Thank you, dear John. I am glad I said "Yes" so long ago.

About The (W)hole Point Institute, LLC

If you want to experience all the richness of the Wisdom WAY, go to The (W)hole Point Institute's website. There you will find more information on all of the (W)hole Shops offered as well as a list of the Certified Master Teachers of Radiance (CMTR). These are the folks who will come to your area to teach live (W)hole Shops, and they are the only folks who are certified by The (W)hole Point Institute to teach the Wisdom WAY. Our website is www.wholepoint.us.

(W)hole Shops are sequential experiences which are practical and above all fun. In these two-day intensive seminars, the students are introduced to the various levels of the Wisdom WAY.

Level One is the introduction to the basics.

Level Two focuses on where and how spirituality and psychology intersect in (w)holes.

Level Three examines the Portal in depth—its terrors, and its surprises.

Level Four focuses on Radiance and Transparency.

Level Five expands the map from a two-dimensional drawing and understanding to three dimensions.

Level Six turns the model upside down and offers/invites the surprise introduction to YOUR Soul Self

Level Seven focuses on Oneness lived.

Level Eight focuses on the Return to the Market Place—walking your (W)hole Self into the world. Reveals the lost last (w)Hole.

All of the (W)hole Shops are founded upon and rooted in the basic Wisdom WAY map, and throughout the (W)hole Shops the student remains the expert of themselves. The emphasis is practical and particular to each person, while expanding in surprising ways upon the basic skeleton of the Wisdom WAY. The method of teaching is designed to include the mind, the feelings, the body, and the spirit of the student. It is also created to touch the brilliant inner child who created so many of our precious (w)holes and the breadcrumb path to (W)holeness.

As individuals move through the (W)hole Shop series, there are many initiatory and alchemical changes that occur. The Wisdom WAY is about profound and deep transformation. It is not just another cognitive theory or process. Students often return again and again only to discover that the wisdom embedded in the model has carried them to even greater aliveness.

For more information, go to **www.wholepoint.us**
or www.sanctuarynh.com.

To contact Alaya, email **Alaya@sanctuarynh.com.**